D1715316

Behind the G-String

Behind the G-String

*An Exploration
of the Stripper's Image,
Her Person and Her Meaning*

DAVID A. SCOTT

McFarland & Company, Inc., Publishers
Jefferson, North Carolina, and London

British Library Cataloguing-in-Publication data are available

Library of Congress Cataloguing-in-Publication Data

Scott, David A.
    Behind the G-string : an exploration of the stripper's image, her
person and her meaning /David A. Scott.
        p.   cm.
    Includes bibliographical references (p.   ) and index.
    ISBN 0-7864-0262-8 (library binding : 50# alk. paper) ∞
    1. Stripteasers.   2. Stripteasers—Interviews.   3. Burlesque
(Theater)   I. Title.
PN1949.S7S36   1996
792.7'028'0922—dc20   96-31884
                                                                CIP

Manufactured in the United States of America

*McFarland & Company, Inc., Publishers
    Box 611, Jefferson, North Carolina 28640*

Contents

Acknowledgments

First and foremost, I would like thank Kate Lynch, who, as the prime mover behind Choice Entertainment in Vancouver, provided me with the first glimpse into the world of the stripper. Kate is one of those very special people with a huge heart and the ability to attract all kinds of people around her. Kate let me spend time at her agency and introduced me to many of the performers who appear in these pages. Similarly, Delilah, the manager of the Pussycat Club in Las Vegas, gave me a free rein to interview the performers there. Delilah was a very gracious hostess and enabled me to accomplish much during my stay in Las Vegas. And Sheri Champagne, a veteran stripper, now retired, has been a close friend and a tireless supporter of this project. I am forever thankful for her friendship and her exuberance.

I am indebted to the late Paul Perry who thought enough of this project to let me interview the performers at his Palomino Club in Las Vegas, Angel Carter who put me in touch with some significant people in Las Vegas, and Damion Guilbault who made some important connections for me in Vancouver. In addition, KOMO TV kindly provided me with some pertinent tapes of "Town Meeting."

My very good friend Richard Gutter loaned me his typewriter and his computer when mine broke down, but I am grateful to Richard most of all for his invaluable criticism of some key chapters in this book. Many people gave me precious emotional support during the writing. First and foremost is my very close friend, Janice Laing, who kept telling me that it would turn out all right when I began to believe that it might not, and Bruce Haden has been an enthusiastic supporter, offering some valuable criticism of several chapters. The encouragement of the following people was important to me and will never be forgotten: my sister and brother-in-law, Elizabeth and Charlie Le Ber, my special friends, David and Louise Masterson, Jerrie and Doreen Netolicky, Glenn and Sandi Allison, Doniella Boaz, and Edward Clements, while the Men's Group,

Darren Berezowski, Alan Boniface, Bruce Haden, Mark Lavelle, Michael Marino, Peter Peach, and Brian Short all gave me much useful feedback about problems that I encountered along the way.

I also wish to convey special thanks to T.J., one of the first male exotic dancers, just for being who he is.

The following people assisted in the production of the manuscript: Janet Bellwether and the late Randy Reimchen transcribed interview tapes; Ian MacNaughton let me use his cabin and his computer; and Judy Holmes gave me access to her printer. In addition, I would like to thank my mother, Jean M. Scott, for her unconditional love and support, my brother, Paul Scott, who made a crucial financial contribution to the project and has been an avid supporter, and Mark Simpson and Norma Cera who made financial contributions to the project.

Finally, I would like to thank Robert Allen for writing what I consider is the best book on the history of burlesque, *Horrible Prettiness: Burlesque and American Culture.*

Introduction

Stripper.

The word creates pictures, and the pictures tend to linger in the mind.

Once invoked, the image of the stripper, now central to consciousness, must be dealt with. Is she a pleasing arrival or a troublesome intruder? Does the mind make her dance or does it encourage throwing stones? Is the pleasure in watching her or is the pleasure in becoming her? Is she troubling because of morality or because of what she stimulates in you? If you find her pleasurable, what are your thoughts about marrying her? If you condemn her, what are your thoughts about getting to know her? How intelligent, artistic, or religious do you think she might be? When she appears in your mind, does she ever get angry, sad, jealous, thoughtful, hysterical, judgmental, clumsy, inane, abusive, smelly, or flatulent?

When questions about the stripper probe her *person* as opposed to her image, the mood shifts. The primary cultural responses to the stripper—desire and loathing—diminish as the focus moves away from her eroticism. Probing her person, we are forced to empathize, and empathy is anathema to both carnal desire and condemnation. Without either response (she thrives on both), the stripper loses her power, her magnetism, and her ability to create controversy. She shrinks from her status as goddess-demon and becomes, well, much like the rest of us. This is the essential dynamism of the stripper: an ambivalent cultural fixation on her image and a collective denial of her personhood.

All eyes are on the stripper. She, in turn, is the eye of a hurricane. Antipathy toward the stripper derives from her provocation of the social order. In Western societies propriety dictates that people sharing public spaces ought to be clothed (one's genitals at the very least) and sexually restrained. There are some obvious practical reasons for such decorum, but for many people, it is a matter of religion and morals. The Christian morality pervading Western culture was crafted from the frustrations, fears, and hatred of lust found in the writings of the Church Fathers.

1

Saint Augustine, for one, the most influential architect of Christian moral doctrine, saw in his own uncontrollable lust the consequences of the original sin of Adam and Eve which freed the libido from its Edenic servitude to the will to become the eternal antagonist of the soul. "For lust is a usurper," he wrote, "defying the power of the will and playing the tyrant with man's sexual organs." If people today—even churchgoers—do not view their libidos with the same foreboding, sexuality nevertheless remains a troublesome issue for most people the world over. Our culturally held agreement about sex is that it ought to remain private and the naked body should only be exposed to strangers in contextually appropriate places, such as locker rooms, nude beaches, and nudist colonies. In the Western democracies, at least, nudity in the theater is also permitted now because it is couched within a veneer of art.

The stripper commits the triple sin of combining eroticism and nudity in a public place, with a meager pretension to art. However, yet another dimension must be considered. With our attention riveted on her body and its motions, a crucial component of the stripper's performance goes unnoticed: her attitude. Notice how she strips off her clothes with abandon, how she positively revels in what she does. She is willful, self-possessed, commanding, and, most scandalously, she is unabashed about it all. There is no hint of vulnerability in her exposure before strangers. She is shameless. It is this component of the stripper's image that is the most grievous, because it signifies that she is somehow immune to social control. To be beyond shame—the internalized punishment for stepping out of line—is to be free of the need to belong. That is a formidable attitude in anyone, but in a woman it is perceived by many to be monstrous. The stripper represents a radical form of femininity, a woman who has transcended the decorum of a female's public presence.

"What you're saying to your audience is, 'Look, you're nervous because I'm taking more chances than you are. That's why you hate me.'" This observation was not made to a stripper, but to another radical image of femininity, Madonna, in Norman Mailer's article/interview for *Esquire*;[1] yet the underlying psychology is the same. Whenever a woman's sexuality goes public, she garners a volatile mixture of attention, adoration, and desire, together with fear, resentment, and hostility, sometimes all in the same person. The image of eroticism unbound sends a seditious message to the libido and sounds an alarm to the inhibitors. The stripper has all the appearance of a modern Eve, brazenly inciting the passions to break free from their subservience to the will of the law, the dictates of decorum, and their consignment to the private realm.

From a different perspective, the stripper's flouting of the rules may well be seen as a form of radical art, a provocation with a revelatory objective. She forces us to reflect on the purpose and the merit of such a decorum. What is so terrible about the human body? Would society really break down if the restrictions on public nudity were overthrown? Who benefits from these social controls? Even pragmatic people—who don't subscribe to the overly zealous concerns of conservative moralists, Christian fundamentalists, and the like—will see the necessity for some kind of limit, knowing all the while that wherever there is a limit, there will be found a libertine testing its resolve. In this light the stripper has all the appearance of a court jester who impishly keeps reminding us of our social conditioning.

The stripper's right to perform is, in fact, protected by our democratic notions of freedom of expression, which, in the United States is enshrined in the First Amendment to the Constitution. However, it has been deemed by the courts that this protection is forfeited where her expression is ruled to be lewd, indecent, or obscene. The U.S. Supreme Court defined obscenity in the landmark case of *Roth v United States* as anything that, by contemporary community standards, appeals to "prurient interests." The key word here, of course, is prurient. Prurient comes from the Latin verb to itch or lust after. The implication of the Court's ruling is that anything that inspires lust is therefore obscene, an interpretation that would have been approved of by Saint Augustine. The stripper thus finds herself in a sort of catch-22 situation. She can express herself all she wants, but she must not appear to inspire lust, when the very effect of even a minimalist performance is the stimulation of lust. How the courts view the matter has depended on the ordinance that resulted in the stripper's arrest, expert testimony as to the prevailing community standards, and what the stripper actually did onstage. Some ordinances explicitly prohibit the stimulation of lust, others prohibit the indecent exposure of the body or particular parts, while still others simply prohibit obscene conduct. In the final analysis, what separates the obscene from the nonobscene is subject to all kinds of interpretations and biases, which in turn reflect the shifting sands of public opinion; and so the stripper lives her life always one step away from arrest.

The stripper is, however, usually tolerated, even exonerated in the courts, where her performance stays within certain limits of nudity and sexual gesturing. The social strategy—a type of truce between the stripper and the surrounding community—is, at least, to contain both her sexual expressiveness and her proliferation. Contravention of the latter category is often taken more seriously than that of the former. As long as the stripper remains in her traditional area—the lower-class part of town—

she may go unnoticed by the law no matter what she does onstage. But whenever she moves into middle-class areas, she almost certainly faces a strident protest. The Minsky brothers, who personified the most innovative and salacious corner of burlesque (and eventually burlesque itself), found this out when they opened several theaters on Broadway, the cultural heartland of New York. The reaction from antivice groups, property owners, religious groups, and civic authorities was a concerted effort to drive them out. The protest, coinciding as it did with an antiburlesque civic administration, was loud enough in 1937 to cause the revocation of every burlesque theater license in the city. While the striptease did struggle on in a much more subdued form, it was almost 30 years before it regained its lost vitality. The Minskys' attempt to transcend their tolerable boundaries proved to be the death knell of their medium.

To working-class and middle-class people the presence of the stripper is seen as a kind of blight on the neighborhood and its values, a cancerous growth that will multiply unless surgically removed. A recent example occurred in 1993 in Port Chester, New York, when a strip club opened up in a shopping mall. The local reaction to the intrusion was predictably one of dismay and anger. As the *New York Times* put it, "Whatever their faults, shopping malls have the virtue of letting people pull right up in the family car at the cleaners or hardware store without risking a seamy sidewalk encounter." Picket lines formed in front of the club and lawyers were hired. Of the protestors, the *Times* article opined, "nothing less than the survival of their village is at stake." One of the protestors even went so far as to say, "This is synonymous with the Civil War. It was fought over racial merchandising of people for profit, and this is the merchandising of flesh for profit." "Sex coming to the suburbs," is how one Port Chester merchant summarized the local anguish.[2]

The stripper is the focus and the target of such protests. It is her behavior that becomes the issue for the courts. But it is not so much the stripper as the strip joint that offends. The stripper is, after all, contained within its walls, invisible to those who wish not to see her. But the club itself, together with its obligatory adornments, has a prominence that is unavoidable. Signs scream LIVE NUDE GIRLS!!! Giant images of scantily clad women gaze wantonly down on passersby; seedy types cluster about the place; the mystery of what goes on inside swells with each rumor and innuendo; and associations with organized crime, and the suspicion of prostitution, if not white slavery, curdle in the mind. The presence of the strip club within the domain of family values is an alien, intrusive, and troubling specter.

In spite of the Minsky debacle, strip joint owners have been tirelessly cunning in their efforts to push the limits on containment. When they were prohibited from having strippers in the same room where alcohol was served, they had strippers perform in an adjoining room behind a glass panel. When showing pubic hair was against the law, merkins were used. Today, the problem of operating in middle-class areas has been addressed with an image makeover. If sleaze is the offense, then dress the clubs in high-status attire and tone down the nudity and the eroticism, at least until a foothold has been established. Since 1990 topless bars have proliferated in urban areas across the continent; some of them offer "valet parking, limousines, shuttle buses, executive dining rooms, and fax-outfitted conference rooms, not to mention topless women who shine shoes and perform secretarial duties." Some clubs have dress codes, cover charges, and extravagant menus. Dancers perform in lavish costumes. In an article on the innovation in the *New York Times,* a topless devotee—a lawyer—enthusiastically said, "Hey, this is elegant—it's not sleazy. You can bring a date here and not give a bad impression."[3]

If the stripper is a demon to a sizable proportion of the population, she is also a goddess to millions. According to *Stripper* magazine, a New York publication, there may be as many as 3,000 strip clubs in the United States and Canada. The average audience on any given day may be conservatively estimated to be about 200 (coming and going). That translates into over 600,000 viewers per night, over 3.5 million every week: a sizable lobby. Obviously, stripping is big business. One club owner boasted earnings of between $30,000 and $100,000 a week in alcohol sales alone in each of his 24 clubs across the United States.[4]

What's the attraction? The stripper represents the perfect sex toy, the dream girl, a man's ideal erotic fantasy, and consequently, the girl who can't be obtained. If she could, she would cease to be a fantasy. If she was available, it would only be to the very few, those who paid her, for instance, if she were so inclined; but even then, she would cease to be a fantasy. A fantasy realized is no longer a fantasy, no matter how it transpired. The fact is that for almost everyone the stripper remains an unrealizable dream. She's an illusion. The stripper's alchemy works differently from the prostitute's, so it is questionable whether the stripper can even be a prostitute. That said, one has to ask why men would willingly submit themselves to the frustrating experience of unfulfilled stimulation of their libidos. Why would they seek out such a tormenting illusion?

This is one of the intriguing questions explored in this book. Other questions pertain to the woman who creates the illusion. It might be deduced that the stripper is akin to other erotic images of women, such as video porn queens, skin book centerfolds, swimsuit models, even models on the covers of fashion magazines; but the stripper, as a viewed image, is also a living, breathing woman. She can tell us what it is like looking back at her viewers. What is it like to bare your body in front of a mob of strangers? Is she really feeling the personal eroticism that we impute to her? Is she really without shame? And how did she get into this line of work, anyway? What does she get out of it? What are the hazards? What is it like being an outcast? The questions are many and the answers are often surprising.

On some level, we are aware of the stripper's complexity, in spite of supreme mental efforts to keep her framed in simple, controllable terms (like goddess and slut). The fact that there is a real person beneath the mesmerizing display of naked sensuality whispers to the mind of hidden depths, of things *un*revealed, that something is working beneath and around and behind, and that deals are being brokered between subconscious minds. Her modern rendition of an age-old motif stirs up linkages between signals and metaphors, arabesques and ancient memories.

This is what Stéphane Mallarmé was driving at when he wrote of the ballerina: "She does not dance but rather, ... writing with her body ... suggests things which the written work could express only in several paragraphs of dialogue or descriptive prose."[5] This book provides those elusive paragraphs.

I am forever indebted to all the performers who shared with me their thoughts and feelings. The following list represents those who consented to the use of their stage names. All other stage names appearing in this book are pseudonyms.

Crystal Blue, Miss Brazil, Denise Bressette, Brooke, Burgeondy, Carmalita, Valerie Carr, Holly Carroll, Angel Carter, Cassie, Sheri Champagne, Chelsea, Cybelle, Dallas, Dayna, Amber Dawn, Danielle Dean, Delilah, Devlin Devine, Egypt, Emanuelle, Emery, Fawn, Shadow Fire, Flame, Brittany Fox, Diana Fox, Gidget, Gio, Jay Jay, Jazz, Jennie, Billie Jo, Jocelyne, Jane Jones, Kali, Kyra, Dynasty Layne, Tyy Lee, Venus De Light, Princess Lillian, Luscious Lona, Claire Love, Tia Maria, Marlo (1), Marlo (2), Marnier, Mary, Mickey, Magenta Moon, Mousanna, Lava North, Rebecca, Rita Rhinestone, Robbie, Crystal Rose, Rosebud, Roxy, Sarita, Seija, Sharday, Shelima, Sky, Ginger Snap, Dee Dee Special, Teri Starr, Judith Stein, Summer, Tammy, Tara, Toni, Tracy Tsar, Brandi West, Karin West, Whisper, Snow White, Whitney, Melissa Wolf.

1

The Business

A description of the stripper's routine, her costume, and the place where she works, may be helpful in understanding some of the terms used in this book.

The stripper's usual routine is a 15-minute show in 4 parts. Each part is normally accompanied by a different song, usually rock and roll or country and western. Sometimes a long song will accompany 2 parts. Strippers create their own soundtracks on cassette tapes and may refer to individual shows by the band, as in "my Pink Floyd set" or "my Mitch Ryder show." The stripper opens her routine by dancing in her costume. Then she unpeels, unsnaps, unzips, and unhooks her way down to her G-string. The third song she performs in her G-string. During the last song, she removes her G-string (where legal) and finishes her performance nude. This basic format has many variations. Some strippers with large breasts, for instance, may prefer to remove their bras last because it is uncomfortable to dance with upper body sway. The interval in which the performer is nude may range from 1 minute to 5, occasionally longer.

The stripper's finale is usually a "floor show." Now completely nude with the possible exception of earrings, necklace, waist chain, and or high heel shoes, she moves in time to a slow song in various forms of recline on a fluffy rug that she has placed on the stage. She may crawl over to the spectators seated at the edge of the stage and play with them. This might mean anything from running one of her stockings around someone's neck, to taking someone's glasses and steaming them between her legs, to opening her labia for someone to see inside. Strippers who "show pink," as this last device is called, are referred to as "spreaders."

Sometimes the finale takes the form of an oil show: sprawled on a polyethylene sheet, the stripper squirts lines of a silky lotion (such as cocoa butter) all over her body and then seductively massages it into a glistening sheen. In those areas where it is illegal for the stripper to perform nude, she will do her floor show in her G-string.

At the end of her show, the dancer puts on her cover-up, a robe or long T-shirt she brought with her to the stage, gathers up the pieces of her costume and her rug and returns to the dressing room.

Some new variations on the traditional format have appeared in recent years. One is table dancing or couch dancing, where the stripper performs right beside a customer's seat for a fee, often on a small portable cubicle that serves to raise her hips to eye level. In this arrangement, the main stage serves only as a sampler to help the customer make his selection, and the performances there are consequently shorter and less elaborate.

As the essence of stripping is relentlessly to tease the limits of the allowable, table dancing has been superseded by lap dancing in some areas. This form essentially brings the table dancer closer to the customer's chair and, following her performance, into his lap. Although the customer is required to keep his hands to himself, at this level of closeness the grey areas tend to fade away.

Another recent innovation is the peep show. Here, the stripper performs in a booth behind a glass panel for one or more viewers who sit unseen by her in darkness. Toilet paper is provided. The length of the show and its level of raunchiness depends on how much money passes through a slot in the glass. This variation has attracted most of the public protest in recent years.

A woman taking a bath was a venerable old burlesque routine, sometimes in a real bath tub placed on stage, sometimes in a gigantic champagne glass. The modern innovations on this motif are plexiglass shower stalls rising from the corner of the stage or Grecian fountains built right into the floor. After, or instead of, her floor show, and often in response to a frenzied audience demand for it ("Show-*wer!* Show-*wer!*"), the stripper takes a sensuous shower (or gambols nymph-like in the fountain) and then dries herself off, whipping the moisture from her hair into the crowd.

The duo show presents the stripper in stereo. Two strippers together on the same stage allows for some semblance of plot structure and the voyeuristic realization of a popular male fantasy: two women stripping each other. The variations on this motif are many, but their essential dynamism derives from the women stripping each other and feigning (sometimes performing) mutual cunnilingus. Three strippers at a time has been tried but seems to have been abandoned, probably because there was too much going on, producing overkill. What has worked much better is simultaneous acts on several stages where the multiple effect is enhanced with a relative absence of ritual. The strippers appear on their respective stages wearing only an open-ended body stocking, remove it during the very first song and then exit, to be followed by their replacements. This concept may represent the last vestige of the traditional ecdysial rite.

The hustle bars or, as some strippers call them, "titty bars," are the forerunners of the table-dancing concept. The stripper does only two songs onstage, one in full costume and one in her G-string. Then she steps down into the audience pit and dances for individual patrons, enticing them to tip her by placing paper currency in her G-string. She will also sit with some of them and subtly hustle them to buy her drinks (often ersatz champagne) at inflated prices. In these situations, the stripper is not paid for performing but makes her money solely from tips plus a commission on the drinks the men buy for her.

The stripper's costume can be anything from a pair of cut-off denims and a T-shirt to an elaborate and expensive dress to something thematic in the guise of Little Red Riding Hood, the rodeo queen, the dominitrix or the Southern belle, to name just a few. Instead of a G-string underneath, she may be wearing a "T-bar." The T-bar, so named because when laid out flat it looks like two T's joined at their bases, is slightly larger than the G-string and is sometimes worn over it. G-string is an abbreviation of geestring, which originally referred to the waist thong that secured the loincloth of the American Indian in the 1870s, and later came to refer to the loincloth itself. Why the geestring was so named is not known.

Almost any horizontal surface will work as a stage, from the floor in a corner of the bar, to the top of the bar itself, a plywood sheet laid across some beer kegs or a pool table, to the real thing: an imposing carpeted platform complete with an array of fixed and moving overhead lights, brass poles, a see-through plexiglass shower stall, and a state of the art sound system. The brass poles (usually two) can be used to swing around, do vertical leg splits against, and to provide leverage for aerial acrobatics. Some of the more traditional stages still have runways. In these holdovers from the burlesque era, the stripper makes her entrance from behind a curtain. More commonly, the route from the dressing room to the stage leads right through the audience.

In the higher status clubs there is a DJ or light man who announces each performer's entrance, cues her music, operates the stage lights, and works up the crowd after her finale. In the less sophisticated clubs there is no DJ. No one announces the stripper, so she performs nameless. Sometimes the sound system in such places is a tape player located on the corner of the stage. Strippers often refer to these places as "dumps."

The audience, which may number anywhere from a handful to about 300, sits in chairs around tables except for (in some places) the seats that ring the stage itself. Whatever the setup, the front row is accorded special status by both strippers and their fans. It is known variously in the trade as Gynecology Row, Gyno Row, Pervert Row, the meat rack, the Sushi Bar, or the sniff seats.

The higher status city clubs employ 10–12 dancers split into two shifts each day. One shift works from about noon to six and the other from six to closing, depending on the club's hours of operation. At these clubs there is often a headliner (or feature), usually someone who has appeared in one of the glossy magazines such as *Penthouse* or *High Society* or who has an unusual act. She does a one week gig and gets paid at least twice as much as the regulars. She may pose for polaroids with customers for a fee and sell merchandise after each performance. At the other end of the spectrum, clubs in the rural areas may have only one stripper for the entire week who performs once an hour or so all day long.

Almost all strippers have an agent who books them week by week into the clubs. The club pays the stripper in cash every Saturday night at the end of her week and the agent his or her commission in a lump sum. Strippers lament that the contract signed between them and the club owners doesn't protect them much in the event of a dispute.

The industry has sought in vain for a more respectable term than stripper. Burlesquer and stripteaser have gone out of fashion, the latter because artful teasing has just about vanished from the act. "Exotic dancer" is the industry's current effort to euphemize itself and it appears to be catching on, at least with some of the media (although many people still hear belly dancer in this term). H. L. Mencken's contribution, "ecdysiast" has won a place as the technical term, much like the Latin terms concealed beneath the common names of flora and fauna, but its proper context remains elusive. Peeler is used by many, strippers included. It is a warmer, friendlier, less controversial word. The majority of strippers prefer plain "dancer." That's about as noncontroversial a term as can be found. Nevertheless, these are all diversions. "Stripper"—sibilant, graphic, and punctuating—says it all.

2

"I Was Broke, I Needed a Job, and I Got Drunk"

How did the stripper find her way into this business? Did she just wake up one day and decide to do it or did she slide into it by degrees? Was it an easy transition in a life already conditioned to sexual licentiousness or did it take a lot of courage? Was it the culmination of a youthful fantasy or was it something foisted on her? Was she born into it or was she sold into it?

To become a stripper is to step across a line. It is the line of propriety that defines socially acceptable behavior. It is the line between what is sanctioned in public and what is relegated to the private arena. It is a benchmark on the scale of assumptions and expectations about people (imagine that the woman you have met at a party and have been conversing with, now confesses that she is a stripper). It is a moral line. It separates insiders from outsiders, those who exemplify the prevailing social order from those who do not. It is the frontier of the realm of the taboo.

To step across this line is to pay a price. The price is paid both internally and externally, to one's sense of morality and to the community at large. The internal hurdles involved in crossing the line are considerable; would-be strippers share in the same social conditioning as everyone else in regard to public nakedness. A brief thought experiment will underscore the issue. Imagine that you are suddenly naked on a busy downtown street. Everyone has stopped dead in their tracks to look at you. You are no longer one of them; you're now a fish out of water, a freak. They will think you must be insane or intoxicated and possibly a threat to them. It will feel like their eyes are boring right through you. You will probably be shaken to the core by a combination of terror, shame, and a feeling of abject vulnerability. Urges to run and hide surface, but where? You have been exposed and your artfully crafted ego is cracking up under the strain. These are the consequences of transgressing the internal prohibitions against being naked in public and they are serious indeed. Just like you, the stripper has to deal with her own internalized controls on public nudity, but with two different variables at play, one that mitigates her situation and one that makes it much worse.

First, the context is different. A strip club is not a street. Its very definition hinges on the expectation of public nudity. No one there is going to be surprised by the stripper's display. No one will think she is insane. Furthermore, there are others there who have already crossed the line and will help the neophyte make her own transition. She is not alone. She has a support group for her walk on the wild side. In fact, she is initiated into a tenured sorority, a tradition with which she can feel some sense of belonging, if not pride. Removing her clothes in front of strangers is a rite of passage. The stripper also has the advantage of being able to prepare herself mentally for her first disrobing onstage. Compared with your experience on the street, the stripper's first public exposure would seem to be not nearly as traumatic.

However, there is another factor to consider, that of intention. In the imaginary scenario above, people would quickly notice your terror. They would see that you probably didn't intend to be in this situation. They would notice your shame and consequently might feel some affinity with you. Your shame would tell them that your inhibitions were still in place and so you were, in fact, just like them. Some of them would probably try to help you. In the stripper's case she clearly intends to be there, and not only naked but sexual as well. She flaunts herself shamelessly in front of strangers. She not only steps through the taboo she makes it look easy, as though she were a product of another culture, or even another time. While those in the audience generally view her with pleasure, the surrounding moral climate casts a pall of condemnation around her. Viewed as a cultural alien, or simply a lowlife, the stripper is denounced as a threat to order, family values, and moral fiber. The price of social condemnation is the stripper's biggest price, because it means that she forfeits her sense of belonging with the culture in which she lives.

To be willing to pay such a price presupposes one or a combination of four possibilities: (1) she's an outsider already (So what has she got to lose?); (2) paying the price is one of two alternatives, of which the other is worse; (3) the benefits of crossing the line outweigh the consequences; or (4) she just doesn't buy into others' opinions of her, so crossing the line is of little moral consequence.

The personal stories strippers tell of the circumstances leading up to their entry into the business are, not surprisingly, all different. Nevertheless, four distinct phases of the induction into stripping are common to most of them and the circumstances of each phase have common traits of their own. The four phases are: (1) a reason or justification for taking the plunge; (2) a contact in the business or someone else who helped shepherd them inside; (3) a catalyst that mollified the internal controls; and (4) some realized benefit from stripping that reinforced the decision to cross over. These phases are illustrated by Tracy Tsar's story. Initially, she answered an ad in the newspaper for waitresses.

> TRACY TSAR: This one club owner used to pull them in off the streets in an amazing way. There was an expensive jewelry store next door to his club and on a nice afternoon he'd just stand around waiting for a good looking girl to walk by. He'd chat her up and bring her into his club and soon she would be dancing. He'd chat you up and he'd send over a couple of drinks and the dancers would wander over to talk to you and between the girls and the drinking and whatever else was around…
>
> He always advertised for waitresses but never needed them. I was broke and I needed a job and I got drunk.

Financial need is the most common justification mentioned. The paycheck is thus, for most strippers, the benefit that most strongly reinforces the decision to step through the taboo. Tracy Tsar's introduction to the business was common to many strippers in that it was a solution to her problem that she otherwise probably never would have considered. The smooth-talking club owner got her to come into the club. Once inside, the resident strippers came over to offer their support. Alcohol served as the catalyst that dissolved any remaining resistance.

That the business of stripping does recruit from the ranks of the destitute might be obvious. Paying the price presupposes a condition of life that is much worse than social condemnation. Dire need with no other visible means of employment or support coupled with the trust of someone on the inside is often the path of least resistance.

> GIO: I started the night before I turned 17 at a place called the Rock Garden in Jamaica, Queens, New York. I did it because of the money. I had a girlfriend who was doing it and I was in college. I worked the whole first semester in the alumni office making minimum wage, which at the time was $1.75 an hour. I'd work 10 to 15 hours a week for $15 to $20, plus they took taxes off, which was totally ridiculous. My parents could not afford to send me money. I was practically starving.
>
> My girlfriend said, "Why don't you become a topless go-go dancer? Then you can work one night a week and make *50 bucks!*"

DIANA FOX: I was working as a cocktail waitress. One day, the owner came up to me and told me that they were putting in a stage and all the waitresses who weren't going to go topless were fired. There I was, straight out of Idaho with a little baby and my husband was out of work. I was lucky to have that job because I was underage. So I had to agree.

So I danced topless and the first time was ... so scary. But I'm extremely near-sighted, so that helped. I just kept in mind that I had to support my baby.

My sister bought me my first costume for my birthday. And I was so uptight about being short, I got these big shoes—you know how they used to make those platform shoes—and I sprayed them pink, because my costume was pink and I got paint on the soles. The first time I opened, I slipped and fell flat on my ass.

CLAIRE LOVE: I got tired of lining up at food banks. I was making $375 a month on welfare. My rent was $335. I had 40 bucks left and I had to pay heat and phone bills and feed a dog and a cat. (I worked at the food bank—you get better food.)

I met a girl in my building—she was a dancer. I did an audition for an agent and it was pathetic. It was scary. The club was open to the public. Secondly, the agent was there with her following and it was very intimidating. I cried after because she didn't tell me if I was hired or not. I thought, "Jesus, I can't even be a friggin' stripper." Until I started dancing I had a very negative attitude about dancers, like society does, because the media presents us in a very negative light.

But the agent phoned me later on in the week and said she'd book me.

SARITA: When I first went to an agent, it wasn't for stripping. Stripping wasn't in my mind. I went to a musical agent, a guy who was supposed to be handling some big rock 'n' roll bands. I played the guitar and I had a repertoire and I wanted to get a job doing that because I needed the money. I had an infant at the time—my daughter is 15 now—and my husband at the time was a fisherman out of work and things were just really shitty. I had no education and I had no real work experience. But I had my own instrument and I could sing in Spanish and English and I could do this crap better than a lot of the people who were working the lounges. Now, this guy promised me this gig in this hotel, but he was at the time trying to get a piece of the strip action and he tried to convince me to do it.

"Well," he said, "You can make twice as much money." I kept saying no, but the first act I ever did was sit on the beer parlor stage in a Spanish dress, play my guitar, sing in Spanish, take my clothes off, and continue singing. It was very weird. I took everything off, but I wouldn't show it. Nobody ever saw anything. I would never do that now, but I was 19 and it was a big hit and they loved it and I thought, "Well, this isn't so bad. I've got a nice body. And I'm doing something *artistic* [said with irony]."

Then something happened to me. I knew I would never get a job doing lounge work because the first person I went to railroaded me into stripping. The message to me was: "We don't value you. We're never going to care whether you do this [sing and play guitar] but we will care and pay you to do this other thing [strip]." So it was like, "Okay [in a resigned tone]."

SHERI CHAMPAGNE: I was working as a chamber maid at the Holiday Inn. I only had the job for 13 or 14 days. That morning—I remember it was Friday the thirteenth—my boss snapped at me: "Get over there and get your bucket and get to work."

I said, "Take your bucket and fuck it!"

My girlfriend was a dancer so I went down to see her where she worked. While I was there, the club owner pointed at four girls and fired them. He phoned all around trying to get some more girls but couldn't find any. He was panicking. And I needed the money.

When I was six years old I used to entertain the neighborhood kids doing bump and grind. I'd set up a little stage by moving two picnic tables together. One bench was the step to get up onstage and the other bench was used for the audience. I'd dance and take my clothes off to a Tijuana Brass tape. I never charged admission.

Sometimes the reason given is not so much financial need as the desire to simply improve one's circumstances—quickly.

MARY: I wanted to go to Mexico [chuckling]. I wanted to make some money real fast.

My girlfriend suggested it to me. She was a bank teller. She just said, "Go and dance. You can do it."

The first time was pretty shaky. It was like, *WOOOOO!* [making her hair stand on end]. I got up onstage and I just turned around, turned my back on people. That was the only time I was ever really, really nervous. After that it was fine. It came pretty natural.

Then when I was in Mexico I found that I missed it. I missed the dancing. I wasn't flexible at all. That came with time and experience and watching other people and going to dance class.

While financial need is by far the main reason for crossing the line, there are a number of strippers who recognized some benefits in stripping beyond the monetary, such as creative expression or an imagined route to stardom. In such cases the aspiring stripper may seek out the business herself, without an intermediary.

JANE JONES: Basically, it was an opportunity to make extra money. I was going to school at the time, taking classes in water analysis. Previous to that, I was a lab technician working in soil analysis and that got me interested in water analysis. But I found out that it was a pretty dead-end career. It wasn't creative enough. In order to get creative in the scientific world, you're looking at 9 or 10 years of university, at least. I wasn't into that. I wasn't willing to put in the time because I felt the return would be too late. I don't want to get my return in life when I'm between 30 and 40. I want to get it between 20 and 30.

VENUS DE LIGHT: I was an auditor for awhile. Then I decided to move to Hollywood to be a star. I saw ads in the paper there for girls who could make $500 a week and I thought, "Oh Wow! Five hundred dollars!" (I was young.) So I went down and auditioned. The audition consisted of taking my clothes off, turning around and putting them back on just to see if I had tattoos or anything. Then he told me to enter a dance contest. It was in the sleaziest, diviest place in all of Los Angeles. I remember I guzzled down about five or six beers so I wouldn't be nervous but I was so nervous I didn't even feel the beer. I went out on stage. It was the kind of place where you danced to the juke box, a show-your-snatch-for-a-buck kind of place. And I won the contest. I won 100 bucks.

After I got offstage I thought I was going to throw up.

The person who plants the idea in the future stripper's mind also represents an all-important external source of approval for the venture. If the "shepherd" is a trusted friend on the inside, as is often the case, say, a stripper or club owner, she or he will be invaluable in making the transition as comfortable as possible given the anxiety-ridden circumstances.

Teri Starr's story is extraordinary in that she started stripping relatively late in life, in her thirties. She had worked before as a professional dancer "with partners and stuff," so she was familiar with the medium, but she couldn't make enough money at it to survive. She turned to hairdressing, but she still struggled to make ends meet. Her connection to the business was a club owner who, as it happens, used to date her girlfriend.

TERI STARR: It was kind of accidental. It was at the tail end of the go-go era in the middle to late sixties. This was in California. They had the go-go. Then they had the topless. And then they had the bottomless. And then they had the real crude rent the flashlights for a dollar and see where you're gonna stick your tip, that type of thing. That's what was happening when I got into it.

My girlfriend suggested I stop in and see her ex. So I did. And he said, "Why don't you work for me? I'll pay you X amount of money." And god, that was a lot more than I made as a hairdresser. So that's how I got into it.

The only thing that even made me consider stripping was that I do like adventure. I like doing different things, different jobs. I'd never seen a strip show. I had to go three times before I could look above those girls' knees.

At that time in L.A. the deal was three or four or five or six girls on stage at once, like what is happening now across the country. After a couple of weeks of getting my bearings and me being almost 40 years old standing up there with somebody who was almost 20 (and often underage), I thought, "I like this. I really do."

Luscious Lona had the good fortune of being "discovered."

LUSCIOUS LONA: I used to jazz dance. I've been a dancer a lot of years. I was at a night club and I was dancing up a storm with a friend of mine. I was dropping into the splits and spinning and doing kicks and stuff. Nothing really refined, but I was half cut and having a good time. I was wearing spandex pants, suspenders, and a T-shirt. And Katie [Lynch], a stripper's agent who just happened to be there that night, came up to me and said, "Excuse me, but what do you do for a living?"

I said, "I'm a waitress."

She said, "Well, you're crazy. You should be an exotic dancer."

So I thought about it and I said, "No way." I took her card and said I'd think about it.

Later a couple of my girlfriends introduced me to a stripper named Dallas and the three of them took me to strip clubs. And I watched the good, the terrible, and the excellent. I watched and listened. I listened to the comments from the crowd about what she did, what she was wearing, how she presented herself. I've been onstage before. I've sung and played guitar and I've jazz danced onstage, so the stage didn't scare me. It was being naked and what people were going to think.

So after nine months of working out, deciding I looked good enough— I had five shows created with good themes and music—I went in for an audition with Katie. I took my cousin with me because we're really close—we're like brother and sister—and I took my best girlfriend for moral support, had two glasses of wine on an empty stomach because I didn't want to eat—God forbid I should have a pot up onstage, right? Two glasses of wine on an empty stomach and I was really nervous. There were five of us to audition and I pulled last spot. The four that went on before me were terrible. There was one lady who was really pretty, young, nice body, but did not know what to do with it. The two after her—one was over 30 and ugly and the other was about 40 pounds overweight—so I'm thinking, "I feel better now. I'm going to go up there and I know I'm going to do better than they did."

So I went up there. I had created a theme of something like a female cat. My hair was frizzed out and I had cat eye makeup on and a leopard skin halter dress, wide black belt with high black gloves. I crawled across the stage to this guy in a suit and grabbed his tie and looked at him. That made my statement. This was to the song "Maneater."

I had every move figured out. Then I danced a little bit. I grabbed a pole in each hand and threw my hair all over the place. I did "Maneater," "Hungry Like a Wolf," "One on One," and then "Every Breath You Take." I did two floor shows because at the time I did gymnastics and could do walk-overs and stuff. That was fine. I got through the show. I got good applause. I was happy. I stood up, took a bow, and just about fell over because the realization hit me: "You're naked!"

I grabbed my cover-up and threw it on, I was shaking so bad. By then Katie was frantic. She couldn't believe the show I'd just put on. She was going, "You lied to me. You've done this before!"

I said, "Katie, sit me down. I'm going to fall over." I started two weeks after that.

As we saw in Mary's story, sometimes the idea comes from a friend who is not in the business, but who nonetheless has unconventional ideas:

SKY: A friend of mine finally convinced me to do it. I couldn't pay my rent. I was on my own and I was 14 at the time. She convinced me to strip at this party put on by some of her friends. But when I got there I almost walked away because I knew everybody there. My ex-boyfriend was there and all his friends. I was so nervous I kept trying to leave. But she grabbed me and took me into the bedroom and poured me four shots of rye. I got blasted. I figured if I don't do it now, I'm never going to do it. I closed my eyes and went for it.

All these guys were offering me mega-money to go with them and I thought, "Bah! Get out of here!" Instead, my friend and I went out and got hammered. I ended up spending all the money anyway.

When the intermediary is a man, his suggestion may have some star-making motivations behind it:

ROBBIE: A male friend of mine figured I'd be good at it. He brought me down to a bar and put me in Gynecology Row! He made me sit in the front row! I nearly died. I mean, I wasn't used to being around naked women like that. The dancer did a roll right there in front of me. I nearly had a heart attack. I couldn't believe that he would actually put me in the front row.

Then he brought me down to another place and put me up as close as we could get again. I felt like an idiot. I thought, "How could he do this to me?" But I looked at the dancer and thought, "She's got it together here." So I thought I'd just go up to the agency and ask about it.

I filled out the application and did an audition a week later. I was pretty bad. Nah, I was the worst [laughing].

Sometimes the business recruits from its margins, from the club waitresses, hostesses, or coat checkers. Already familiar with the sights and sounds of the stripper's world, they are also conversant with the strippers themselves. Eventually, paychecks are compared, encouragement to go for it prods, and the transition is now just one crucial step through the inhibitions.

DEVLIN DEVINE: I was working at a strip club as a coat check girl. They had stricter morality laws at the time. It had to be like a dinner club if they were going to have nude entertainment. Then I got fired and I got a job at a natural foods restaurant. I worked there for a long time. One day the lady who had been supplying the girls at the strip club came in for lunch and I just started talking with her. I was making minimum wage or something and she supplied hostesses as well as strippers where you'd wear sexy little outfits and serve drinks.

I was not a sexy girl, but I thought, "Well, I'll go in there for the money." So I worked there as a hostess for a little while. But there was a lot of stress going to these large halls where 200 men were drunk out of their minds and grabbing you all the time. But I made really good money in tips. They'd take 10-dollar bills and stuff 'em in here and grab your boob and you had to, you know, smile and be charming and I just wasn't into it at all.

So I just started dancing. I thought, "Why not? Instead of working all night, work for 15 minutes." So then for a year it's almost a blur because I drank so much wine all the time. There was just no way I could get up there straight. I just couldn't. It wasn't me. It wasn't my personality at all. And then I got a grip on it.

I'm still nervous. Every show I'm nervous. Reality hits me all the time when I'm up there. I don't think I'm meant to be in this profession.

JOCELYNE: I was first introduced to dancers when I worked in a coffee shop in a hotel. They worked in the hotel pub and they'd come in to the cafe to eat and they'd tip me really well. I wasn't of age yet, but I'd peek through the kitchen and watch them doing their shows. It really blew my mind. I thought it was gross. Once in a blue moon, a dancer would come in and say to me, "You should be a dancer." But they didn't allow me to associate with the dancers other than in the restaurant for some weird reason. One of the rules was that I couldn't go to the dancers' rooms.

Then one day a dancer snuck me into her dressing room and I tried on some costumes and stuff.

Meanwhile, the man I was in love with had moved to another town to work and one day he called me up and said, "All right! Come on down!" I don't know how he did it, but between the time I got on the bus and the time I arrived, he lost the apartment he had for us, lost his job, and the next thing you know I was in this small town, 17 years old, didn't know anybody at all, and he was treating me like I was just some girl he was seeing once in awhile. He was staying with his aunt and she wouldn't let me stay there with him. So I had to get a hotel. Meanwhile, I only had $200, so the money started running thin. The hotel was $35. The room was so bad, I cried when I saw it. I had never seen anything like that.

I was tanning out on the roof one day and this girl was tanning beside me and she kept getting up and leaving for about 15 or 20 minutes and then coming back. Finally, by the second day, I just had to ask her where she was going. She didn't want to tell me because she was afraid I would not want to be her friend anymore. Eventually she said, "I'm a dancer in the pub." I just laughed.

Two weeks later she had me onstage doing a show. She played a trick on me. She knew I was interested, but she knew it would take a long time before I'd have the guts to do it. I was quite naive and young and gullible. She told me that she sprained her ankle and that they were going to fire her if she didn't do her next show and that the only way she could keep her job was if I did the show for her. And of course I just fell right into believing it.

I wanted to do it so bad, and I was glad it was happening, but I was scared and freaked out at the same time. I said to her, "Make sure you have a costume on and you're right beside the stage just in case I chicken out." She said, "Yeah. Yeah. Okay."

So the next thing you know I was up there doing my show and I looked over and she was still in her jeans and T-shirt.

Some avenues lead to the ultimate exposure of the body on stage by degrees. Some strippers had performed in other dance forms and others started out in wet T-shirt contests or in mud wrestling.

JAY JAY: I've always been a dancer. I was belly dancing when I was nine years old. My mom used to take me to this Greek restaurant where they had this belly dancer. After dinner when everybody was dancing I'd stay in the coat check room with the coat check girl. One day I was copying the moves of the belly dancer and someone grabbed me and pulled me out in the middle of the room and that's how I started.

My mom is a professional designer and she made me a belly dancing outfit.

Later I decided to try out exotic dancing. That was scary. For the first couple of months I was on the phone every other week to my agent—"I can't do it." I think it was the floor work. I could handle taking my clothes off, but having to crawl around on the floor made me uncomfortable.

MARNIER: My friend and I would do these wet T-shirt contests. I would just take my top off. I was too paranoid to take anything else off. That's what we lived on, money from wet T-shirt contests. Gradually I got down to my T-bar and then I got down to nothing and I figured it wasn't as hard as it looked.

CARMALITA: I was in the first year of university and I was really broke. My parents are well off, but I wasn't into taking money from them. I just hated that. I wanted to be independent.

One day I was flipping through the newspaper and I saw an ad for mud wrestlers. So I started off mud wrestling. At the club where I worked they had two levels. On top, on the weekends, they had mud wrestling and sometimes Jell-O wrestling and whipped cream wrestling and what not, and then down below they had strippers from Monday to Saturday.

At first I was really shocked at seeing the strippers because when you're a mud wrestler you're in suits or it was topless and you're always covered in mud so you don't reveal much. But I just gradually got used to the sight of these girls taking their clothes off. And I talked to them and found out how much money they made. They were a really nice bunch of girls and that's probably the thing that made me not mind it so much. I think if they were bitchy and mean and that sort of thing I would never have started.

But they were friendly and said, "Why don't you try it?" They were always giving me encouragement like, "Here, you can use this costume," and "Do this," and "Don't be worried about it."

One night a couple of girls didn't show up for work so it was, "Okay, get Carmalita from upstairs and she's got to go on." So the first time I went on with none of my own tapes, none of my own costumes. It was just do it. I was scared. It was nerve-wracking.

Even if one is recruited from the margins of the business or from some preparatory medium and has had a long time to get used to the idea, or even if support comes from trusted friends on the inside, stripping can still be a traumatic experience. Alcohol and drugs (usually marijuana and or cocaine), therefore, are often used as a means of anesthetizing the shock of exposure. Jocelyne, for instance, confessed to smoking marijuana for that show she was tricked into doing, even though she never liked what the drug did to her. As she explained: "It twists my mind. Like, I don't know where I am or what I'm doing. But I got stoned before that show. For some reason it helped. It helped me to escape reality, to give me enough guts to do it."

PHOEBE: I was fourteen years old and I applied for a job as a waitress at this strip club. They did me up on Grand Marnier, grass, and coke and I got up on stage that very same night and did a set to Pink Floyd's *Dark Side of the Moon*—the whole album. I pulled my pants down and tripped over them. I fell off the stage and cracked my nose. That was ten years ago.

Instead of numbing the senses with drugs or alcohol, the neophyte stripper may call upon some internal source of support, the memory of a consoling voice of authority, for example.

TARA: I was living with my aunt and working in a photography studio part time and at a dress boutique part time—and spending all the money I made there on dresses—and then I wanted to get my own apartment and I saw an ad saying "Dancers Wanted." I liked to dance, but I didn't know it was nude dancing. They said, "You have to take your clothes off." And I went, "Oh!" I left then, but I thought about it.

When I was about 14, I lived in San Diego and there was a place called Black's Beach—it was a nudist beach—and I asked my Dad, "When I'm older, is it okay for me to go there?" and he said: "Sure. Why not? There isn't anything wrong with the human body." And that just kept going through my mind...

The first time I went on, I was scared. There was a big stage and I was very nervous. My knees were knocking. I got up there and they announced, "This is a new girl." So they were all clapping. Then I took off my top and I was like, blind from one end of the stage to the other. I thought if I can't see them, they can't see me.

In Shadow Fire's case, the stimulus which was to remain an indelible source of comfort for her was a dream.

SHADOW FIRE: I went from wet T-shirt contests to dancing. But there was something before that too: a dream. I had a dream. If it hadn't happened to me I probably would not have stuck with it or believed in it as much as I do.

I went to sleep one night and in my dream there was a knock on the door. I walked up to the door and opened it. My half-brother was there. Then suddenly I was in a car accident and I was flying through the air and it looked like I was going to hit the ground. I was terrified, thinking, "Oh my God! I'm going to go *splat!*" Then suddenly my body shifted and I was flying. It was incredibly exhilarating. I couldn't believe how real it was. I woke up in this place and some friends walked in. Then we walked upstairs, except that they went up the stairs and I danced up through these plateaus. This symbolized accelerated progression to me. At the top was a building, which I left and got into a car.

The whole thing threw me right out. Here was a Mormon girl who'd been kicked out of her home and was on welfare and had this dream and shortly thereafter got into wet T-shirt contests.

The next day there was a knock on the door and it was my half-brother…

Kyra's story below illustrates the possibility that the stripper does not concern herself with the opinions of others, a disposition that has triumphed over public opinion. For some people, the craving for experience is a higher criterion than conformity. This hunger for adventure is a latent drive in everybody, but the rigors of earning a living, providing for a family, and retaining a veneer of responsible citizenship are powerful incentives for investing our wildest dreams in, say, the movies. That is, until life delivers a shock that destroys, even temporarily, the ordinary sense of reality.

KYRA: I was living with a man and I was hair dressing and one day I got the news that I might have cancer. It was just a tumor and they removed it, but it started me thinking about a lot of things. I was 21 and just plodding along, you know, just plodding along…

I think after that I just decided that I was going to do everything—whatever it was that came up. I wasn't going to fuck around with bullshit anymore, because I had done it for so long.

I know inside of me that that changed the way I think about a lot of things. I think that's the number one thing that gave me the whatever to do it, to get onstage. Now I have this thing of, "What the fuck, I'm here, then I'm gone." And if I do something like stripping, it's not going to make a difference in anybody's life but my own.

It took me six months to quit my job. It took me a year to leave my boyfriend. I went with $250 and stayed with a girlfriend who had a baby and another roommate. Soon I ran out of money. I didn't want to live there and they couldn't afford to have me there, anyway. I didn't want to call my parents and ask for money and I *didn't* want to go back home. I was totally broke for a week. And this girl told me about strippers and how much money they made. And that you could go to a place and stay there for the whole week in the hotel.

And I thought, "Gee! I could do that for one week, maybe two, and get enough money and find a job!" So now it's two and a half years later and I'm still doing it.

For most strippers, the fact that they survived their first time onstage is an extraordinary rush that makes the next attempt that much easier. Then, at the end of the week, the paycheck solidifies the crossover. Spending the money adds the icing. But there are other benefits to this vocation beyond the money and a sense of accomplishment. As these are the subject of the next chapter, I would like to mention here only one that conveniently allows a place for Marlo's story. For the histrionic types (many of whom may be noticed in the anecdotes above), stripping provides an extraordinary opportunity to display their attributes and be applauded for it. Exhibitionists might fall into the third category above, those for whom the benefits of crossing the line outweigh the consequences.

MARLO (1): I had been a dressmaker and I needed a job. I answered an ad in the paper from an old customer of mine. We had talked over the phone for a long time. But she had never seen me. When I went over there and she saw that I was black she told me the job had just been filled. But I phoned the next day and the job was still open.

This was when I said, "I give up." Why should I slave 16 hours a day and then turn around and have somebody deny me just because of the pigment of my skin? So that's when I started practicing dancing with my girlfriend. She showed me how to take my clothes off slowly and then I did it for her friend once. The third time I did it at her boyfriend's birthday party and they thought I was good. They thought I was getting the hang of it. I still didn't think I was ever going to be a stripper because how could anybody who doesn't even like taking her clothes off in front of a man be a stripper? So I got an idea.

There were these guys across the street who used to look into my apartment with binoculars all the time. So I thought, "Am I ever going to fix these guys!" I was basically pissed off at them, but it was still a good idea. There was a railing on my balcony so they couldn't see the bottom half of me, so I got on a table so they could see all of me [laughing]. Did I ever give them a show!

They were there every day after that.

About a month later I went to an agent and told her I was a professional dancer. I made a costume and had everything ready. She booked me on an oil rig. I got $800 for the week. A rich guy there tipped me with a $50 bill once and then once again. He stood under my window for at least half the night. I kept saying to him, "Go home. You're going to freeze to death!"

He said, "It would be worth freezing to death for you."

3
The Up Side

When I'm on the stage, I'm living the fantasy.
Gio

Most strippers will say that the sole attraction to this controversial line of work was the money. And for many, the decision to work as a stripper was made during a time of financial crisis. Is income security the stripper's real motivation or is it merely a rational explanation for doing something brazenly rebellious, if not deliciously perverse?

A certain view prevails in the mainstream that stripping is the outward expression of an inner drama, that it is less an act than a purging of a resident demon. The majority view of stripping holds that it is neither a vocation nor an art form: it is an aberration. Women who strip have forfeited their right to belong in the mainstream; they are outcasts. To be willing to pay such a price, one must be either insane or hopelessly incorrigible. Either way, from the point of view of the moderate majority, the stripper is considered to be intrinsically tainted.

Before we examine some possible psychological motivations underlying stripping, much has to be said for the surface rewards. If there were no indwelling demon, the money *would* be reason enough. The average stripper can earn between $800 and $1,300 a week and headliners (or features) can easily double that. Mitzie Dupree, "The Ping Pong Queen," claimed she made $4,000 a week "with a bottle of Dom Perignon a day written into [her] contract"[1] before her arrest on obscenity charges in 1984. A woman with no abilities or attributes other than a reasonably nice figure and the courage to step through her inhibitions can immediately have the earning power of a young lawyer.

In addition to the money, there are several nonmaterial rewards that might be expected to accrue from *any* stage show. First and foremost is ego gratification. Onstage, the stripper becomes the center of a small galaxy, a star surrounded by gazers.

25

SARITA: Unfortunately, I belong to that group of people that needs adulation. I was born for it. I was born to be in show business. It isn't just the money. It's the adulation. You get addicted to it. I've seen girls start out who were really shy and fearful who planned to do it for some quick cash, for a short period of time, maybe to pay some bills. I've seen them go out there and get hooked on it, seen their personalities change. I've seen them go snake. The audience applause changes them. They take on a pseudo-personality. They lose sight of who they are. They become somebody else. They become prima donnas.

The ability of the vulva to attract attention has few rivals. Because society demands that it be covered up, its appearance in public is an anomaly, and one that inspires a host of reactions. Its beauty, its mystery, its meaning, its desire, its danger, and its intrigue—even an unappealing dancer will stop conversations and turn heads when she finally removes her G-string. One of the starker realities of life comes into play here: an unattractive woman can still redeem herself in the eyes of men by exposing her genitals.

Since genital attention is gratuitous, the measure of a professional stripper lies in her ability to entertain over and above the expectations of the audience, and by so doing, to create raucous applause. The men will clap politely for most shows but they may bring the house down for something exceptional. The trick is to stimulate at least one other area of the viewing brain than the purely sexual, to traverse the path to the ultimate exposure with humor, acrobatics, theatrics, or imaginative costumes, with in a word, style.

On some level, the stripper recognizes the burden of tension in the audience. Their collective desire for her conflicts with the reality of her unavailability and searches for avenues of socially acceptable release. The professional stripper strives to create rapport with her audience so that their applause will seem to them a worthy gift to her, when it is just as much a way of blowing off steam. The more dynamic her act—the more she appears to be providing for her admirers—the louder and longer is the applause.

Once in a while the stripper earns a standing ovation and there's nothing quite like it.

GIO: Nothing compares to the standing ovation. Especially when I know that I did a good job. When I know inside myself that I didn't make one mistake, that everything came together, the costume worked perfectly, the sound was perfect, the lights were good, there isn't any comparison. You can't compare a sexual orgasm to that kind of thing.

I wish more girls had the opportunity to understand that it can be that great. All they have to do is be able to conceive of how high you can get from applause.

LUSCIOUS LONA: I put together a Tina Turner set. She was hot at the time. She had just come out with the *Private Dancer* album. I did "Better Be Good to Me," "What's Love Got to Do with It," and "Private Dancer." I had a black cape that was just long enough to cover my bum and then black bra, G-string, a couple of studded belts, and studded little hand pieces in leather. I did a cape show to "Better Be Good to Me." The cape was black on one side and red on the other and under the strobe light it looked really effective.

So I did this and I was thinking, "Hey, like, I'm doing a good show. I'm feeling great about this."

I had a smile from ear to ear. I was right into my music and into the crowd. It was a packed house: 350 to 400 people.

They were really good for my first song and then the money started to come onto the stage. I did a shower show as part of my floor show and there was about an inch of water on the stage because my hair holds a lot of water and I was spraying it ten feet on either side. Suits were water-spotted everywhere. Water was flying all over the place and there was more and more money and every time I rolled over, more bills stuck to me. There was everything from quarters, handfuls of quarters, to $20 bills, and it was still coming...

I got to the end of my song, "Private Dancer," ... stood up ... and they were quiet! Nothing! ... For what seemed like an hour! My mind was racing. "What'd I do?

And then suddenly they all stood up and started screaming! I was so blown away, I dropped down on my knees.

Stripping gets no notice as a theatrical medium anymore, but to the stripper it is a wonderful opportunity to explore various persona. She can play the vamp, the coquette, the rock star, the rodeo queen, the Barbie doll, the Southern belle, the Grecian goddess, the *femme fatale*, the dominitrix, the virgin bride, the nun—the possibilities are endless. In Venus De Light's words: "You get to play Miss Dress Up again."

BILLIE JO: A dancer can be anybody she wants to be up there. If she wants to be Alice Cooper, she can be Alice Cooper. If she wants to be hard like "Pain and Passion"[2] or soft like girls who do these "Like a Virgin" songs—all done up like teeny boppers—whatever she wants to be up there.

For me, it lets out a lot. If I'm angry, then I can put on something like "Rebel Yell" and do a whip show or I can come out with a sword like I'm a warrior; or if I'm in a really good mood, I'll get into something like a tribute to Elvis.

If you can portray what you want to be, instead of just getting up there, walking around, and taking your clothes off, the audience will see that, too.

I like expressing my music. It's just like being a singer. When I'm dancing, my body is my instrument.

And then there's the power trip:

> GIO: When I'm up onstage, it's a power trip. It's an ego trip and I play it for all it's worth. I am smart enough to recognize where the power is. The minute I am off the stage, I revert back to my normal self. When I'm on the stage, I'm living the fantasy that I can control all these people in the room, that they're all paying attention to everything that I'm doing up there.

As she begins to find her stage legs, as anxiety turns into excitement, the neophyte stripper rediscovers the pleasures of dancing. One could watch strippers for a long time and not see the dancing. With our eyes on their bodies and our minds held fast to the anticipation of the final act, the dancing is seen only peripherally. Of course, consciousness given to dance appreciation is consciousness unavailable to sexual fantasy.

The pinnacle of dancing is probably ballet, which is an Everest away from striptease. Trying to imagine an overtly sexual ballet is problematic: the mind oscillates between sexual fantasy and the appreciation of grace. After all, sex is something we descend to; art is something we exalt. As George Santayana observed, "High art cancels lust."

The tension between sex and art has always been pivotal to exotic dancing. In more modest times the entertainment value of burlesque was the cover for its titillation. Now, the clamor for open genitals threatens to eclipse any pretension to style or grace. The majority of strippers would prefer a G-string law to shift the emphasis away from genital exposure and back to dancing as a performing art.

While for the man in the audience the interest is heavily sexual, for the stripper the dance is the thing. Most strippers love this part of their job. (Many have at some time studied jazz and ballet; some are simply born boppers.) The thrill of movement, the taut arabesques, the music pulsing through their veins, and their personal trademark on the infinite variety of styles makes dancing fun, creative, and loaded with verve.

Dancing in its simplest, most primitive expression is synonymous with freedom. It mocks the very cool, rigid, defensive way we normally behave. Dancing is joy; it is a leap into life's rhythms. Nude, the dancer is an expression of freedom at its starkest. Could it be that dancing in the nude produces a special euphoria? As Emery enthused, "I love dancing. I love dancing to death. When I leave this business, I don't know what I'm going to do without music and dance as a daily part of my life."

Stripping is the freest dancing there is. Whatever choreography informs the show is completely at the whim of the performer. She can sleep through it or she can create mayhem.

In an occupation devoted to the glorification of the body, self-worship is an ever-present pitfall. One stripper told her agent, "My boyfriend and I are so beautiful that when we stand nude together in front of the mirror and look at ourselves, we come."

One of the core ironies of this business is that while so much attention is paid to the body in the pursuit of electrifying men, the men who compliment strippers on their bodies are written off as geeks. This is not to say that, from the right sort of person, a stripper will not appreciate compliments about her body, it's just that it's so gratuitous. "Of course you like my body! I'm a stripper, remember?"

But narcissism can be healthy. The daily aerobics, skin care, hair care, and the workouts all add up to physical fitness. Though their bodies come in a variety of forms, they all share a degree of supple resilience. A few strippers are true gymnasts, bringing the word home again to its original meaning of naked exercise.

Together, the money, the approval, the artistic expression and the physical fitness are not enough for the vast majority of women to seriously consider stripping as a career. Social condemnation is too high a price to pay. But social belonging withers as a motivator when things get desperate. There are some rebels and some eccentrics in these pages who took to the stripper's stage with an eye for adventure, but, for the majority, the job represented some form of security. When daily life reduces to a seemingly hopeless struggle to maintain bare essentials, everything one has becomes negotiable, including one's social approval. The stigma of the social outcast is small change compared to being down and out.

Economic survival ought to be sufficient justification for being a stripper, but somehow it just isn't. The woman spreading her legs mere inches from a stranger's nose and smacking her lips about it does not present a very convincing picture of a labor of necessity. From the point of view of the social insider, nothing but an aberrant drive of some kind could possibly account for this behavior. In the shadow of Freud it is easy to think that someone so artfully naughty must be dealing with a peculiar unconscious drive. We might easily intuit that the stripper is working out some unresolved issue or enduring childhood trauma.

It is taken as a given in the general population that early influences on the future stripper could not have been ideal. She could not have come from a good home, for instance. Rather, we think of her as having emerged from a shadowy place brooding with alcoholism, violence, neglect and, most probably, sexual abuse.

A prevalent assumption about strippers and prostitutes (who are often lumped together) is that they must have been sexually abused as children. Some veteran strippers, after hearing the story over and over again in dressing rooms all over the country, have also come to believe this is true.

> MICKEY: It is very common among dancers. I've noticed that a lot of dancers were sexually abused by their fathers, stepfathers or neighbors. I would venture to say six or seven out of ten. I was shocked at how many girls confided in me. "Oh yeah? It happened to you, too?"

> TRACY TSAR: I remember one really sad girl I worked with. She'd get up on stage and you could see her deteriorate before your eyes. She'd start dancing and she'd start to get uptight and she would get nervous and more uptight and she wouldn't be rhythmical and you'd see her get more and more tense. And as she got more naked, she'd become just a vibrating mess.
> We used to say to her, "Why don't you quit?"
> "I can't quit. It's the only thing I know how to do. I want to be a dancer. I love to dance." And she obviously hated every minute she was onstage.
> She had this horrible tale about being abused by her father as a young girl and every time she was out there dancing, she saw him in her mind's eye. She used to torture herself onstage. It was very sad.

The quick persuasiveness of the sexual abuse hypothesis is that it roots an aberrant occupation in an aberrant childhood. (It also allows us to feel some pity for strippers, to look down on them from a position of superior mental health.) This hypothesis is, however, too simple an explanation for too complex a subject. For one thing, surveys indicate that between 20 and 35 percent of females in the United States and Canada have been sexually abused.[3] Obviously, these women did not all become strippers. Until a comparative study reveals a significantly higher incidence of childhood sexual abuse among strippers than women in the general population any assumptions about strippers are purely speculative.

Another theory is that inside every stripper is a little girl vying for the attention she never received from her father. Strippers themselves see some merit in this theory. They remember fathers who were absent physically as well as emotionally: alcoholic fathers, unaffectionate fathers, fathers who were always too busy with work, and fathers who were never on the scene at all. Sometimes it was just that there were so many children in the family there wasn't enough affection to go around. Other influences may also come into play, as demonstrated by the following interviews.

KARIN WEST: A lot of girls are looking for something from the business that they're not getting. They're looking to be loved. A lot of girls had shitty relationships with their fathers. My father was my stepfather. My real father left when I was ten. He was a complete jerk.

There is a point when she's young that every little girl really needs to be told by her father, who is the primary male image in her life, that she's pretty and that she's loved. And if her father does not tell her this, she'll start looking for it in other men as she grows up.

When I started to realize this, I began asking girls about their family life and there were so many in the business who had no strong male image in their early years, it was outrageous. It was true for about 90 percent of them.

MUSIDORA: I had a pretty rough childhood. I had good parents but I've had a lot of tragedy in my life. My father was a very strict man. He used to be really rough on us. No sexual abuse, but he beat us often.

He had diabetes and choked to death on his pills.

I had a sister who was terminated some years ago. A crime of passion. She was annihilated by a jealous wife. The wife went to an insane asylum after. Her husband, the man my sister was involved with, was no prize, let me tell you. I didn't like him from the word go. When I met him the room took on a gray hue. I very rarely see auras but I saw his and it was black. I pulled my sister aside and I said, "What are you doing with this guy? He's going to hurt you more than you know." She was furious with me and wouldn't speak to me for two weeks.

Maybe this is my subconscious way of getting back. Like, getting up onstage is saying, "I've got power over you guys."

JANUS: My Dad kicked me out because he felt I was being a slut. It was a very violent ending. I think it stemmed from his repressed rage at my mother. He attacked me with a hammer. He hit me with it and then I got it away from him. Then he choked me. I was about to pass out. For the first time in my life I saw red. I woke up on the floor and we were in a deadlock and I was about to shatter his manhood. That's when we split. That's also the day I started smoking.

LUSCIOUS LONA: I had a terrible childhood, absolutely rotten. Up until I was 19 I had the worst inferiority complex. I thought I was plain and unattractive. I had an older sister who let me know that I couldn't dance, I couldn't sing, I couldn't do anything I tried to do. I was a straight A student because I totally immersed myself in my school work. I had no friends. My father was rarely home because he was a fisherman and my mother was usually busy with my younger sister.

That memories of a lack of affection and a distant father are common to strippers has been supported by an important study to which we will return shortly.

The most obvious assumption about strippers is that they are exhibitionists. (Who else could possibly delight in such a thing?) This label attaches itself easily in our minds because it seems merely descriptive. It is one of those words that, having been conscripted for psychology from common usage (as were narcissist and fetishist), now has a foot in two camps. The word exhibitionist now describes a person afflicted with a particular psychological syndrome and, by extension, any person whose behavior is in some way similar. As a result, in its wider sense, exhibitionist carries with it implications of psychopathology.

When it is applied to strippers, the label has further implications. For one, it places all the power with the audience (and with men in general). The assumed compulsion the label imparts depends on voyeurs for its expression. The voyeur can actually feel some gratification that he is doing the stripper a favor.

For another, if the show is all about exhibitionism, then there is no room for courage or joy or artistic expression and little room for style. The voyeur (viewer) applauds her only to encourage her to continue.

The term "exhibitionist" makes unorthodox behavior understandable, even though it conveys no real understanding of its meaning. The assumption is that psychologists have an explanation for it and that is enough.

Fundamentally, the label dehumanizes. It's now them and us: we who are the psychologically healthy and they who are the affected. By linking antisocial behavior with pathology it makes a subtle contribution to the maintenance of conformity.

Just what is an exhibitionist? What do psychologists comprehend in the term? And do strippers qualify?

Within psychology the label has gone through many refinements since its coinage in the late nineteenth century. A current definition has it that true exhibitionists "practice exposure as a means of sexual relief in preference to all other means."[4] The salient feature of this behavior *so defined* is that it is almost (if not completely) unheard of in women.

There are numerous case histories (as well as criminal records) of male flashers the world over, but very few of females. It is generally accepted among Freudian psychologists that the flasher is reacting against unconscious feelings of being castrated, that the commotion he causes by baring his genitals upon the unsuspecting public is reassurance of the power of his penis.

David Allen explains, "Since genital exhibiting for women cannot act as a reassurance against feeling castrated, it is clear why feminine exhibitionism as a perversion is in both theory and fact virtually non-existent."[5] The flasher has no real female counterpart.

However, the absence of such *behavior* in women should not necessarily preclude the presence of a similar *impulse*. Perhaps the same impulse that drives a man to expose himself to strangers—by virtue of the fact that it filters through different biology (not to mention upbringing)—emerges in women as different behavior. Instead of the flasher, what emerges in women is the *femme fatale* or the Circe,[6] who seduces without any intention of completion: "The Circe syndrome in women is closely related to the impulses toward genital exhibitionism..." The unconscious formula here is: "I am castrated and have an ugly genital part. Very well, then, Circe-like, through beauty and seduction I will turn men into rooting pigs, ugly and castrated like me."[7]

Superficially, the relationship between the stripper and some of her viewers appears to replicate that between a Circean presence and a captive audience: burly men wilting before the naked aplomb of the dancer, the drunken descent into rowdiness, the catatonic submission to the stripper's pranks, the crude comments, when the men become either hopelessly enthralled or regressively bestial.

What a wonderful place then for a would-be Circe. The stripper's stage offers the *femme fatale* a relatively safe place to do her thing and endless meaningless men to grovel at her feet.

However, the validity of rooting an occupation (whether it be doctor, garbage collector, or stripper) in a hypothetical drive is questionable. At the moment we have a tenuous thread linking male exhibitionists with Circean women and the latter again with strippers. The thread comes home: strippers are exhibitionists. And yet there is something profoundly dissatisfying about this equation. Though both expose their genitals to strangers of the opposite gender, strippers and flashers differ in critical ways. The essential link between them is our assumption that they share a similar resident demon, a similar compulsion. But how do we measure such a thing? According to some social scientists, the answer is that we should do it with a great deal of skepticism:

> Primarily ... it seems problematic to argue backward from people's present behavior to prior psychological predispositions. Most of the studies on prostitution, for instance, are replete with this type of "psychologizing." Further, the literature on exhibitionism does not delineate clearly the range of behaviors covered by the term. As indicated by [Leonard] Blank and [Robert] Roth, "The line between conventional and aberrant expression for this behavior is a blurred one."[8]

What is needed is a comparative study of strippers and clinical exhibitionists, which brings us to the research of Edwin Wagner, a psychologist at the University of Akron, Ohio. Wagner set out to find indications of the exhibitionistic content of the unconscious in both clinically diagnosed male exhibitionists and strippers. Using Rorschach ink blots and Wagner's own invention, the Hand Test (a series of cards with pictures of hands in various gestures that the subject is asked to interpret), he tested 7 strippers, 12 exhibitionists, and a control group of non-strippers and non-exhibitionists for "exhibitionistic, voyeuristic, sexual and aggressive tendencies."[9] Though he refers to both groups as "exhibitionists," Wagner is careful to point out some crucial differences:

1. The strippers were all female and the exhibitionists all male.
2. Professional stripping is legal and, while sometimes frowned upon, it enjoys a certain amount of social acceptance; exhibitionism is not only legally proscribed but is regarded with distaste and contempt by the vast majority of society.
3. Interview data indicated that the stripper's feelings, while she performs, vary from mild elation to bored detachment; the exhibitionist usually experiences heated and anxious excitement.
4. The stripper deliberately chooses her profession—at least partially for financial remuneration; the exhibitionist is compulsively driven to expose himself for purely emotional reasons.
5. Stripping is a continuous, routine mode of earning a living; the exhibitionistic performance is sporadic, impulsive and avocational.
6. The stripper shows off secondary sexual areas while the exhibitionist almost always exposes his penis.[10]
7. Strippers presumably strive for attention, admiration, attraction; the

exhibitionist reportedly has a somewhat hostile need to startle, frighten, and impress his victim.

We can add to this list that the stripper's audience is there voluntarily while the exhibitionist's is not.

Wagner's findings have a few surprises. His interpretation of the strippers' responses to the Rorschach and Hand images is that they showed *more* exhibitionistic tendencies than the exhibitionists themselves. However, the exhibitionists scored higher than the strippers on the sexually disturbed and aggressive scale, while the strippers showed no significant deviation from the control group of other women. Wagner concludes, "Strippers are no more aggressive or sexually disturbed than other women."[11]

A shortcoming of Wagner's research is that his samples were noticeably small. In addition, his strippers were interviewed and tested in the strip club between shows, hardly a neutral or clinical setting.[12] Wouldn't anyone's responses to Rorschach blots have more sexual content in a strip club than, say, in a church?

Wagner is also guilty of arguing backward. He concludes that strippers' "pronounced exhibitionistic tendencies," indicated by the test results, "probably contribute[d] to their choice of vocation," without demonstrating that these tendencies were present before they became strippers. While he allows that "the explanation for the greater number of exhibitionistic responses among strippers [compared with the exhibitionists] may be ... vocational (the stripper exposes herself constantly),"[13] he does not go the necessary step further and allow that vocation may be the reason for the disparity between strippers and other women. Who's to say that anyone working in that environment for that length of time (an average of 8.3 years in Wagner's sample) would not develop similar responses to the tests? Without the results of tests conducted *before* these women became strippers, the inference that inordinate exhibitionistic tendencies led them to the stage is unscientific.

Perhaps the most widely read study of strippers in the post-burlesque era was that undertaken by the two sociologists, James Skipper, Jr., and Charles McCaghy.[14] In this study the inference of exhibitionistic tendencies rests on the strippers' accounts of their personal histories rather than on psychological testing. The researchers found several common factors in their sample of 35 strippers. On the average their subjects' physical development, awareness of their physical attractiveness, and first sexual experiences all occurred at an earlier age than for women in the general population. They also left home earlier.

The distant father influence gets a lot of support here. Skipper and

McCaghy report that 60 percent of their sample came from "broken and unstable homes, where they received little attention and affection. A characteristic feature was the absence of the father from the home, or if he was present, his disintegrating influence on family relationships."[15] (They estimate the corresponding figure for the general population to be less than 30 percent.)

Skipper and McCaghy construct a sequential model for the choice of stripping as an occupation. The future stripper (they theorize) comes to realize that her sexual attractiveness brings her the attention and affection she did not get at home. Consequently, she gravitates toward jobs involving the display of her body (70 percent of their sample had worked either in show business, as artists' models, waitresses, or barmaids before becoming strippers). A financial crisis develops in her life. A friend or someone she has met introduces her to the business and informs her of the economic rewards. In view of her circumstances and her skills training, there is little choice but to give stripping a try.

Beginning with the point of financial crisis, this model is consistent with many of the personal histories of strippers presented in Chapter 2, but the evidence for a general prior psychological disposition toward gaining affection through the display of the body is speculative at best. For one, the authors studied their strippers in the late 1960s and compared them with two studies of the general population of women conducted in 1953 and 1962. It is quite conceivable that "early coital experience" and "early independence and departure from home" were (and remain) a reflection of the social upheavals of the 1960s, in particular the so-called sexual revolution, and not anything significant to strippers. We cannot be certain, from the information presented here, that in their teens strippers were more sexually precocious than their contemporaries.

Another factor to consider is that polls, such as Alfred Kinsey's landmark study of female sexual behavior—the 1953 study referred to above—have been criticized simply because people do not always answer honestly about their sex lives. It has been suggested that people will tend to give a more conservative overview of their sexuality in conservative times (such as the 1950s) and insinuate a more active sex life when the pendulum has swung the other way (as it did in the following decade).

Skipper and McCaghy conscientiously point out that, in view of what passes for socially acceptable dress for women, it is difficult to define the line beyond which one can with certainty level the charge of exhibitionism. Nevertheless, they are moved to observe: "There is, however, a consistent pattern among our subjects of using their physical attributes for affectional and economic advantage prior to their entrance into the occupation."[16] In view of the fact that marriage still offers an economic advantage to most women, and that in most modern cultures physical attractiveness is considered to be a major component in the making of a marriage, the authors' assessment could probably apply to most females almost anywhere.

A comparison of the Wagner study with that of Skipper and McCaghy illustrates that arguing backward from present behavior to motivations rooted in childhood is speculative at best. In Wagner's hypothesis strippers act out the methods they used to get attention in childhood. In Skipper and McCaghy's hypothesis they are compensating for the attention they did *not* get. Perhaps it is a bit of both, but is any other occupation fundamentally different? Do not doctors, lawyers, sports figures, and politicians also seek approval through their respective vocations? Is writing a groundbreaking paper on thermodynamics ("Look how smart I am") fundamentally less exhibitionistic than stripping with style ("Look how attractively adept I am")? Or, to view the issue from another angle, if strippers are driven by exhibitionistic urges, then are garbage collectors driven by a neurotic compulsion to clean up the world? Are doctors fixated on the body? Do all shoe salesmen have a foot fetish?

The difference between the vocation of stripping and those of doctor, lawyer, shoe salesman, and garbage collector is that stripping is apprehended as deviant. That is to say, it is not culturally sanctioned. Deviant, in this sense, has come to mean more than simply a deviation from the norm; the term has acquired the additional implications of the disorderly, the immoral, the unhealthy, and the contaminating. On what constitutes deviance, however, there is no universal agreement. It merely reflects a particular culture's way of defining who are the insiders and who are the outsiders, who are the morally correct and who are not. The transition of Christians from the status of deviants in Imperial Rome to the very arbiters of Roman morality is only one example of how such cultural perceptions can change.

The stripper is viewed as deviant because disrobing in public is not socially sanctioned behavior, especially for a woman. But deviant behavior must also imply a deviant psychological makeup, otherwise we would have to explain how a healthy person can willfully choose to behave in a deviant way. To admit that normal, healthy people might remove their clothes in a public place puts tremendous pressure on the underlying cultural assumptions that make such behavior unacceptable. To even suggest that a stripper may be as psychologically healthy as the rest of us tends to legitimize her behavior. The easiest resolution of this conflict is to view the stripper from the point of view of culture and to search for the sources of her deviance, not in the validity of its definition but in her psyche. This bias may explain such lapses of scholarship as allowing that years on the job may account for strippers' higher test scores measuring exhibitionism as compared with clinical exhibitionists, but not as compared with normal women. The bias facilitates the leap from observations of present behavior to the conclusion that an exhibitionistic predisposition was a causal factor in the choice of stripping as an occupation.

The issue of exhibitionism is most intriguing where it concerns strippers, because the need for approval that we accept and expect in all performers (let alone all people) becomes subverted by what strippers make us observe. In the hypnotic and disturbing glare of exposed genitals the conventional suddenly becomes clinical, self display becomes exhibitionism. The stigma attached to stripping is so entrenched in our culture that it is almost impossible to view it objectively as just another occupation.

Speculations on the psychological motivations of strippers (as opposed to lawyers or doctors) serve to reinforce the prevailing assumption that stripping is rooted in pathology when a much simpler approach serves to resolve the issue. Let's imagine for a moment that exhibitionism never existed, either as a pathology or as a concept. Surely strip shows would still exist, simply because there remains a market for them. When we stop watching the dancer for a moment and look around us, we might see that the need for genital exposure does not reside in the stripper but rather in the men who are willing to pay for it.

What do strippers have to say about this subject? Do *they* think they are exhibitionists?

> CRYSTAL ROSE: No. In the 12 years I've been a stripper, I can think of only 2 that went to nude beaches or things like that. Most of them are very conservative.
>
> I wouldn't do it without the lights and the music and the makeup and the props and the action because it just seems kind of ridiculous otherwise.

> MELISSA WOLF: I could never go to a nude beach and take my clothes off. I could never do that. I don't know how people do that. Millions and millions of strange people stark naked on a beach suntanning. I would be too shy. I couldn't do that. That's weird, eh? And I get on-stage and I can flaunt it and spread it and do whatever.

> KYRA: The first time I went to a nude beach was last summer. I took my clothes off. I felt like an idiot. I stood up and walked over to buy a beer and I put my shirt on. I am basically a really shy person. If I'm changing in front of a man and I don't really know him, I'll tell him to turn his head.

MOUSANNA: Not all of us are. But here's a funny story. Working in Florida I met a group of college kids. They came to the club to see my show. Well, we had such a good time, they invited me to their house for a late-night party. When I got there I wanted to take a shower. So I took a shower and one of the girls came into the bathroom. Instinctively, I wrapped the towel around myself and she just looked at me. And we started to laugh. Here I had been taking my clothes off in front of these people all night and here I was feeling so modest at the end.

Sarita (a 10 year veteran, now retired) has a motivational theory of her own that is part exhibitionism and part rebelliousness.

SARITA: It's the "fuck you" psychology: "I hate men and I'm going to make you bastards pay." And there's "You told me I was a bad girl all my life. Well, fuck you. I'll show you who's *really* bad." Anger plays a big part. It's not very well understood by the people who possess it nor are they really and truly conscious of it. But it is there. Scratch the surface and you are going to find some very hurt and angry little girls. It goes back to somewhere along the line a little girl finds out that she can press buttons just by virtue of the fact that she's a girl. All of us go through that: "Hey, I've got something that men pay attention to, that I can press buttons with. It's called my *sexuality*. I can cause all kinds of upheavals. I mean, I can go and ask for an abortion and cause a great ruckus in our society. I can go and take my clothes off and have people freaked out."

The energy applied to making strippers psychologically different serves only to deflect attention away from our own personal dramas. The fact remains that everyone is the product of a dysfunctional family. No one has ever been unconditionally loved for who he or she truly is. At some point in our upbringing, judgments against the expression of certain heartfelt emotions were installed in us and a dispossessed self created with which we struggle the rest of our lives. The stripper can't help but be a mirror for many people's dispossessed selves, since unbridled sexual expression has been forbidden to all of us. Our issue with the stripper is really a reflection of our attitudes about our own sexual selves.

Some strippers, such as Sarita, have a sense that their vocation provides an opportunity to work through some unresolved issues. Jennie, another 10 year veteran (also retired), who has a bookcase lined with titles like *The Complete Illustrated Shakespeare*, *The Women's Encyclopedia of Myths and Secrets*, and *A Psychiatrist's World*, plus glossy art books on Bosch and Matisse, says it's all about erasing the tapes in the mind.

Before we can develop a voice of our own, she says, we are overwhelmed with the voices of others. All the dos and don'ts of the adult world, tied as they are to love and pain, become persistent echoes in our ears. "Stop!" they say. "Don't do that!" "You'll hurt yourself!" "Don't be stupid!" "You can't do that!" "You're bad!" "Why can't you do it right?" "You'll never make it." "Be a good girl!" Over and over until each is etched on a circular tape in a seemingly endless bank; the voices of authority become an unappeasable fixture of the mind. Before too long the self becomes lost in a cacophony of denial.

One way back to the true voice of the self, Jennie says, is to "play the tapes out," to steep yourself in the experience of the implied taboo. Do everything you're not supposed to; become an outlaw; get down and dirty; and naked.

Stripping affords an excellent opportunity to play the tapes out, she says.

> SARITA: All women have deep-seated anxieties about their bodies, and how attractive they are to men. We all have deep-seated anxieties about how guilty we really are as women. Are we bad girls? There is a guilt syndrome in women who do this kind of job related to being a bad girl. Something is operating there: "I'll do this *because* I'm a bad girl," or "I'll prove to myself that if I do this, I'll be able to live with it, to neutralize it, to see that it's no big deal." In other words, face your fear. Once you do it, you can make nothing out of it.

The first step through the taboo on public nudity can be terrifying. It is not just a step into the feeling of being naked in front of others, it is also a formidable step into the feeling of being completely vulnerable. Many strippers have a sense that their ordeal is somehow therapeutic. The business of stripping has all the makings of an odyssey, a trial by fire, where the exertions of the outer world are refracted in an inner journey.

> VENUS DE LIGHT: I figured if I could get up onstage and strip I could do anything. I was too nervous to get into auditioning for shows and stuff because I was too inexperienced. So I figured this would give me the experience. If you can take your clothes off in front of people, you can do anything.

> JENNIE: I went through various stages of growth the same as everybody else. I became very much aware of myself as a woman. I became very much aware of myself as a sexual being. And then I lost that awareness of myself as a sexual being. I just became a being. The sexuality did not matter. What mattered most of the time was what I was feeling in my heart. And that had nothing to do with the audience. A lot of times I would forget that I was an entertainer.

Dancing ended up being an awakening for me. I consider it very important that I was a dancer in my development as a human being. It gave me a tremendous amount of strength. It also woke me up to a deeper insight into what life was all about, into the struggles of life, and not to accept that it was defeating but to embrace it because it's really a beautiful place. But you have to learn that.

I remember being onstage one day. A lot of changes were taking place in my own consciousness and it was like I woke up from a big, long dream. I was standing there looking out at the men in the audience and suddenly my heart just ached for them. And it ached for me, too. I looked at us both and I thought, "Boy, have we got a long way to go here." I thought, "At least I can leave. They're still going to be here." I knew that my life lesson at that point was somehow to learn compassion for people and myself. It was like, there they are. They're sitting in that miserable little room. All they've got is their beer, their cigarette, and their wife or their girlfriend and their argument or their buddy that they're fighting with. They have a few good chuckles, but basically their bodies are fucked.

SHADOW FIRE: I didn't believe I could do anything on my own. I had a low esteem value. I've never felt worthy of anything. In becoming a dancer I felt worthy. I felt that I was somebody who made a difference. I was somebody who mattered. People needed me. When I was on that stage I had their attention, which was something I lacked when I was younger.

MISS BRAZIL: I've become far more confident. I like myself more. My body looks much better. I carry myself well. I feel healthy. My dancing is getting better and that pleases me to no end. When I can do things that I couldn't do at one time, when I practice and practice and practice and I do it, there is a great feeling of accomplishment. I've learned so much in the business from meeting all these different people. All my experiences—bad and good—have taught me a lot.

GIDGET: I've learned a lot about men in their *true* form. I was very naive and very innocent when I started in the business and now I know what men are really like. And there's not too many of them I trust. I've seen married men come in and let their hair down and I just know what they're like now. It was a good education for me.

I was from the old school, a Southern Baptist. You were a housewife and a mother and that was it. Husbands did whatever they wanted to do and the wife stayed at home. Now I'm very independent. I wouldn't get married now, not if he was the most perfect guy in the world.

CRYSTAL BLUE: I'm really good at reading lips. When I get offstage I can tell you what those two dudes over there were talking about while I was dancing. My hearing has also gotten better. Again, I can be dancing onstage and I can hear two dudes over there talking about my breasts or, you know, whatever.

I'm 21 years old and it's made me older in a way in my brain because I have experienced a lot of things that most 21 year olds won't experience until they're 25. I've done a lot of traveling. I've met a lot of different people.

I know how to read people. So if I was to meet someone and he was a goof, I would know right away. It's the same thing with the dancers. If one of the girls is a goof, if she's a thief, or she talks a lot about the wrong things, you know and you stay away from her.

I'm harder now because of the reality that, at 18 years old, taking my clothes off was just pushed in my face and it's like—Wow! [sighing]. This whole big balloon has just burst and I'm finding out all these new things. So it's made me mature a lot.

I control my feelings a lot better. I'm an extremely sensitive person— I'm an Aries. I will not let people hurt my feelings. I'll just shut it out and not let it bother me. That's come now.

JENNIE: I don't feel it's necessary to have to justify being an exotic dancer. We are who we are. For each one of us to set ourselves free from who we are we have to discover ourselves; and it's however you choose to discover yourself. Through suffering you decide. You want to do one of two things. You can continue on a road to a dead-end street or you can grow. It's when you realize that you are in control of yourself that you decide to make that change, that you are responsible.

After all the money, the applause, the fantasy, and the whims of the inner journey, there is another reason for being a stripper: it's a buzz.

It's the buzz of showbiz, the pizzazz, the snap and sizzle of life after dark, the glitz and the gusto: it's all of these, but with an extra twist. This is a life whose sails are set for commotion.

Strippers live life on the edge, without refuge or anchor, spun out on a reckless adventure that has unlimited possibilities for jangling the nerves.

It is life in the wild. Its hook is the lust for adventure, to live life up-tempo, to hobnob with the outlaws. It's like joining the circus or living in a border town: the days are hazy and the nights crackle with intrigue.

Exotic strangers come to town—idolizers, misogynists, masturbators, geeks, desperadoes, dealers, bikers, pimps, hustlers, high rollers, rednecks, roughnecks, ribalds and rogues, as well as all those drama queens who sashay across the same stage: each one the agent of a new trip, a new angle, a nuance of plot. The stripper's life is a soap opera, but in fast time, compressed time. Each day has 100 episodes and nothing gets censored. There's juice here.

It is in this emotional buzz that the up side and the down side are reconciled. On the other side of the obstacles, abuse, risk, and exposure is the intensity of involvement with them. Interesting problems make for an interesting life. Adversity makes the nerves hum, and occasional pain is never boring.

In the trade-off between trouble and exhilaration the stripper must hone her wiles and her guiles or she won't survive. The ones who are still dancing by their late twenties have healed many wounds, and it shows. You can see it in their faces, their eyes, and the way they move.

The veteran stripper puts out an aura that gathers from a place deep within her where experience forges character. It is at once an aura of self-possession, resilience, and serene confidence, what might be called a streetwise spirit or élan; and it is not without its resigned humor about the follies of man and men. According to Kali, "You can't live a stoic life and expect to be a personality. You've got to have some battle scars." While Miss Brazil stated, "Being onstage is the most powerful feeling I've ever had in my life. It fills me from head to toe. I feel strong. I could lift mountains. After a show I'm up. My eyes are brighter. I feel taller. I feel … invincible!"

4
The Down Side

I swear to God. This is hell on earth. It's a crazy fucking life. It is
not the real world. It is not reality. I don't know what it is. It's
like the Twilight Zone. You walk into a bar, you walk into the
Twilight Zone. And it's hell on earth.

Cassie

Every stripper has a moment when the down side of the business rises
up and engulfs her. It can happen the instant someone in the audience
makes fun of her or it can build up gradually from the little things and
finally overcome her when she is exhausted and lonely on the road.

The little things include pimples, hemorrhoids, herpes sores, unsnipped
tampon strings (which glow under the black light), toilet paper that has
somehow become trapped under the G-string and menstrual discharge during the show. More serious are crabs and other infections picked up from
the floor of the stage. Sometimes costumes don't behave as they should:

MICKEY: A costume maker should also, at least, have been a dancer.
Otherwise, she will not understand what it means to have something get
stuck or get caught. She doesn't know the humility of it. You can fake
your way around those things—that's the art of improv—but it doesn't
have to happen.

I have this full skirt that has a little zipper in the back and what I
usually like to do is undo the zipper as I'm spinning around and then
when I stop, the skirt spins down to the floor. It looks great. But the zipper wouldn't come undone and there's no way I can get this skirt off
without undoing the zipper. And this was in, like, Bum Fuck, B.C.,
right? Funky place, but nice management. They don't care if it looks
good or not, just as long as you're doing your job.

So I got this guy on the side of the stage working on it and he can't
get it. The material's stuck inside the zipper. So I thought, "Piss on this!"
and ripped it off, threw it in the corner, kicking it and stomping on it.
Everyone thought it was funny. Meanwhile, I was just furious.

CRYSTAL ROSE: In San Francisco I had this beautiful costume made. It was all red sequins. All the sequins were sewn on one by one and it was lined. It was just gorgeous. And I was going to unzip it and the zipper got caught. And I'm up there trying to ad lib and one of the girls noticed that I hadn't taken my dress off yet. And this is like almost the end of the second song. So she ran backstage and I had to back up to the split in the curtain, moving sensuously, trying to maintain some kind of professionalism onstage [laughing] while she ripped the zipper down.

That's a nightmare. That's a big fear of strippers.

Performance injuries are common. These include rug burns (the bane of the profession) and miscellaneous bruises. Bruises develop from banging into the stage poles (on the swing), crashing down into the splits and from almost any other dance or acrobatic maneuver. Carrying suitcases full of costumes from town to town produces welts on the side of the legs.

Some strippers throw themselves so totally into their work that they are constantly on the edge of losing their balance.

CHELSEA: The first two months of dancing are hell. Rug burns, bruises from the poles; I had bruises up and down my thighs. It was like I got bruised by some maniac. I have scars on my knees from rug burns that will never go away.

EMERY: The only time I actually did get money thrown at me, it was supposed to be a compliment, but I hurt myself on a $20 bill. I didn't see it on the stage which had a plexiglass floor. I went to kick—one foot was already up and the other one came out from under me. I did this: "Whoa!" [holding her arms out and rotating them rapidly for balance]. I got my balance but I threw my back out with such force that I slammed against the pole. I felt my back go out and I just decided to sit for a few minutes. I looked around and there were three $20 bills lying there, one close to me and two over there by the audience. The guy who put them there stood up, grabbed the two twenties near him and shot out the door.

LUSCIOUS LONA: I was getting ready to do my show: "The Lady in Red." She's all done up, she's in a perfect head space, she's going to do "I Am the Warrior." I walked onstage and I thought, "Lona's going to make her entrance like God!"

I walked across the front center stage and fell on both knees. I was so embarrassed. I whipped my shoes off because I figured there was something on the stage and it might still be on my shoes, and I did my show barefoot which threw me right off. By now, my knees were swollen and beginning to bruise. I was really upset. I was practically in tears. I got offstage and I looked at the bottom of my shoes. This bitch had done a banana show before me and you know how, when you peel a banana, there are those fine hair-like pieces? Well, one of them had been left on the stage and it had curled up on the bottom of my shoe. So I literally slipped on a banana peel! [laughing].

GIO: I injured my foot once. I rested my back on the floor and put my feet up on the wall, which was tiled with little mirrors, and I sliced the end of my toe off. The bar was in the meat cutting district of New York. The neighborhood smelled like stale blood. It was disgusting. The guys would come in with blood all over their aprons and hard hats. And they loved it because it was blood, right? They took me into the manager's office and poured half a bottle of Vodka on my toe and then took me to the hospital.

CASSIE: One time I bent over and dropped my pearl necklace. I did not want to just pick it up. I decided I'd do spins all around the stage and pick it up as I spun by. I went to do that and I stepped on it and went rolling across the stage. I rolled off the necklace, my shoes came off and I hit the floor with my bare feet. I was going 90 miles an hour backwards. Then, all of a sudden, it was *grip* right now, right? I took three hard steps backwards and the third step was off the stage, into Pervert Row, into a guy's beer glass, exploding the glass. It hit him and each guy on either side of him. I went flying into the guy's lap. He pushed me back onstage and I landed right in beat with the music.

MAY DONNA: I've gone onstage with major injuries. I was out partying one night and I fell down a flight of stairs and sprained my ankle. I just put a big bow around it and danced on it. I hopped to the stage on one foot and got up and danced.

I don't know what it is, but it seems that when you get on stage, nothing hurts anymore. You don't think about any kind of pain. You could have the worst headache or the worst pain in your side, but once you get up there, you just don't think about pain anymore.

The audience often takes it for granted that the rigors of the job manifesting as bruises are sexually related. Fatigue or thigh bruises may be interpreted to be the results of a wild sexual adventure the night before, sniffles as cocaine irritations. Men ask strippers leading questions about all these, but it is possible they are fishing for ways of bringing sex and drugs into the conversation. Lives of sex, drugs, and rock and roll are a stigma the stripper shares with the musician, the paths of both frequently crossing.

These job hazards, while rankling, are not the stuff of hell on earth. What Cassie is referring to in the opening epigraph is audience abuse. Most of the abuse in this business arises from the unique relationship that is created in (and which also sustains) the strip club: that between a gang of clothed men and a naked woman who is a stranger to them. If we take this relationship at face value, the very symbols of clothed and naked tell us who is defended and who is vulnerable, who is the potential aggressor and who is the victim. Five shows a day, six days a week, an average of 100 men per show who are usually consuming alcohol and may be stoned on something as well, 1,500 shows a year—she's nude, gorgeous, teasing, and elusive—the odds on some form of aggression quickly stack against her. It is not obvious because the more serious incidents are rare and the others remain discreet. Some seem so much a part of the locker-room atmosphere of the bar that they are perceived (by the men, at least) as being less offensive than good old-fashioned ribald. When a man yells out, "Fuck your costume. We just wanna see your clit," most of the men in the bar will laugh even if it's only at the audacity of the remark. Meanwhile, the remark has a very good chance of wounding the dancer.

Here's a sampling of what strippers hear from the audience.

Show me some pink.
Show me your change machine.
Show me your coin machine.
Show me the man in the boat.
Let's see what you had for breakfast.
Let me see your cunt.
Let me smell your pussy over here.
Turn up the smell.
Baby, your ass looks like chewing gum and I sure like to chew.
Nice tits.
Nice ass.
Nice schmeebs.
Nice hoop.
We wanna see your pussy.
We wanna see your box.
We wanna see your piss flaps.
Hey Baby, if you show no flap you get no clap.
Show us your tits.
Drop your gear.
God's been a bit cheap with you, eh?
You're nothing but a hole for me to shoot my wad into.
Pussee!

You've got a big twat.
Can I buy a house to go with your rug?
Do you wanna get married?
Can I buy you a condo?
Hey, I can see your breakfast from here.
Get the fuck off the stage.
Are you ever ugly.
You got no fuckin' tits.
You slut.
What the fuck are *you* doin' up there?
Where's the beef?
Greenpeace![1]

Some of these afford the stripper the opportunity for some stand up comedy or to outsmart the heckler into embarrassed silence. Toni, for instance, gleefully remembers the time a young man in the audience screamed out, "Sit on your face!" "Sit on your face!" she called back. "Are you kidding? I don't even sit on toilet seats."

JENNIE: There was a young guy who kept bugging me. I guess he thought that that was the thing to do. It was my first song and he was going, "Show me some pink! Show me some pink!" And I was thinking, "Like, this is my first song. Get off my case."
Naturally, when stuff like that happens I never take anything off. (I'm very stubborn.) So my second song came along and I was still not taking off my clothes. Third song, he was still doing it. I knew if I wanted to get paid, I had to take my clothes off pretty soon. And he knew that, too, but he knew he was getting on my nerves. So between the third song and the fourth song the music stopped and I looked at him and I said, "Excuse me, but it's 12:30. Isn't it time you went back to school?"
I knew that that would be the thing to say to a 19-year-old because they're so very proud of their age, of being able to get into the bar. He acted just like he'd been bit. He started screaming about what a bitch I was. I just stood there and crossed my arms and waited for him to leave. The audience loved it anyway because it was still entertainment.

SKY: This one guy was just being a gross pig. He kept saying to me, "Show me some pink, bitch."
So I looked at him and spread my legs. "Do you see this?"
He said, "Yeah. It's a cunt."
I said, "Great reflection, eh?"
Melissa Wolf, who was seen shaving herself in *Penthouse* (June 1985), has sometimes been asked from the audience who her barber is. Her stock reply to that one is "Bic, of course."

Some dancers, in response to "Show me some pink" stick out their tongues. And black dancers have been known to say, "Black girls don't have pink." Then there's the wordless reply.

TRACY TSAR: One time there was this guy sitting in the front hassling every dancer. One of the girls—he was getting really lewd with her—just kept smiling at him and then suddenly she leaned over and picked up his pitcher of beer and said, "Cool off!" and dumped the whole thing in his lap. All the dancers thought it was hysterical.

While these jousts are entertaining and, on the surface, satisfying—the men get what they deserve—they convey a sense of trivializing what can only be described as a variable alloy of ignorance, vulgarity, and maliciousness. It may not spring to mind immediately, because the entire context of stripping is so beyond (if not beneath) our sense of ordinary reality, that what goes on there is almost completely open to speculation. And indeed, in many ways it is a different world with different events. Our expectations are that the strip club is an enclave of rough trade anyway, so this kind of behavior is not surprising. We are happy for the strippers to have had the last laugh (as are most of the audience), but we don't sympathize with them much because, after all, they chose to be there, they wilefully chose to excite the rowdy passions of men.

What is not different about the stripper's world is the human dimension of feelings, the basic drive for self expression, and the need to be accepted by others. If raucous comments do not appear to wound it is because the stripper has become hardened to them. The transition from chamber maid, sophomore, or lab technician to stage-wise sex goddess takes many years. The payoff is being able to maintain rapport with the audience in the face of disruption, but the price may be an overburden of stress, pressure, and, ultimately, desensitization.

To the unseasoned, the sensitive, and those strippers who have been pushed beyond the breaking point, the jibes hurt. The least harm they do is interfere with their rhythm.

BROOKE: The comments really kill me sometimes. More than once I've asked myself, "Why am I here?" I don't deserve it.

One time a fellow said, "Oh, really nice show!" and his friend went, "Yeah. Too bad about the tits."

And it was like: "I'm going to punch your lights out!" You know, I wanted to, so bad. But I just walked away. And I went upstairs and I started crying. I felt like going back down there and saying, "Look. I was born this way. It's not my fault, so don't insult me."

Cassie corroborated this opinion by saying, "When I get those kind of remarks, I feel like killing them. Like, literally killing them. Like, if I had a gun I'd take great pleasure in blowing them away."

The remarks are not delivered dispassionately. They spring from a well of deep-seated sexual angst. The stripper is aware on some level that she rouses powerful forces. All women know instinctively that exciting men they do not know can have dangerous consequences. And to intentionally excite a man so as to reject him effectively removes the woman from the protection of the law. Compared to their place of origin, the remarks are fairly innocuous. That's why some stage-wise strippers caution against the disparaging rebuttal.

> PANDORA: I don't crush them. I've learned to stay away from male egos. They feel so betrayed and so belittled. Because other guys are listening. Don't ever put them down. You've got to make it a joke, but so the joke's on both of you. The intelligent ones might catch on that you put him down, but the average ones will think, "Aw, she's cool. She's got a good sense of humor."
>
> You never know what makes people tick any more in this world. You don't put people down because that guy might be going through a crisis with his wife, his girlfriend, or his parents and that could be the thing that makes him snap. And he might hurt you.

In a sense, the strip club is like adjoining locker rooms in a high school. The boys have discovered the chink in the wall or the keyhole view and a precocious young woman on the other side is giving them a show. The boys are bonded together in mystery, wonder, and desire—and unspoken powerlessness and anxiety. Who's in charge here? Clearly, it is the boys who are transfixed. A case can be made for the fact that the girl is as much tied to the need for the audience as the boys are to the view, but for some reason she is always able to depart the scene before they do. It is more likely that the boys will think they are being done to than the other way around. After a while their anxiety will begin to burn hotter than their desire. But about all they can do to reverse their powerlessness is to break the spell, to destabilize the woman verbally, humiliate her, make *her* the victim. The boys are now bonded together in aggression toward a common enemy.

The only tangible differences between this scenario and a strip-club is that the strip club patrons are older, and there is no physical barrier between them and the performer. Otherwise the psychological underpinnings of the relationship are exactly the same. The men desire a woman who has exaggerated all her faculties of sexual attraction but who has left little room for anything but ultimate rejection. More physically painful tortures have been devised by human beings, but surely none as diabolical. The men have all grown up in a society that rewards rational control and punishes emotional vulnerability. The men's base feelings are that they would like to have sex with the woman onstage. But to express that truth risks almost certain rejection. And rejection is one of man's greatest fears. Rejection in adult life stimulates all the devastating feelings of the child whenever the mother withdrew her love. Then, as now, the meaning of rejection is, "I am not lovable as I am."

To avoid paying this price, men make a near impossible compromise between vulnerability and defensiveness, with oafish results. From the opening line and the one-liner through snide remarks to coarse and violent talk, the message is the same: "I'm attracted to you; I'm afraid you'll reject me; I'm afraid I'm not worthy of you; and, at all costs, I must keep my cool." The avoidance of vulnerability is reflected in the macho use of "tits," instead of breasts, "cunt," instead of vagina, "piss flaps," "fuck," and the rest. The words call to mind the erogenous zones and the sexual act, but they are stripped of their tenderness and intimacy. They make their user look tough, in control—not out of it; cool—not burning with desire. They put the owner of the body parts referred to (and much desired) on the defensive, thereby deflecting attention away from the tender, vulnerable submacho truth.

While the psychology inherent to the strip club has always been the same, its context has shifted. The show used to have a sizable degree of humor. Striptease (as it used to be called) acquired its first legs in the variety show. Back in the heady days of burlesque, sex and comedy were bedfellows, providing relief from each other and also flavoring each other's acts. Eventually, of course, the sex effectively muscled the comedy right out of the show. In the interim, while burlesque waited for the moral climate to shift, comedy's *raison d'être* was more artistic cover than release valve, but the release it did provide is significant. A good case can be made for the therapeutic value of the earlier burlesque shows for this reason.

By turning sexual anxiety into comedy, burlesque offered a harmless outlet for energy that otherwise might have been expressed as hostility. It is important to understand this alchemy of turning anxiety into humor because it was the essence of burlesque and serves to explain one aspect of its subconscious attraction, and also to explain the difference between burlesque and modern day stripping. The very words tend to give it away: stripping is burlesque stripped of its humor. This is one of the major irritations of the older dancers. Humor used to be the bridge between the performer and her audience; together they shared in the joke, together they shared in the release. The implied rejection was not as brutal because the men in the audience could feel some connection with their stage idols. In the older days when vaudeville and burlesque overlapped, the male onlookers could also feel a vicarious connection with the male bit players who starred alongside the women in the various skits that often made fun of man's perpetual failure to captivate the woman of his dreams.

Now that the humor is almost gone from the act, as the tease evaporates and the shows get more explicit, many older dancers are noticing that the men are leaving the clubs and bars in a much more serious mood. And they are becoming ruder and cruder. It isn't funny any more.

A stimulated libido will find some way of expressing itself. If it can't go down through orgasm then it will try to go up through laughter. If it fails to find the humor, it may just break out in violence. By dropping the humor from her act the stripper has unwittingly passed a portion of control over to the men in the audience. If the catalyst for release doesn't come from the stage, the audience has to provide it for themselves. Left to their own designs, the men regress to the most primitive guffaw, the cheap shot, or the childish snicker.

Furthermore, as she becomes more serious, the stripper becomes more distant and apparently more likely to reject any advances. And the more distant she becomes, the easier she is to target, for when the stripper and her audience no longer share the joke, she must become the butt of it.

The dancer's message, "Be attracted to me, but remain in your seats," exalts the role of the woman in the rite of seduction, while forbidding the role of the man. In this light stripping looks like an impudent (and sometimes defiant) reversal of the rules of the game. These rules make it clear that the woman is the object and man is the possessor. All the action is toward the woman: man talks, woman listens; man gives, woman receives; and woman attracts and man moves toward her. The woman may tease and play coy, but the man at least gets to chase her. All these mimic the sex act itself where the man's sperm swims toward the fixed and waiting egg.

If the natural response of the male is repressed, either by the woman or by the man himself in memory of something traumatic, hostility may surface. The frustrated urge to move toward the woman may invest itself instead in spearing remarks or worse: makeshift missiles and even physical attack. In *this* locker room scenario, there is no barrier between the audience and the exhibitionist. If the laughter grows stale, if the libido becomes bound up with anger, if the alcohol swamps the social defenses against aggression, *this* precocious young woman is vulnerable to all kinds of abuse.

It is not uncommon for men to throw things at the stripper. Sometimes there is a very thin line between something thrown *to* her and something thrown *at* her: money, for instance. With paper money there is no doubt that the intent is to tip her, but quarters double as missiles. Sometimes when she is on the floor with her legs spread open the men sitting at the edge of the stage try to roll quarters into her "coin slot." Coasters also fall into this category. Often they have messages of adoration (love poems and the like) on them. But everything else that enters the stage area is a deadly weapon. These include ice cubes, rolled up napkins, pickled wieners, french fries, chicken bones (anything available from the kitchen), hats, shoes, prophylactics, glasses, and ashtrays.

Many strippers will shrug off such missiles and continue with their show. Others will erupt if *anything* short of serious money or a dozen roses litters their stage.

MARY: One time I was dancing away and I was having a really good time. Then these two guys started throwing quarters at me from Gynecology Row. So I took the money and gave it back to them and I said, "I pity you." And I smiled.

So I was dancing again and—two strikes you're out eh?—he hit me again. I looked at these guys and I said, "I don't have to take this shit!"

And they looked at me and both of them said, "No. You don't have to." So I got up and walked off.

Now, in the back, there was this great big hulk of a man. He was about six foot two, muscle over muscle, and he was going [in a husky voice], "Hey! How come you're not dancing?"

I said, "Those guys over there are throwing coins at me."

He walked over and started going *Bang! Bang! Bang! Bang!* He picked them up and whacked them on the head, saying, "You ruined my entertainment." *Bang! Bang! Bang!*

TIA MARIA: I remember a time before I was married. I was just going to do a show and this guy came up to the stage and he had a green fluorescent dildo and he asked me if I could use it in my show. I was very polite. I said, "No thank you. I don't do that sort of thing."

So I went up and was doing my show and I saw it flying from the back of the room. It hit the stage and bounced off, and this guy, who was very drunk and about 400 pounds—he was enormous—came over and picked it up and he walked over to the stage and he said, "Hey, Honey, can you—" And I hit him. I just hit him as hard as I could. It was like, anything anyone had ever said to me, this guy got it. I was so insulted. Just that he placed his hand on my stage which is *my* territory. His mouth dropped and he was shocked. It was really funny because you could have heard a pin drop in the room.

SARITA: I've had things thrown at me like condoms with a wiener and mayonnaise in it. Can you believe it? One of the worst experiences I ever had was at a hoity-toity place, a respectable establishment. I used to have thematic acts and one of them just didn't go because I was too naive to know that there was racism and that that place was a redneck bar. I put on some Middle Eastern music and I went out with a Middle Eastern style of act. The music was Afro-Arabic but see, to those guys, because they didn't know anything, because they were so dumb, they thought it was East Indian. They called me raghead and nigger. One guy threw a can of black shoe polish at me and hit me in the back. I went down on my knees because I lost all sensation in my lower body for a moment. They were going to lynch me! I'm serious! It was that bad! I practically crawled out of there and went to the office and talked to the owner. The owner said he would do something about it, but he didn't. I had to go to the hospital; then I went home. I was docked all my pay.

JENNIE: When I first started dancing I always used to do this move: I used to slide off the stage onto the stairs. It was a pretty tricky little move. One night this guy leaped over, put his face right onto mine and said to me: "You're nothing but a dirty little cunt whore bitch. You're just a fucking little cunt."

So I thought, "Holy shit! What's this guy saying to me?" I lay there for a minute and thought, "What's the best way to react to this?" And I clearly remember thinking: "Have a temper tantrum."

So I had a temper tantrum. I jumped up and said, "I'm not going to tolerate this type of behavior!" I really had a fit. I turned around and did a lot of yelling. Then I walked away, saying, "And furthermore, I'm not doing my show," so I'd be the star.

So the guy threw a beer bottle at me as I was walking away and it hit me on the back of the head. That's it. I turned around. I said [in a booming voice], "Throw that guy out of here!" The ultimate star trip, right? The bouncer grabbed him and threw him out.

BURGEONDY: I had an ashtray thrown at me, one time. There are scars all over my bum now from it. It looks like bruises because every time I do the splits it bruises the scar tissue. And it all started because he wanted me to take a beer like Mitzi Dupree and empty it in my crotch. She had been there before and the guy had put a beer and an opener on stage.

The guy said to me, "Look, bitch. Just 'cause you ain't black don't mean you can't do it!" [Mitzi Dupree, a stripper from Los Angeles, is African-American.]

And I got all upset. I was crying and I threw the bottle of beer on the floor and he called me everything in the book. At the end of my show, I went over and told him off and walked away and he threw the ashtray at me. It hit a table and shattered into long, pointy pieces. Customers got cut. One guy got glass in his eye and now he can't see.

I called the police and the bar manager. This lady went up to the guy who threw it and said, "You'd better get out of here. She called the cops." And the guy wasn't even from the town. Like, nobody knew him.

The hotel owner wouldn't pay me because I didn't complete my contract, so I had to hitchhike to the hospital. It was a Friday night and as I was trying to walk out to the lobby, an Indian broad jumped me. I was in the hospital six and a half hours getting glass pulled out of my butt. Every time they tried to pull a piece of glass out, it would break. I've still got a piece of glass in my bum.

Taking to the stage is like beaming into another world. Fundamentally escapist, the performing artist leaves behind the laws of physics and enters a fantastic realm. For the dancer, grace in motion becomes an oasis within a wasteland of strife. This lends added emphasis to May Donna's statement: "When you get on stage, nothing hurts anymore." The men who take the dancer out of her trance by bombarding her with something also remind her once again of her pain. Interruptions are serious offenses for this reason alone.

Invasion of the stripper's stage or personal space is an ever-present possibility. Though the limits of this space are not well defined—when she, for instance, removes someone's glasses to steam them between her legs, or places her legs on someone's shoulders in Gyno Row, or walks into the audience to masturbate a patron's tie—it is absolutely forbidden for anyone to touch *her*. This fact alone could tempt many a would-be hero, but some men just lose it. Alcohol can turn a man into a beast or a boy.

LUSCIOUS LONA: The first time I was grabbed onstage was in Calgary. It was his mistake. I have a horrid temper. I have a real long fuse but a very bad temper. I had been doing a very good show. There were probably 250 people there. They were tipping and I don't believe in taking tips with my tits and all that shit, but I'll take them with my hand and thank the guy.

I reached out to take the tip with my hand. He grabbed my wrist, pulled me towards him and, with the other hand, he grabbed my tit. I felt so dirty and so appalled. He failed to notice the studded black belt I had around my waist, which was in seconds wrapped around his forehead. He was ripped open and bleeding. I put on my cover-up and I was going to proceed off the stage and kill this motherfucker—I was mad!— but the bouncers took care of it before I had to do anything else.

But the feeling! It was so embarrassing to be touched in front of all those men. It hurt. You're embarrassed, you're hurt—but you feel dirty. I was touched once on my hair and it still sent a cold chill up my spine.

AMBER FLASHING: I've table danced in Toronto. I could tell these two men were not from the city. This one guy, when I turned around on my table, bit my ass. Needless to say, I picked up my $5 and put my top back on (you kept your G-string on there) and I said, "You'd better leave. Get the hell out of here!"

He picked up his beer and said, "No. I'm drinking my beer."

So I grabbed his beer out of his hand, because my adrenaline had started going, took his hat off and poured beer over his head and threw his hat back at him. I said, "No. You're leaving now!"

He went to grab his beer again and I thought, "The gall of the guy!" So I just picked up his bottle and hit him over the head with it. He left.

BRANDI WEST: One of the only real problems I've had was when I was working in Calgary. The club was owned by a woman and her sister ran it and we had a light man who weighed about 90 pounds. I was doing my show and a guy came up to the side of the stage and I thought he was going to tip me—they tip quite a bit in Calgary—so I walked toward him and he jumped up on the stage.

I said, "Hey! Hey! You can't do that!" And *bang* he had his clothes off. Like, I've never seen anybody take their clothes off that quickly. And I realized this guy was serious and I called Sharon, the lady behind the bar.

By that time, the guy had me down on the floor and he had a hold of my leg and I was pushing on him. Sharon came up and grabbed a hold of his hair and this little light man grabbed his leg and we had this big brawl on stage [laughing].

Now it's funny, but at the time it was a very shaky experience. I would have liked to have been in the audience because I know it must have looked just hysterical. They got him dressed first and threw him out.

Another time they had a band set up behind me and there was about this much room to dance in front of them and they had this chain around the stage. I was doing my floor show and I went into a back bend and this guy dove head first over the chain. The bouncer had him before he hit the ground. He was a guy from New Zealand. He came back the next day and apologized. He said he had been really loaded and he had never seen a nude woman before.

I stopped doing back bends from that angle. I always do them from the side now so I have a view.

KYRA: This guy was giving me a tip and I wanted to take it. It was $5. I didn't have a G-string on. I wanted to just take it in my hand and the

guy that was sitting across the table from him—I had my back to him—
grabbed me. He grabbed me and he molested me with his hands all over
my breasts and my body.

I hit him in the face about four times and he let me go. I started crying and I ran offstage and everyone was booing me. The place was
packed. They said, "Don't let one guy ruin it for the rest of us!" It was
my last 30 seconds of my last show for the day.

I went down later to give the DJ shit for not stepping in and he told
me that the guy pulled a knife when he tried to throw him out. The DJ
had to fight him off with a chair. The cops came and one of them asked
me, "What did you do? What did you do to provoke the guy?"

I looked at the cop and I said, "I don't want to talk to you anymore."
And I left.

I've had guys reach out and try to touch me and then be real innocent
and surprised when I've turned around and slapped them right in the
head: "What'd I do?" [in a child's voice].

I said, "You don't go around touching people without their permission.
You don't do that. You don't do that anywhere."

They have the feeling that they can do that onstage. It's funny. I don't
know if that will ever change. I really don't. I wonder if that will ever
change.

A climate laced with this kind of abuse from hostile men and the rest
of the audience would make anyone think twice about working there. But
this is only a part of it. The stripper has a life backstage, too. Here she
must deal with flashers, voyeurs, and rapists, not to mention murderers,
as well as agents, bar managers, and DJs—the vast majority of whom are
men—and the other dancers themselves who present challenges of their
own. She must ply her way through a miasma of deception, rumors and
sexual politics. She is constantly besieged with sexual advances from audience types, male agents, and club owners who have been known to use
their pass keys to enter the dancer's room while she sleeps. She may be
pressured to spread her legs more, to be more raunchy onstage. And, in
spite of signed contracts, the club owner can fire her for the simple reason he doesn't like her body or her attitude, or because she won't date him
or one of his friends.

Other dancers will steal her costumes, tapes, and jewelry. They will
try to seduce her boyfriend. They will talk behind her back. They will crit-
icize her dancing, her body, and her holier-than-thou attitude. They will
put it out that she has herpes or AIDS or that she is a sex change. They
will say she has "an ugly pussy."

The hazards and abuse don't end at the strip-club door. They follow her down every avenue of her life where her occupation becomes known. In this, the stripper shares something with the policeman: both bear a stigma that makes them stand out at parties. The image is not as easily shed as the costume. Once people find out what she does for a living they shun her, often making disparaging remarks about her.

Finally, the stripper's job can be devastating to her love life. This might seem too obvious. How could any man put up with his lover prancing around in the buff for a gang of rogues? The answer is that he does not. Once he has secured his position as the stripper's lover and the novelty of that conquest has dimmed, he becomes very demanding about putting an end to her stripping. Jealousy can erupt in the relationship at any time, and it can get ugly.

Nevertheless, it must be made clear that in the strip club it is not open season on the dancer. Most of the men behave themselves and many, instead of reversing the rejection, actually seem to invite it, to wallow in it. To some men, any attention from a woman is better than none at all, even when it makes them look foolish.

The hazards in this business are, generally speaking, rare. They also appear to be selective. While some strippers hardly ever get abuse from the audience, they nevertheless have continuing conflicts with agents, club managers, and DJs. Others, who may get along reasonably well with the people in the business, cannot help attracting abusive men in their personal lives. Still others seem to find themselves in conflict only with other strippers.

But the stripper's life is a saga; it is a story made up of one page per day. Gossip, besides being cruel at times, has a necessary survival function. Strippers readily pass on information about anything or anyone that could be dangerous. (A common saying among club DJs is that the three most modern methods of communication are telephone, telegram and tell-a-dancer.) If a stripper gets attacked on stage or in the club, the story is told and retold until it has become an anecdote in bold relief in the lives of many other strippers. As such, it becomes an integral part of the stripper's folklore. "If it can happen to her, it can happen to me." Though it may never befall her, by its whispered presence, by its implication of her constant exposure, it is nevertheless a hazard as real to her as it was to its victim. Some strippers carry knives. A few carry cans of mace in their purses.

ASPASIA: People can be so ugly sometimes in this business, for no reason. It's in their nature. In the night world, it's dark as it is. There's a lot of alcohol and it affects the way people think and the way they act. Mishaps are more likely to happen in that kind of atmosphere. It's far more dangerous to be in this business, as well as mentally taxing. You're out in the open. If and when somebody ever wanted to, they could shoot you or knife you.

None but the daring, the desperate, and the eccentric enter here. The twilight zone of the stripper's world exacts justice in strict proportion to guts and luck. For some, the saga ends abruptly in nervous breakdown, suicide, or simply resignation: she just can't go on anymore.

It all adds up to pressure.

DEVLIN DEVINE: There's so much pressure out there—pressure on the girls to be a certain way, to dress a certain way, to get a certain response, to have a certain kind of music...

There should be room for creativity and individuality, but there doesn't seem to be much room for that anymore. It's just like a body factory now. I see all these girls and they're all the same to me. They all do the same thing, they all have the same moves, they all dance to the same music. And it's no fault of theirs; they're just going with the flow.

And pressure about age. I'm only 24 and already I feel pressure.

CARMALITA: Most of the time, it's a really easy job. I mean, you go up there for 10 or 15 minutes and dance to music you like. Except, I couldn't dance for long periods of time. I could dance for about two or three months and then I'd need a break. I think more than anything, it is the mental pressure. Society is always against the human body, against nudity, against everything—especially women's libbers. It's like the human body is bad, sex is bad, all this is bad and I never felt it was. There was a lot of stress on me. I didn't think it was bad, yet society, my parents, and everybody that was important to me were against it. So I would need to take a break and do normal things for a while.

KALI: You're always questioning whether you're good, if you're a hot item. If you don't get booked in the places where you'd like to be working, you think, "I must be the shits. I must be terrible." So there's a lot of self doubt. You suffer physically all the time, but you heal. The heavy suffering is mental.

I wasn't a real mad dancer. There's lots of dancers that shouldn't be up there. They're angry. Why are they doing it then? I guess you just get tired after a while. You can pretend only so much. Because it is pretence. When you're up there, you're doing your job, you're entertaining; you're supposed to be of a different mind. But then that can peter off and you'll think, "Look at that geek." Something will twist in your head and you'll think, "This is really ridiculous. What the hell am I doing up here?"

TRACY TSAR: You get a warped view of men. You get a warped view of life. You get a warped view of yourself. It's not easy to stay mentally healthy.

SARITA: I'll tell you, and this is the honest-to-God truth, I hated every single solitary minute that I was onstage.

5
Getting In and Out of Character

When I lower my gown a fraction,
And expose a patch of shoulder,
I'm not thinking of your reaction,
I'm not even feeling colder.
I'm thinking of a landscape by Van Gogh,
Or *The Apples* by Cézanne.
Or the charm I found in reading,
Lady Windermere's Fan.
And stand here shyly, with nothing on
at all—well, practically nothing—
clutching an old satin drop and looking
demurely at every man. Do you believe
for one moment, that I'm thinking of
sex? … Well, I certainly am.
                    Gypsy Rose Lee, quoted from her stage show[1]

The tease in Gypsy Rose Lee's stage show was twofold: will she or won't she (take it all off); and does she or doesn't she (really have her mind on sex)? One tugs at our anticipation; the other teases our suspicion. By the end of the show she will have revealed most of her body, but we will still have only her cryptic monologue with which to see into her mind. She alludes to faraway places: landscapes by Van Gogh, still life by Cézanne, a play by Oscar Wilde. These suggest that she might only be going through the motions, that her body is there for all to see, but her mind is off on a jaunt—at least until her finale when she stands there "shyly, with nothing on at all—well, practically nothing," and can't avoid the thought of sex any longer.

So closely do we associate nakedness with sex that we cannot fault those who think the stripper's experience up there is a sexual excitement *for her*. More than this, she positively seems to delight in what she is doing. Coupled with our mind-set about exhibitionism, we just assume that here is a woman who simply exults in being naughty.

61

So convincing is the stripper's performance that men ask her, in all seriousness, questions like, "Do you finger yourself to get in the mood?" and "Do you come onstage?"

On the other hand, we might assume there is some *acting* going on up there simply because it takes place on a stage. There have been several clues to this possibility all along, scattered among the strippers' anecdotes. Gio, for instance, speaking about stage power: "When I'm up onstage, it's a power trip... The minute I am off the stage, I revert back to my normal self."

But the stage is not necessarily the giveaway to an act. Many performers take to the stage and have us believe that they are *not* acting: for instance, Bible thumpers, psychics, and politicians. As opposed to dramatic actors, these performers operate without story line or plot structure. They appeal directly to the audience and present themselves as genuine, that is, not playing a role or wearing a mask.

Strippers fall into this category: people enter the strip club not in a state of disbelief begging suspension (as they do when they sit down to watch a play or a movie), but expecting to see the revelation of a woman's sexual self.

We don't even give it much thought. There is no hint of flimflam in her act: the nymphean mischief in her eyes, the cant of submissive readiness, the glistening pucker, the silent moan, and the naughty grin; the vicarious hands jiggling her breasts, tweaking her nipples, caressing her thighs, and stroking her vagina; the writhing snake-like postures, the legs thrown open with bravado, the frenzied hip rolls, and the rollicking motions of mimed intercourse. What we see is a woman whose entire body has become an instrument of the erotic.

We think the stripper's performance must be congruent with her feelings. We don't think of her as playing a role or wearing a mask. After all, she's naked—what can she hide? The entire theme of her performance is disclosure, not masquerade.

As she spreads the lips of her ultimate disclosure (as though to let the whole world see inside her), could it be, as Gypsy Rose Lee suggested, that she is really thinking about Oscar Wilde?

The mask is an old and powerful force. As a covering for the face or even as a metaphor, the mask foreshadows mysteries and make believe, magic and lies.

The best masks are the invisible ones, the ones that are so convincing that they are taken for the real face. This is the essence of drama: if the act is convincing enough, the audience becomes seduced away from its collective assumption that what they are seeing is fiction. They come, by degrees, to be involved in the drama as though it were their own.

All the actor has to do is duplicate the physical expressions—the analogues—of the feelings he or she wishes to emote. It is not necessary for the actor to feel them. (This goes for the politician, the Bible thumper and the psychic, to say nothing of the stripper.)

The stage mirrors society where everyone presents a face to the rest of the world that is in varying degrees of conflict with the true self. Sometimes our social mask is the self we would like to have; or sometimes it is merely protective of an inner sensitive being.

The irony of this conflict is that if one conceals the protective social face with a theatrical mask, the inner self can become free to play. In the words of Oscar Wilde: "Man is least himself when he talks in his own person. Give him a mask and he will tell you the truth." Which is another way of saying, I can be myself as long as you don't know who I am.

There are then two masks to consider here: the stage mask and the mask of the persona or the self as it is presented in society.

The stripper's stage mask is less a physical mask than a facial highlight. It is painted on with cosmetics to accentuate the eyes, cheeks and lips. It is basic street paint as you might see at any singles bar, but a thicker, glossier chrome for the stage lights.

Mary Wigman, the celebrated dancer-choreographer, used to say that rather than a second face, makeup gives the dancer a second skin. In other words, the interface between the dancer's stage mask and her persona is as thin as a smear of rouge. Rather than conceal her, the stripper's cosmetic accents actually seem to betray her to us. It is not the *mask* of eroticism we think we see up there, but its very *face,* and therefore the resonance of its very soul.

Nevertheless, a thin smear of paint can work a sublime transformation. In collusion with an exotic costume and a bewitching bouffant, the most modest of masks can turn an ordinary woman into a sorceress. The importance the stripper places on her facial mask is underscored by a statement made by Sally Rand, one of the most famous striptease artistes of the 1930s. When a reporter for the New York *World Telegram* dropped in on her for an interview, he caught her in the middle of making herself up. Suddenly self-conscious, she said to him, "I'm sorry you came in on me like this, with my face bare of makeup. I don't mind if you see any other part of me bare, but not my face."[2]

The hypnotic potency of the stripper's mask (animated by her persona) lies in its being otherworldly. The refined beauty, the exotic costume, and the anomalous nudity zap the viewer out of his (or her) normal waking consciousness into a close erotic focus. The enthralling vision is the ticket to a world of dreams. What the viewer does with her in his own mind removes her even further from who she really is.

That the stripper is often unrecognizable shorn of makeup, in her jeans, out of character, on the street, is common parlance among the people she works with, including the DJs and club managers.

> LAVA NORTH: For the most part, when you leave the club, no one recognizes you unless you dress like a dancer. A lot of girls wear their Spandex pants outside. They wear their baubles and beads and six inch high heels and they flash "I'm a dancer!" as they walk down the street. I dress right down. I've walked into clubs like this in the morning, got all done up for my shows, and then, when I handed my key back in at the end of the day, they said, "Who are you?"
>
> One day I came in with makeup on, as opposed to my hair in a pony tail and no makeup, and the girl asked me, "Who are you replacing today?" And I said, "I'm the same girl who came in yesterday."

Beneath the glitzy packaging and animating through it is the stripper's persona. How she comports herself onstage will determine the success of her act measured in applause.

What the stripper, the Bible thumper, and the politician have in common is that each is a role fashioned on a limited range of human expression. And each is as remarkable for what is expressed as for what is left out.

The politician's role is built on courage, dedication, confidence, and empathy, but must not include any fear, weakness, confusion, guilt nor, advisedly, lust, even though such occasional feelings are both common and appropriate to all human beings.

The Bible thumper can get away with anger (directed at sin), fear (of God), hatred (of evil), and tearful reverence, but let him entertain confusion, anxiety, despair, or lust and he will completely discredit his performance. (Of course, he has the advantage of making everything all right again by saying he is sorry, that is, by appearing to feel remorse.)

The role of the stripper, on the other hand, is almost completely hinged on the expression of lust, with some acceptable nuances of insolence, joy, playfulness, or vulnerability. There isn't much room for anything else in her performance; almost anything else will unhinge her from her role and break the spell.

Especially damning to the stripper are shame, boredom, fear, anger, and—possibly worst of all—intelligence. She must cloak all of these behind the mask of desire.

CHELSEA: Sometimes you just don't feel like it. It's a very weird sensation when you're up onstage and you don't really want to be there. The first show is always like that. Especially when you're out of town. You know, you just woke up an hour ago and you've done your face with bright lipstick and it seems so strange just looking at everybody in an alien way. They're all sitting there drinking beer and you're thinking, "How the hell can they be sitting in a bar drinking beer at 12 noon?"

MATA HARRIETTE: As soon as I'm downstairs by the DJ I just go into character. I start smiling and being sexy and charming and acting like a real goof, because you can't be intelligent in this business.

I'll give you an example. This happened about a month ago. The manager of the club came up to me on Monday and said that he wanted two girls to do a stag for these bankers and that it was all arranged. I was going to be working with this little girl who's really, really sweet, but incredibly—not stupid—but when you talk to her, you think she's got a problem. Like, even the manager said, "Is there something wrong with that girl?" So these bankers came in and saw my show and came up to me after. We talked about me doing the stag and (I thought) arranged everything. Now, when I'm onstage I'll play a certain character, but when I'm talking business, it's business. We got it all worked out, and then I saw them talking to the other girl. The manager came up to me the next morning and said that they decided they didn't want me to dance for them. He said, "Everything was fine until they talked to you."

FAWN: I think Fawn can be dumb sometimes. "Don't talk to me, because I'm dumb." I don't like people to see who I really am. So a lot of times at work I'll pretend to be really stupid so I can protect my real self.

A couple of weeks ago I was really tired. I hadn't slept all night and I was not having a good day. It was my last show and I was feeling upset about a few things and somebody threw a chicken bone at me. I just let it all down and started to cry. And that's *me* crying, the real me. Usually I try to pretend those things don't bother me. A lot of people are taking their frustrations out on you and if they can tell it's going to hurt you, they're going to do it more. It's pretty dangerous.

Some strippers say that they switch off a part of their inner life before going onstage. Cassie, for example, says that she switches off her emotions, while for Devlin Devine, it is her mind: "Turn on my pussy, turn off my mind." In Miss Brazil's case, it is her consciousness of the audience: "When I was afraid of the audience I used to close them off. Sometimes I would even drop a thin veil in front of my eyes. It's easy to do. You glaze your eyes over by concentrating so much on one point that the background gets faded out."

Once we get an inkling that the stripper's exterior is somewhat in conflict with her inner experience, a couple of questions come to mind. For instance, does she feel naked onstage?

On the face of it, asking a stripper if she ever feels naked onstage seems akin to asking a cowboy if he ever feels dusty. And yet, when you think about it, being naked ought to be just like being clothed (or habitually dusty): one could be expected to lose consciousness of it after a while.

This is not readily apparent to the strip joint voyeur whose own consciousness is overflowing with the fact of the dancer's nudity. In his clothes (and in the strip joint, now unavoidably conscious of them) he cannot help but empathize with what he assumes are the dancer's feelings, with what *he* would feel like if the roles were reversed and he was up there stripping for a room full of women.

Being naked is metaphorically linked with being exposed—one can mean the other—and yet they are not synonymous. One can feel exposed without feeling naked and vice versa. In most cases though, being naked in front of strangers is an experience weighing heavily toward feelings of exposure.

FAWN: Oh yeah. Real naked. I mean, how naked can you feel? You're naked in front of a whole bunch of people and you're up there where everybody can see you, under the lights.

You just sort of wake up to it once in a while. Usually you block that part out. You don't think about it. But once in a while you think about it and it's scary.

SKY: Yes. If I don't wear something like a neckband or a headband or something, I feel naked. I always keep something on. Insurance, I guess.

RITA RHINESTONE: Yeah. It's funny. One of the things I found about performing in western Canada is that there's no setting. Like, there's often no type of stage, so the times I've felt naked in the sense that it didn't seem appropriate, that rather than feeling nude or feeling like I was making a presentation of physical beauty, but just felt I didn't have my clothes on, was vulnerable in that way, was when the setting was not up to any sort of professional standard, such as when the lighting was bad.

The most shocking thing to me in that part of the world is that they have no curtains or anything, so when the show's over, the girl crawls around naked on the floor and picks up her stuff—with no music—and then walks through the bar. Those moments when it's no longer a performance, it's just being caught not properly dressed.

GIO: I have felt embarrassed a couple of times when a tampon string showed. But now, even that doesn't bother me.

The first time it happened I was working for this company called Strip-a-Gram and I did a strip-a-gram in a Wall Street office and I had forgotten to cut the string. You didn't really take anything off (in those days, top, bra and panties stayed on) but the string was sort of sticking out from underneath the panties. I spread my legs to do a back roll and the guy went, "Oh, look! She brought me a tea bag!"

I grabbed my clothes, grabbed my ghetto blaster and went running into the elevator. I didn't even get paid.

After a while I realized it's a natural body process and it's going to happen now and then.

If you love us, please don't mind
If now and then we bump and grind!
We will shimmy and we will shake
But please don't think we're on the make![3]

If the stripper generally does not feel naked, can it be then that she does not feel sexual?

DALLAS: If I'm really high and I'm into my music, maybe. And if the crowd's really good.

TARA: If I'm horny, I can get down and dirty. It depends on how often I've gotten it. I think I make more money when I really feel it.

REBECCA: Yeah. Sometimes. Yeah. I feel more sensual, I don't know about erotic. I'm not thinking erotic thoughts, but I feel sensual—or sexy.

LUSCIOUS LONA: It's not sexual to me at all. It's a head trip and it's an adrenaline rush, but it's not sexual. I work on the manipulation using my eyes, using the lyrics to the songs, the way my clothes come off. I'm manipulating *them*. But you have to have constant concentration when you're doing that.

I know girls who do get sexually aroused onstage and they tend to lose the crowd. The crowd's watching but there's no crowd-dancer contact. To get yourself stimulated onstage you have to shut off the crowd, and I just can't do that.

CRYSTAL ROSE: There are dancers who will *tell* you they do [laughing]. But it's a whole different story from what you hear in the dressing room. We talk about guys asking us, you know, "What are you thinking onstage?" Basically, we tell them we're thinking whatever they think we're thinking. It's all an illusion.

Like guys say, "I wish my wife was as good-looking as you." Well, if she had a ton of makeup on, all the right lighting, the right music, and a makeup mirror she'd look great too. We'll lie to the customers about that because that keeps 'em coming back. Backstage we laugh about it.

What's going through your head as a performer—you know, you have a routine down to that music and you have to do certain things at certain times and your facial expressions, your hand movements, your body movements, what you're taking off, what you're doing, is all running through your head at the same time. And you're cuing your music to what you're doing at the same time. And your facial expressions have to hide all that. You have to look as if you're aroused and *into* it. It has to look easy. And it's not.

KYRA: It is all an act up there. When you're looking at some guy real sexy, you're not thinking, "Oh. Gee. Wouldn't I like to screw you." No. You're thinking, "God! I can't stand what that guy has on his T-shirt."

I'm always going up to guys to read their jackets and the things they have on their hats, and they think I'm paying them some special attention; but I'm not. I'm actually doing something different [laughing].

You're being a real hypocrite when you're up there. You're looking at some man and you're pretending that the look of that man is just making you want to rip your clothes off. What you're really thinking about is what's going on in the soap opera that you were watching. You can't wait to get back to your room to see the rest of what happens to Julia, or whatever.

The difference between me and an actor is that people aren't that dumb. When it comes to somebody reading Shakespeare, they're not going to think that Hamlet or Romeo and Juliet really died.

I mean, I've had guys ask me, "What do you do to get yourself in the mood? Do you play with yourself before you go onstage?" and "What do you think about while you're up there? Do you lay back and think about that gorgeous man on top of you just fucking you like crazy while you're there naked with all those men around?"

See, they put that into my mouth, into my mind. I get all this input from all these people around me and I'm always defending myself. And you know why? It's because people are stupid.

"Some do, some don't" could very probably answer most of the questions in this book. The gray areas of this extraordinary phenomenon are long on possibility; so many personalities, so many motives, so many reactions. The generic stripper exists only as an idea in our minds. The construction of all-encompassing themes, after all is said and done, merely gives us oblique reflections of something that is multifaceted, multi flavoured, and subject to change.

For instance, why should a stripper take so much care to be not entirely naked? Is it to retain some small measure of security? Is it to trick her own mind into abandon because, after all, she won't be *completely* naked? Or is it cunningly to underscore her nude facts by contrasting them with ornamental reminders of clothing? Does she keep on her earrings, her waist chain, or her spiked shoes for the sake of modesty, guilt, or craft?

The diversity of personalities we are dealing with here is reflected in the answers to the question about feeling erotic onstage. Some clearly do, and some decidedly don't. Some say the feeling is sexual; others say it is more *sensual*. Some veteran strippers maintain that to put out the real thing tarnishes the whole performance, destroys the purpose, and loses the crowd. Others confirm that once in a while an authentic erotic mood may slip through to flavor the show, unbeknownst to the audience.

The erotic is so anomalous to the everyday that it is as though we are all double agents, living between two very different worlds that both demand complete allegiance to the exclusion of the other. The interrelationship between these two realms was the subject of Murray Davis's book, *Smut*. Expanding on the ideas of the philosopher-sociologist Alfred Schutz, Davis differentiates the two realms and proceeds to demonstrate how each interferes with the other. "Most sex theorists agree that people lead split-level lives, experiencing everyday reality and erotic reality as two distinct realms. Nevertheless, components of one realm sometimes appear in the other."[4]

This is especially true where sex and work collide. For instance, reviewers of pornographic films "must watch them in the bright light of everyday reality, which washes out much of the shade and color of their sense." This is also true of editors of pornographic books, who must put their minds to the task of rewriting authors' submissions with more explicit words.

One might add that the reluctant erections in many pornographic films attest to the fact that the male actors often have to be chafed back into the erotic realm.

An example of how sexual arousal interferes with the analytical process is provided by the very candid disclosure of James Skipper and Charles McCaghy regarding their interviewing of a stripper for their controversial study.

> Backstage, it was difficult for us to feign indifference over her appearance when she ushered us into her dressing room. As she sat clad only

in the G-string she had worn onstage and with her legs on the dressing table, we became slightly mesmerized. We had difficulty in even remembering the questions we wanted to ask let alone getting them out of our mouths in an intelligible manner.[5]

According to Davis, not only work but talk also is of the everyday reality.

> Copulators who direct their sexual interaction verbally also threaten to shatter the fragile goblet of erotic reality ("Roll over and put your head down there").
> Manipulating their environment through work and talk, then, is part of the everyday world that lovers are trying to forget. Erotic reality is often too delicate to contain these alien processes without disintegrating. Thus erotic reality and everyday reality must each be whole and self-contained. Those shifting from one gestalt to the other usually want to go all the way if they want to go at all.[6]

The operant words here are "delicate" and "fragile." Taking an erotic mood onto the strip-joint stage is like singing a lullaby to a den of thieves: neither can survive very long.

Where the strip joint is clearly an erotic domain for most of the audience, for the stripper it is a place of work. Whether the setting is a squalid lower-class bar with its creepy blank shaded faces and its lonely geezers talking to their drinks, or a modern, up-tempo techno-pop showroom with its endless sports on video and thunderous music, the stripper's arena is hardly the place to nurture her own desire (ketchup and vinegar smells notwithstanding). Besides, there are many more important things to think about. The concentration on the moves, the sequencing and timing, the involvement with the music, the constant measuring of audience rapport, and the defenses primed for duck, fight, and run do not leave much room for feeling sexual.

But let's take our research into a laboratory where the physical evidence of erotic moods ought to be more conspicuous. If stripping were *ipso facto* an erotic experience, or one which is capable of sustaining an erotic mood self-induced in the dressing room, we might hypothesize that *male* strippers would perform visibly aroused.

In fact, male strippers do go through the motions with half erections, the prominence of which makes women scream and men uncomfortably silent. (A legend among them earned the name "Stick" because his penis, through some quirk of biology, stayed stiff throughout his whole show.)

The truth of the matter used to be a hollow rubber dong slipped over the performer's real (and flaccid) penis and kept in place with invisible thread. Nowadays, the performer (Stick, for instance) gives himself an erection in the dressing room and "ties it off" with a rubber band around the base and concealed beneath pubic hair. The ostensibly randy man hurling himself around a room full of ecstatic and admiring women is actually feeling a small measure of genital pain.

Now that our eyes are open we will notice that female strippers often twirl their nipples into prominence between thumb and forefinger as they remove their bras.

Establishing stripping as something belonging to the stripper's "everyday" and not to her "erotic," does not mean that the erotic never intrudes. As some of them said: "Once in a while…" or "If I'm really high…" or "It depends."

On the job, a stripper can slip into her own erotic fantasies, just like a bus driver, accountant or nun, especially if she gets bored. Having done the same old routine in front of the same old faceless crowd many times before, she can easily find herself thinking about the soap opera she was watching just before her show, or her lover, or some other seductive imagery. The fantasy is not likely to last long or to plumb her depth of feeling, but once in a blue moon, say during her floor show or that chance standing ovation, perhaps she will rediscover a delicate and personal epiphany.

When the stripper does slip into an erotic mood (no matter how fleeting) it is her moment of maximum irony. The erotic face masks an erotic self, but is not of it, for it, or because of it. If the feeling endures, it may begin to flavor the act simply by diffusion or possibly by boldness— recalling Oscar Wilde and the truths that are revealed through masks. In the rarest of moments the stripper, under cover of her persona, may actually manifest her personal eroticism onstage.

Conversely, the everyday can also intrude on the erotic. Many strippers report having to go through a transition period between coming home from work and making love to their boyfriends or their husbands. That it is not *her* sexuality that is seen onstage; that it is a construct serving male fantasy is illustrated by the fact that most strippers won't strip for their lovers. Loving sex at its best is defenseless, intimate, and without ego. Stage stripping is none of these. For those strippers who are not averse to performing for their lovers, one can assume that while the motions are similar, the inner experience is much more present, less defended, and probably sexually charged. Crystal Rose, for instance, said, "I've had husbands who've wanted me to dance for them at home and I just won't do it. I mean, it's like, you want me to come home and *perform?*

(Laughs). Pay me." Diana Fox had a similar opinion: "Up there, when you take off your clothes, you're an actress. You're actually two different people. You're not really going to do that with your intimate lover—well, maybe sometimes—but not like that."

The model of masked eroticism described above, from "the nymphean mischief in her eyes" to her "rollicking hips," does not describe any one stripper. In fact, many of them will not be seen in that description at all. Rather, they appear bored, aloof, disinterested, disconnected, resentful, stoned, spiteful, or just too good for anyone in the audience. And so convincing are they that it becomes obvious, with a little reflection, that they are not acting. Now all of these may have their erotic components, or triggers, for select viewers, but the bottom line is that the simple fact of a woman removing her clothes is enough to project an erotic veneer.

Nevertheless, for many other strippers, young and old, the act is less than a consonant removed from art; they embrace it that seriously. Professionals at heart, they take to the stage with the intention of making a presentation, a performance that remains independent of their current moods.

One may ask which of the two profiles—the acting or the nonacting stripper—is more effective?

First, a clue comes from Luscious Lona, who observes that getting sexually aroused onstage tends to lose the crowd; and secondly, from Fanny Brice, the burlesquer, who said, "Men always fall for frigid women because they put on the best show."

The irony of the act is that if the actor begins to feel what he or she is portraying, the act may be lost. The other side of Oscar Wilde's aphorism about the mask is that telling the truth dissolves the public face. You can't *act* like you're carrying groceries when you really are. You can't act being sexual when you are feeling sexual. You can only *be* sexual. The result may be that the audience senses something is amiss.

This answers the question about the stripper as a *femme fatale*. If she were a true *femme fatale* she would have trouble with the part onstage. Imagine for a moment Joan Collins in her role as the deadly Alexis Carrington playing the part of a stripper and all her power disintegrates. Such a calculating woman wins by tendering mere crumbs of herself, never the whole cookie. No *femme fatale* worthy of her Circean glimmer need hit the stage to ply her trade. On her way there she would encounter ample willing victims to make stage life superfluous. Those strippers who do play the part onstage may be acting out a wish fulfillment they harbor for their daily lives. And then again, some of them (especially the younger ones) may think that this is what is required of them.

So we may conclude that (1), stripping is not in and of itself an erotic experience; (2), feeling erotic is not necessary to the stripper's performance; (3), the eroticism that one is likely to see in the stripper is not her own, but an act; and (4), Gypsy Rose Lee was merely reassuring her fans (the hallmark of a professional tease).

With a regular juggling of roles between the stage and normal living, the boundary separating them can very easily become blurred. The lore of the theater contains horror stories about actors who became possessed and consumed by the parts they played. But these are myths about the possession and consumption of our private selves by our public masks. While a particularly powerful, swashbuckling role can be seductive, the variety of roles available to the actor always contrasts with the one who plays them.

The stripper, however, has only one role to play and, unlike the actor, is defined by it. The public sees it less as a part in a play than as something arising directly out of her being. Where an actor is judged on the quality of his performance, the stripper—and the person who plays the stripper—is condemned for the role itself. When the stripper leaves the stage and becomes a person again, she finds that no one will allow her to leave her role behind. Everywhere she goes people see her as a gypsy from the erotic zones.

On the other hand, because she has only one part to play, it could be expected to acquire a force of its own. Even though, as Venus De Light has said, "Burlesque is the toilet of entertainment," there is a measure of glamour wherever there is adulation. When this glamour is not reflected in the bleak realities of one's life, it can become seductive. The social mask begins to look more and more like the stage mask. Strippers may come to be known almost exclusively by their stage names. Some wear their stage makeup everywhere as well as the costumes that won't get them arrested (such as Spandex pants and tops).

> ROBBIE: A lot of girls are really insecure about themselves. When they're onstage, they're another person and that's what makes them strong. Some girls will not even leave work or show their face in a bar unless they are in full makeup. I usually come in looking like a slob. I'm not insecure about how I look without my makeup on. It doesn't bother me.

Not only can the stripper's act interfere with her personal life, her personal life can also intrude on her act. As we saw in Tracy Tsar's story about the stripper who kept seeing visions of her father as she disrobed, relics of the self can surface fitfully—and fatefully—onstage.

An act that is so divorced from everything we take for granted in upright society cannot be so easily sustained without practice, or intoxication.

For most strippers the process of getting into costume parallels an inward process of getting into character. As she brushes on the finishing touches of her makeup, the stripper's "self in the world" is being painted into a corner of her consciousness. As she fastens her G-string (the stripper's badge, her trademark) and adjusts the rest, all her voices are silenced except for the one voice that will direct the show. Not quite the doubling of personalities that prostitutes confess to (stripping obviously isn't as intimate an act as prostitution), the switch seems more a glazing over of certain areas of the personality inappropriate to the act.

Intoxication is mentioned here because most strippers are stoned on something, be it alcohol, marijuana, hashish, or cocaine. There are one or two junkies on the circuit but heroin is not a stripper's drug; ultimately, it works against the principle of motion. In this medium numbness does not work as well as dreamscapes or crystalline energy rushes. The strippers who do shoot heroin are always searching for new hidden veins or have to wear long gloves onstage.

The one element seldom mentioned in the narratives about how they first got into stripping was the fact that many of them had to get very high to cross over the threshold. Devlin Devine speaks for many of her sisters that first time when she says, "There was just no way I could get up there straight." Or as Jocelyne said, "It helped me to escape reality." Although there is the odd teetotaler among them, for the vast majority of strippers, sweetening the experience with something or other has been, since day one, a means of coping and probably a means of forgetting certain things.[7]

Everything must be in place when she hits the stage. The master choreographer turned seductress must be in charge and all the agents of decorum, the internal finger waggers, must be silenced (or stoned).

But lots of things can pop her balloon: rude remarks, missiles from the audience, or inadvertent menstruation; all the little elves who remind her she's naked—anything that brings her back to her self in the world of decorum, for instance, seeing someone she knows in the audience.

DYNASTY LAYNE: Depending on the person. People who knew me before I was a dancer who always thought of me as just a sweet innocent little girl—that bothers me. Because they're seeing me exposed. They're seeing a part of me that they've never seen before. I always worry that it will change their opinion of me.

CRYSTAL ROSE: Very difficult. I think one of the most difficult times was when a childhood friend of mine came to see me perform and I really wanted to do well. And I wanted him to see striptease the way I saw it. It was funny, because he told me, "I should have married you so you wouldn't have to be doing this." It was really painful for me because I didn't feel that I was doing anything wrong. I enjoyed what I was doing. But you can't make people see what they refuse to see. It still hurts me today that he chooses not to see this business in any other light.

When faced with parents, relatives, friends of parents, coworkers of parents, what can be unsettling for some strippers can be positively traumatic for others whose job has been kept a carefully guarded secret from their families.

Though it isn't likely to happen, the possibility of parents sitting in the "sniff seats" is a situation that could easily divide the stripper's consciousness against itself, both because of her own judgments about those who sit there and because of the proximity of the moral judges in her own life.

But some strippers do share a closeness with at least one of their parents that transcends even the stigma of stripping. It is courageous for a mother to enter such a male dominated enclave to witness her daughter in action.

LUSCIOUS LONA: She showed up Monday, with her boyfriend. She told me she was going to show up Friday, which would have been great—a full crowd. I would have been working harder. Monday is not a great day for me. First show of the day you're tight, you're tired. There were only about 15 people there. So I thought, "Okay. I'm going to go out there and do a relaxed show and I'll just do a little more spreading to make up for it. I did my show, walked offstage and went: "Shit! There's Mom!" I couldn't believe it!

She was in tears. She said [laughing], "Every time you bent over, I felt like powdering it."

Getting into character can become a smoother process as the years go by. But the inner reality always has the option of refusing to play along. For some strippers the conflict between the layers of being becomes almost unmanageable, especially in the face of the harsher realities of the job, at times of down-side depression, and the more severe professional burnout.

DIANA FOX: Yeah. It's always there. When the people are very shy, it's hard to warm them up. Your ego starts to intercede and that's when you can't work the role. And you feel a lot of insecurity. It's an inner conflict. You're paid to be an entertainer. You're an actress. You can't break the role. You have to do it. But sometimes, all of a sudden, you're in yourself and you're sitting there naked and you're going, "Wow! I was in Idaho one time, feeding my goat. Wait a minute!"

BROOKE: Usually I don't think deeply because that's when I start getting into trouble. I just accept my job as it is. Part of me wants to be the part of society which is prejudiced against us. And part of me argues, "No. It is okay. What you're doing is good. Forget what everybody else says." And yet the other part of me is saying, "No. You've got to stop doing this. You have to be accepted by everybody, not just by yourself." It drives you crazy after a while. I have had sleepless nights when I've had these two parts of me fighting each other.

DEVLIN DEVINE: The hardest thing in this business to deal with is my conscience. I'm really not cut out for this business. It's just the money that's keeping me in it, and I have so much more I want to do. And it's so easy not to do it because I'm doing this. Guys in the audience always say to me when I'm walking offstage (and this is really hard to take!): "What are you doing here? What are you doing in this business?"

I always get defensive and look at them and say, "Well, what are *you* doing here?" But inside I know what they are saying. Because I know I should be doing something different. I can feel it inside me. This does not fulfill me. That's the hardest thing to deal with.

And I think that every girl gets to a certain point where she realizes that you can't be fulfilled with that. At a certain point there's no more challenge. You've had millions of men tell you this and that about your physical being. And that's just not important, you know? I don't even like to hear it. I don't even like people telling me that because, you know, it doesn't matter.

EMERY: I've probably returned to the dressing room three or four times in nine years and said, "I had the strangest feeling just now. Why am I doing this? Why did I just go downstairs and take my clothes off in a public bar?" The whole idea is fairly strange when it comes right down to it.

For some strippers the conflict is with their sense of religion.

MISS BRAZIL: I'm beginning to realize that striptease is not a good thing. It stems from Christianity. I'm a Roman Catholic, obviously not a practicing one, but from what I read in the Bible, one should not be doing things to entice the lust in men, because lust, according to the Bible, is a negative thing unless it is love.

Thinking about things like that and looking at the business around me and seeing a lot of people in the audience who are, I don't know, "far away," it's odd. It's an odd feeling you get after so many years in the business. You wonder if this is all the right thing to do. Especially with the animal shows that are coming in. You wonder if it's *all* just trash.

DENISE BRESSETTE: I follow the Mormons, mostly. They've got really good beliefs about family and love and being united. They're also very healthy people. Every time I see one of their commercials, it hits me. Their main focus is family life. You can't allow your other ambitions to come ahead of that need. If I was a mother, I wouldn't be doing this. I'm not going to start a family until I finish with dancing.

DEVLIN DEVINE: I'm a very spiritual person. It conflicts with my job. On the one hand I try to condone it by saying that I'm making people feel good. When I dance, I really try not to portray women in a bad light. I'm not lewd and I'm not suggestive. I try more than anything to be sensual and to look people in the eyes and be humble. Maybe if you saw me dance, you'd understand it better. Women aren't all little bouncy things, bouncing around everywhere and getting into doggy positions two inches from men's faces; that's not what women are about!

GIDGET: I was brought up in a very religious family. I was a Southern Baptist. The first time I went onstage I thought I might be struck by lightning, I felt so guilty. I used to think, "God's going to punish me for dancing." I just knew I was doing something terribly wrong. But as the years went on, I found out that it wasn't all that bad. A lot of people were doing it and that's how they were making their living.

It must also be said that some strippers do not rely heavily on a "second skin," preferring instead to exploit their modest girl-next-door looks. Some go flashily into the world; and some go homespun onstage. Most pick up something of the character somewhere in the bar and then leave it there when they go home.

6
The Sublime Vision
Part 1: Projection

In the previous chapter strippers revealed that their thoughts and feelings are usually incongruent with their outward expression. Not only do they not, as a rule, feel sexually aroused onstage, but they also rarely even feel naked. That they exhibit a sexuality that is not their own is substantiated by the ones who confess they won't strip for their lovers because it is work, not intimacy. That their physical appearance onstage is a radical departure from how they normally look is underscored by the people who do not recognize them when they are dressed for the street. What the audience sees is a cosmetic mask embellishing the stripper's real appearance and an act that belies her real self. The stripper is a facade, a modification (if not a travesty) of natural human femininity in both form and substance. That the men believe it *is* her sexuality is verified by the ones who ask her what she does to get in the mood. This is the stripper's alchemy and she does it effortlessly; in fact, as will be seen below, some strippers are surprisingly unaware of the full effect they have on men.

The dynamics of the strip joint gestalt then will be seen to arise out of two sets of interlocking relationships: that between the stripper's subjective self and her performance, and that between the stripper's image as it appears in the minds of the men and the men's own subjective selves.

It might be thought that what the stripper does would be synonymous with what the men see, but this is not the case. That they are at variance is illustrated by the following research. *Spotlight,* an erstwhile periodical for strippers serving the Pacific northwest, conducted a survey in 1982 of both strippers and their audience to find out what each thought was essential to a good performance. Each was asked to rank in order of importance a list of items (selected by the magazine) pertaining to the show. This is how the results compared when averaged out for each group:

Audience	Strippers
1. Slim figure	1. Dance ability
2. Cute bum	2. Friendly smile
3. Pretty face	3. Good music
4. Nice legs	4. Slim figure
5. Dance ability	5. Variety of interesting costumes
6. Friendly smile	6. Pretty face
7. Large breasts	7. Sense of humor
8. Showing pink	8. Nice legs
9. Good music	9. Cute bum
10. Sense of humor	10., 11. (tied). Acrobatic ability;
11. Acrobatic ability	large *breasts*
12. Variety of interesting costumes	12. Showing pink

It is not difficult to see the disparity between the two lists. The men placed all the emphasis on body criteria, while the strippers tended to view these as secondary to their creative and empathetic ("friendly smile") sides. The *Spotlight* article's author concluded: "The majority of dancers thought audiences wanted to see good dance ability and smiles! Little did they know attention was elsewhere."[1]

One is pressed to ask, to what degree are strippers aware of the disparity between the image they project and the image that is seen? Does their list reflect their suppositions about what men think is important to the show or their views about what *ought* to be important to the show? What do strippers think are the reasons men watch them?

DENISE BRESSETTE: A lot of people come for a lot of different reasons. Some people like it because the music's not too loud. You can sit and have a beer and you don't have to scream at each other to be understood. Some people come because there's good music.

A lot of people find talking to dancers very stimulating because they have a lot of things to talk about, because they have been introduced to so many walks of life. They're open-minded.

Some people are perverts.

Some people just find it entertaining.

JAY JAY: If I thought about how they were thinking of me, it would bother me. But I don't. I think of them as looking at me for my dancing ability or my smile. A body is just a body. It's how you present yourself. I don't like to think of them as looking at my nudity. I know they do, but I just don't think about it that way.

I feel good when I'm dancing. It really means a lot to me to do a good show. Then, my boyfriend might turn around and say, "They don't care. They look at it totally different than you do." And that takes away from what I'm striving for. If no one's appreciating it, what am I doing it for?

MAGENTA MOON: You can get up there with a lot of enthusiasm and then you start thinking, "All they want to see is my twat and my tits and they don't even really care about the tits anymore."

RITA RHINESTONE: If you're performing and you're doing it well enough, then you get a reaction from the crowd that's completely appreciative and completely understanding.

Sometimes, you've got the crowd and titillation or eroticism is the least of it. But the female nude does have a lot of impact onstage. People can be mesmerized by it. And I think some of that is the power of the female nude as the symbol of creation. There's a lot of fear around that. Also, the man sees himself onstage. If you're a good performer and you achieve that superhumanness for the moment, then the man sees himself in the female form. When a performer creates that moment of being super alive and superhuman, expressed so fully, so vividly, then everyone in the crowd identifies with that person; everyone in the crowd feels more possibilities in life.

I think a lot of art is like that. The people are watching and the performer is expressing what the people are feeling.

When it is a woman onstage, and she has achieved that for the moment, then, whatever she's expressing, any man will identify with her; but if she's nude, then there's that double shock. Some of the power that's there when men are watching women is that extra jolt.

I think there's a common misconception that the men are all drooling and being bestial and the women are forced to grovel and crawl around the floor, or something. There's aspects of that, but it isn't all like that. There's degrees of transcending that—or not. My experience was that men are certainly capable of comprehending everything that dancers have to offer and appreciating it—in whatever context.

LUSCIOUS LONA: I know why they like me. That's why I do well. If I objected to why they like me, I wouldn't do it for a living. I know they like Luscious Lona. They don't know Lona. They don't know that part of me and I don't want them to know that part. *They* don't want to know that part. They just want to know the fantasy that's up onstage, that's sexy and looks like she wants everyone in the crowd and wants to be with everyone in the crowd. It's an act. It's manipulation of 150 men at once [laughing]. It's great.

SARITA: There's all kinds of elements involved in why men watch strippers. There are men who want to see women degrade themselves because it takes their anxiety level down—whatever's making them afraid to be intimate with a woman. They can go away convinced that women are just objects.

Then there are men who are simply curious. That's natural. Curiosity about the mysterious feminine form or the feminine mystique. You know, different bodies, looking at different anatomical parts. For the younger men.

There's a lot of guys who go hoping they're going to date one of the girls.

There are men out there who are obsessive womanizers, but can't get a woman, so they become obsessive voyeurs.

SHADOW FIRE: There's a saying in *The Prophet* by Kahlil Gibran: "Modesty is a shield for the eye of the unclean." There's no reason to be modest except that people do not always see with clean eyes. It's all in what you look for. If you look to see lust, you'll see it. If you look to see beauty, you'll see it. If you look to see art, you'll see it. If you look to see lies, you'll see them, too.

Here is further evidence of the disparity between the image presented and the image perceived, but it is clearly one of degree, not substance. Some strippers acknowledge the erotic emphasis in the show and gleefully play to it; some acknowledge it with dismay; some dissociate from or simply deny it in the service of their public face or their own internal moralizer; and some seem to think that the men in the audience who gaze at them carnally are only a small minority. A significant fact that underscores the gray areas of this business is that many strippers who acknowledge the erotic emphasis of the show also do their professional best to entertain over and above gratuitous self-exposure.

To be sure, the spectrum of opinion on the stripper's side is mirrored by a similar spectrum on the men's side. The men are not unanimous in being genitally focused. While more men in the *Spotlight* survey rated showing pink the single most important feature of the show than any other, a very high number also rated it least important (which explains its eighth place finish). In addition, many men in the survey did choose dance ability, friendly smile, and other aspects of the dancers personality as their number-one focus.

However, the cumulative weight of opinion on each side of the image does reveal a differing sense of priority. The professional stripper conceives of her show as a creative dance performance utilizing the vehicle of her nude body while the audience sees it as an erotic spectacle that sometimes makes the transcendent leap into entertainment.

Having established that the stripper's performance and the visual image of it are not synonymous, we may proceed to conclude that what makes it different on the receiving end has less to do with the stripper than with the men. That is, what the men see is partially shaped by their own subjectivity. The image—what we understand as the stripper—is as much a construction of the male mind as a role played by a woman. What does the male psyche contribute to the image of the stripper? What does she satisfy in that psyche?

On the surface such questions seem naive. The male obsession with ogling so saturates the fabric of Western social life that it is simply taken for granted. It is, and always has been, accepted as part of the furnishings of life: man looks, woman attracts. Ostensibly, this simple formula greases the wheels of human evolution. It is as though a man's vision of the goddess, though seen in the eyes and savored in the mind, is actually riveted in the genes.

And yet, while the stripper apparently capitalizes on this endemic male appetite for the look, the abuse she attracts indicates that she is viewed with much more than elemental desire. Some men seem to focus a great deal of animosity on her. In light of the fact that the stripper is a modified, idealized form of natural femininity, how is the ambivalent view of her to be explained? Why would a market exist for such an image?

To answer these questions, it will be necessary to start at the beginning, that is, at birth. What follows is a brief overview of developmental psychology. The model used to map the development of the genders from birth to adulthood is from Dorothy Dinnerstein's book, *The Mermaid and the Minotaur.* It has been selected from the many available expositions on the topic because of its unique focus on the attitudes each gender inherits about the other from its upbringing, and, in particular, men's ambivalent view of women.

Human life is forever marked by its origins in a state of fusion with the mother and the ensuing drive to come to terms with the state of separation that begins at birth. While separation occurs abruptly, consciousness of its conditions, its boundaries, and its relativity develops only gradually, over the course of several years. Thus, while a de facto separation occurs at birth, the infant lives in a state of emotional contiguity with the mother for some time. Consequently, the mother's effect on the infant is profound and lasting. The mother makes the first and fundamental imprints in the impressionable wax of the neonatal consciousness. This means that the first relationship with another human being, the first struggles with another's will, and the first experiences of love, approval, authority, obedience, belonging, vulnerability, pain, and pleasure have all occurred with a woman.

One basis for our species' fundamental ambivalence toward its female members lies in the fact that the early mother, monolithic representative of nature, is a source, like nature, of ultimate distress as well as ultimate joy. Like nature, she is both nourishing and disappointing, both alluring and threatening, both comforting and unreliable. The infant loves her touch, warmth, shape, taste, sound, movement, just as it loves dancing light, textured space, soft covers, and as it will come to love water, fire, plants, animals. And it hates her because, like nature, she does not perfectly protect and provide for it. She is the source of food, warmth, comfort, and entertainment; but the baby, no matter how well it is cared for, suffers some hunger or cold, some bellyaches or alarming sudden movements or unpleasant bursts of noise, some loneliness or boredom; and how is it to know that she is not the source of these things too?[2]

The child is, moreover, physically dependent on her ... far into a period in which it is mentally developed enough to be, in important ways, aware of this dependence. The human baby, because it is immobile longer and at the same time very much brighter, has a capacity for *feeling* powerless unlike that of any other baby animal.[3]

While physical fusion with the mother becomes a dim cellular memory, the mother's all-encompassing embrace, her emotional bond—her love—tempers the transition into life on the outside. But as the infant's motor abilities improve and its consciousness expands, its innate drive toward personal autonomy conflicts more and more with its gravitational pull back toward the mother's embrace. Inevitably, the will of the infant clashes with the will of its mother and her status as omnipotent provider turns to that of omnipotent authority. The essential resources of love, approval, emotional support, freedom of exploration, and even nutriments, given so selflessly before, can now be withheld to manipulate behavior. Mother's selfless love reveals itself to be contingent upon the infant's obedience.

This woman, moreover, is the overwhelming external will in the face of which the child first learns the necessity for submission, the first being to whose wishes the child may be forced by punishment to subordinate his own, the first powerful and loved creature whom the child tries voluntarily to please.[4]

Through woman's jurisdiction over child's passionate body, through her control over what goes into it and what comes out of it, through her right to restrict its movements and invade its orifices, to withhold pleasure or inflict pain until it obeys her wishes, each human being first discovers the peculiarly angry, bittersweet experience of conscious surrender to conscious, determined outside rule.[5]

The state of fusion (which has a postpartum as well as a fetal significance) is perceived retrospectively with both nostalgia and apprehension. On the one hand, it is viewed as a time of innocence, safety, and belonging in the keeping of a benevolent, all-powerful presence, a time before the installation of ego defenses on the vulnerable, sensitive, uncomplicated state of being. It is perceived as a time before obligations, necessities, responsibilities, commitments, abuse, conflict, fear, anger, guilt, disappointment, rejection, and meanness: a state of harmony, spontaneity, and sensation marked by a feeling of floating with the rhythms of life. It is possible that such adult notions as arcadia, utopia, and nirvana arise from preconscious memories of personal fusion. It is also possible that the pleasurable side of primeval fusion resonates in later life with more nostalgic weight than in fact it is worthy of. The harsh realities subsumed by a life of separateness stimulate wistful longings.

The other perspective on fusion, filtered through the ego defenses of the self-reliant adult, is that it was a state of abject helplessness, complete dependence on and total vulnerability to another's will. Instead of harmony, this perspective sees absorption, subjection, and abuse. The primal sense of belonging is seen to have a price attached to it. From this view, the pleasurable side of fusion is a deception, a hook to further the real agenda of manipulation and control.

Total dependence on the mother, coupled with the intervention of her more powerful will, results in ambivalence between resentment of this dependence and the feeling that without her one will die. The theory holds that the girl resolves her personal sense of ambivalence by transferring the positive feelings to her father. The boy, however, "cannot use his father in this way without giving homoerotic attraction a dominant place in his love life. If woman is to remain for him the central human object of the passions most deeply rooted in life's beginnings, his relation to her must embrace, at a primitive level, *both* the worshipful and the derogatory, the grateful and the greedy, the affectionate and the hostile feeling toward the early mother."[6]

But the boy is left with a further conflict that the girl does not share: he and his father are now rivals for the same woman. The boy, obviously at a severe disadvantage in this contest, learns to control his feelings to avoid reprisal from the father as well as rejection from the mother. He resolves the conflict by moving toward solidarity with his father (and the male club), a move given some impetus by the boy's own negative feelings for his mother.

While the original state of fusion is ancient history to the self-actualized adult, desire, sex, and love tend to reawaken the old ambivalences. Female rejection, a widely held male fear, and the frequent unavailability of sexual partners, resonate with the neonatal sense of frustrated belonging. Manipulation, the métier of the dreaded *femme fatale*, is essentially the false promise of the pleasurable side of fusion to further other ends. Sexual intercourse, which holds within it the potential of supreme pleasure in fusion, also compels the complete dissolution of the egoistic defenses. Sex reawakens the primeval memory of absorption and maximum vulnerability. Orgasm, which may bring about a brief unconsciousness, has often been referred to as the "little death." Intimacy demands the release of one's self-imposed controls on deep feeling and augurs the loss of autonomy. In adult life, women signify to men both the resolution of their very primitive urge for union and a threat to their self-control and independence. "The threat to autonomy which can come from a woman is felt on a less rational, more helpless level, experienced as more primitively dangerous, than any such threat from a man."[7] In addition, women "can more readily re-evoke in him the unqualified, boundless, helpless passion of infancy. If he lets her, she can shatter his adult sense of power and control; she can bring out the soft, wild, naked baby in him."[8]

The threat presented by women push men to retreat in two directions. One is to exclusively male enclaves or spheres of activity: "secret societies, hunting trips, pool parlors, wars ... refuges in which they can recuperate from the temptation to give way to ferocious, voracious dependence, and recover their feelings of competence, autonomy, dignity."[9] Another is away from deep feeling in heterosexual love. "One way to do this is to keep heterosexual love superficial, emotionally and physically. Another is to dissociate its physical from its emotional possibilities."[10]

This is not to say that women do not share such fears. Having their origins in a similar state of fusion as men, women struggle with a similar conflict between self-determination and sexual fusion. Women fear rejection, manipulation, and losing themselves in another, just like men. Women also view men with ambivalence. However, because women are the same gender as the mother, they do not apprehend her as an "other," the way men do. While the neonatal girl, like the boy, separates physically and personally from the mother, she does not separate from her categorically. While boys rebel against the mother, girls identify with her. Girls internalize the role of the mother and so retain a sense of gender continuity with the omnipotent source. In women, desire for another does not invoke the same sense of conflict between the maintenance and the dissolution of interpersonal boundaries that it does in men. Women are thus theoretically less anxious about the revitalized sense of primeval fusion that sex evokes.

> In the sexual recapitulation of the infant-mother interplay, [woman] has more of a sense than [man] does of embodying the powerful mother within herself; a greater part of her than of his reliving of the infant role is vicarious, through the other person. This makes her less afraid of being plunged back into the atmosphere of helpless infancy, and therefore typically better able to fuse intense emotional and intense physical intimacy…

> Infancy has not taught her, as surely as it has taught him, to feel simultaneously the boundaries of herself and the current between herself and what attracts her.[11]

However, the relative difference between the male and female fears of the opposite gender is not as significant as each one's relative ability to compensate for it. Males form a dominant class in Western social systems (if not most of the world). They control the economic and political sectors and are preeminent in the arts and sciences. Women are an underclass, disadvantaged in their access to available resources, including, most critically for our purposes here, the market for images, ideas, and opinion. Because Western culture has been shaped and defined largely by men, it could be expected to reflect men's psychology and its constituent anxieties much more than women's. That is, the male's fear of the opposite gender is more likely to become a fixture of culture than that of the female.

But the male fear of women, as such, is not a culturally recognized syndrome. Its presence as a topic in academic discourse is meager and what there is never achieves much prominence. It is hardly ever (*if* ever) the focus of talk shows, television documentaries, magazine articles, or self-help books. It is rarely discussed among men. So the male fear of women, although endemic, remains invisible.

This is because it has been sublimated to forms of expression that turn fear into more powerful dispositions. In her seminal article on "The Dread of Women," Karen Horney wrote that the male's first line of defense is to objectify the fear:

Always, everywhere the man strives to rid himself of his dread of women by objectifying it: "It is not," he says, "that I dread her; it is that she herself is malignant, capable of any crime, a beast of prey, a vampire, a witch, insatiable in her desires. She is the very personification of what is sinister."[12]

Objectification converts the subordinate state of fear into the superior states of judgment, criticism, and censure. The displacement of fear onto women's "dreadfulness" roots its cause in the external present instead of the internal and obscure past. Fear sinks beneath the properties attributed to women (emotionalism, deceit, and ambivalence) on the one side, male condescension on the other and is forgotten in the resulting commotion.[13] The evidence for the male fear of women, therefore, will be found beneath its objectified manifestations.

Such evidence is not difficult to find. One of the privileges enjoyed by the dominant class is that it can turn its anxieties unselfconsciously into art. (Horney, along with many other psychologists, believed that all the creative endeavors of the male—his art, literature, and mythology—are byproducts of the eternal conflict between his desire for and his fear of women.) The verbal evidence has been repeated so often that it has earned its own anthology. The *Home Book of Quotations* has devoted an entire section to the topic of woman as a curse. A selection of these quotes strung together, unencumbered by author's credits (from Homer to Tolstoy), testifies to an enduring historical resentment of women.

O woman, woman, when to ill thy mind / Is bent, all hell contains no fouler fiend.
A man shall walk behind a lion rather than behind a woman.
There is no other purgatory but a woman.
Women are the gate of hell.
Weren't not for gold and women, there would be no damnation.
The world is full of women, and the women full of wile.
All wickedness is but little to the wickedness of a woman.
There is no evil so terrible as a woman.
What an inviting hell invented.
When toward the Devil's House we tread, / Woman's a thousand steps ahead.
Of all the plagues with which the world is curst, / Of every ill, a woman is the worst.
He seldom errs who thinks the worst he can of womankind.
There is more death in women than we think.
Nothing is worse than a woman, even a good one.

There are many wild beasts on land and in the sea, but the beastliest of all is woman.

Women are one and all a set of vultures.

In point of morals the average woman is, even for business, too crooked.

Regard the society of women as a necessary unpleasantness of social life, and avoid it as much as possible.[14]

The following example, which did not find its way into the volume, has the flavor of settling the matter once and for all: "If all the world were paper and all the sea ink, and all the trees and plants were pens, and every man in the world were a writer, yet were they not able with all their labor and cunning to set down all the crafty deceits of women."[15]

Examined closely, the anecdotes reveal their emotional underpinnings. Although they compare women unfavorably with various horrific images—like ferocious beasts, purgatory, hell, damnation, evil, plague, and death—their emotional tone is not one of fear but supercilious contempt. They have the flavor of invective rather than that of a poetic catharsis of dread. They represent the transformation of fear into the much stronger position of censure. The words are the literal analogues of cages and quarantines; they circumscribe the threat within a configuration of superior judgment. (There is no equivalent section of the *Home* devoted to women's anxieties about men.)

In mythology and representative art the fear appears as the female demon. The Ancient Greeks, for instance, gave us Circe, the prototypical *femme fatale*, whose magic wand turned men into hogs; Echidne, who was half goddess, half serpent, and ate men raw; and, of course the proverbial Sirens who lured sailors to their doom with enchanting songs. From Hebrew lore came Salome, the prototypical dancing girl whose dance cost John the Baptist his head; Delilah, who betrayed the indomitable Samson; and Judith, who beheaded Holophernes after seductively lulling him into carelessness. With one possible exception, all of these images were the fictional creations of men. And while Salome may have been a real historical figure, the story that made her an enduring legend—historians agree—probably never happened. It, too, appears to have been projected from a deep-seated male conflict about women.

The salient feature of most mythological female demons is their duality of identity. They are either physical composites of the attractive and the hideous, exemplified by the Sirens' maiden faces, enthralling voices, and their menacing clawed feet, or they are a seductive presence masking a perilous agenda. In either case, they are one and the same: the mythological monsters are allegories of the *femmes fatales*. A modern example of this genre is the René Magritte painting *La Gâcheuse* (*The Spoiler*), a disturbing rendition of a female upper body, nude and shapely, topped off with a menacing skeletal cranium. This choice of juxtapositions effectively mirrors the male conflict: woman's protean personality—a voracious and predatory nature (symbolized by the gnashing jaws of the skeleton) concealed beneath a beautiful and seductive facade.

The collection and display of anecdotes united in their rancor toward women and the prominence achieved by female demons in our lore—a prominence far beyond that of (in Paula Stern's observation) "exceptional, independent women like Rebecca, Sarah, Deborah, or Ruth"[16]—testifies to their status as established genres. As such, they cease to shock. Their repetition falls in with the rhythms of civilized life. We become desensitized to them and the feelings that are ignited by them. Whether or not we consciously agree with their perspective, we do not react to them with antipathy because they strike a long-established chord. They meld easily with our inured conception of the battle of the sexes. We accept that the differences between the genders create frustration and suspicion, and we buy into the animosity without questioning its deeper underpinnings. But this acceptance cannot help but reinforce the messages these anecdotes and legends promote. Their repetitive invocation of the attributed dreadfulness of women serves to deflect attention away from the underlying fear and to provide a cultural catalyst for the transformation of fear into hostility, distrust, and the social control of women.

While much space here has been devoted to the emotion of fear because of its relative obscurity, it is but one side of the male's ambivalence toward women. Desire, too, has its own process of objectification. Opposite the female demons in our mythology, art, and dreams stand the goddesses. The goddess and the demon represent the two sides of the primeval ambivalence: the omnipotent and benevolent gratifier of one's needs—the pleasurable side of fusion—and the manipulative, controlling, consuming threat to one's autonomy, one's sense of self. However, the effects are not strictly dichotomous. The presence of the demonic side overshadows that of the goddess. The demonic is perceived to reside as a latent threat *within* a seductive shell (in effect masquerading as a goddess), and hence, more closely allied with a woman's soul, with her true nature. That is why the images that serve the respective themes appear as they do: the demon as a composite of sensuality masking danger, the goddess as a monolithically sensual being. The goddess's form and content must remain mutually consistent; if she fails to convey the message that she has been purified of any intent other than the gratification of her viewer she will pass into the ambiguous state of the demon.

The properties of the goddess reflect the resolution of the adult male's gender conflict. Conceptually, the goddess is physically enchanting, available, unambivalent, sexually willing, and a tireless servant of one's personal preferences. These properties represent the pleasurable side of fusion raised to an ideal and the vulnerable side dissolved. They presuppose the absence of any of the demonic properties of rejection and manipulation. The man remains in complete control of the situation, the woman in it, and his own emotions. He may experience the pleasure of harmonious fusion with her without being vulnerable to the loss of his autonomous self. Obviously, an *image* of a goddess can only deliver on some of these concepts. The rest must occur in fantasy.

The quintessential male fantasy image may be described as the ever available, infinitely gratifying, monolithically sexual, and physically ideal goddess. And she has three incarnations: the one perfect love relationship (in which monolithic sexuality has been compromised to allow for intimacy, conversation, and play, which gratify the man nonetheless), that is, the perfect wife; the one perfect sex partner; and an endless supply of different sex partners, each one an embodiment of the ideal. If the goddess image soothes the male fear of intimacy, this last fantasy must be the most soothing one of all. An endless supply ensures that intimacy with any one partner remains superficial. On the other hand, their monolithic sexuality makes them unidimensional and ultimately boring. So they necessitate an endless reproduction in new forms.

One might expect that, considering the anxieties men have about women inherited from their formative years, there would be a vast market for goddess images. The tension generated by desire, fear, and control finds its path of least resistance and its safest resolution in fantasy. Fantasy appropriates images of the goddess and makes them come alive. In fantasy one adds the properties that the image cannot convey, such as gratifying the man's every wish.

The alchemy of sexual fantasy is essentially the alloying of an ideal form with an ideal psychic content. This motif has been immortalized in the legend of Pygmalion, the obsessional king of Cyprus. Frustrated in his affections for the beautiful and elusive Aphrodite, Pygmalion fashioned an ivory image in her likeness and placed it in his bed where he prayed to it continuously. Such was the power of this ritual (or the pity of the goddess) that Aphrodite eventually entered into the idol and brought it to life as Galatea, with whom the king sired two children. The enduring romance with this legend hinges on its wish fulfillment: mere mortals can be gods on earth; and form can be bestowed with vitality—but a vitality as skillfully crafted as the form.

The first step in the alchemy of sexual fantasy is to find the right form (or image). Pygmalion found his in the goddess of love; modern man can find his wherever women appear: "live"—on the street or the stage—or "mediated"—in art, photography or film.

The second step is the separation of the form from its indwelling personality. The removal of the female's subjective self ensures the absence in the re-created image of any moods that are not sexually willing, compliant, or tend toward the demonic. The re-created goddess will be able to reject, manipulate, smother, or otherwise dominate only under the auspices of her new master. Pygmalion carved her image in ivory; the mortal man will simply capture her in his imagination.

The third step is to suture the ideal self to the ideal form, to revitalize the image with a life force appropriate to the wish fulfillment of the moment. Made available, the image is now monolithically sexual and infinitely gratifying. *She* is no longer animating her; her *viewer* is. The result is woman reborn as sex goddess—the perfect body animated by the flawless disposition—to be used, discarded, and re-created in an endless variety of forms.

In erotica and pornography the first two steps in the process have been taken care of already. The female images are selected for their form and choreographed to appear ready, willing, and available. All the viewer has to do is reanimate them in his mind according to his personal preferences.

This is true of many other images of women that are not pornographic: images of beauty, for instance, in which sexual expressiveness has been played down to further other ends. These would include cover girls, beauty queens, swim-suit models, and various movie stars who are neither nude nor as explicitly sexual as, say, the porn queen. They are goddesses of beauty as opposed to goddesses of sex, but they are equally as much idealized forms, surfaces devoid of substance, and screens for projected fantasies.

All goddess images are united in their lack of ambivalence. They cannot reject or manipulate; they cannot absorb or dominate; they are never contrary, difficult, or judgmental; and so, to the adult mind-set of the Western man (at least), they are comforting. They offer a catalytic resolution of deep-seated conflicts in fantasy. What remains to be explored is how the stripper fits in with her sister images.

On the surface the stripper appears to replicate all the essential properties of the goddess. As a variation on the theme of the ever available, infinitely gratifying, monolithically sexual, and physically ideal goddess, she embodies all the requisites of a screen for fantasy. What makes her unique among such images is her integration of the themes of nudity and dancing in a live medium. The fact that the stripper appears in a live format, as opposed to a mediated one—like a photograph or a video—endows her with some peculiar properties that put her in a class all her own.

While still an image, like her photographic and cinematic sisters, the stripper is also, uniquely, still a woman. As such, the stripper appears to be *really* available. The men cannot help but think that here is a figure that not only embodies the traditional codes of the goddess but is one that might actually be procured *in the flesh*. Of all the goddesses, the stripper may be the only one to arouse authentic hope in her viewers. Hope is almost as good a fuel for fantasy as desire. The stripper's alchemy percolates when she (often unconsciously) meets the eyes of a viewer and lingers there for a moment as though she is interested in him. Many veteran strippers know the extent to which they can play on this hope without crossing the line into conspicuous manipulation.

But a few strippers have no scruples at all about making the men grovel, and it is this latent potentiality that reveals the stripper's most significant feature: her aliveness implies the presence of the demon. Beneath the facade of the infinitely gratifying and the monolithically sexual, lives a symbol of original ambivalence. The stripper, while clearly a woman reborn as a sex goddess, retains the ability to reject and manipulate, even absorb and smother. As such, her embodiment of goddess imagery paradoxically contravenes its traditional formulation. The stripper is a radical, an outlaw.

The stripper produces a suspension of disbelief necessary to the alchemy of fantasy, but it is one that teeters precariously on dissolution. The viewers see the image and are persuaded by its monolithic sexuality, as long as the stripper stays in character. In the exposition of the origins of the adult male's fears of women, the point was made that a woman's spontaneous, unbridled sexuality may evoke old memories of a mother's uncontrollable independence. (This is one reason for the infinitely gratifying component of the goddess. Without this mollifier, monolithic sexuality may become overpowering, and hence, demonic.) Photographic images offer the resolution of this conflict by their apparent capture of woman's sexuality in a freeze-framed form, thereby allowing it to be reanimated in fantasy to a degree controlled by the viewer. Even a video, which presents an animated sexual content, offers a view from a safe distance, its eroticism confined within the boundaries of the television screen. In contrast, the stripper's unmediated format brings her dangerously close to the viewer and thus she brings to the image an unusually vital charge. (Couch dancing represents the probable limits to which this concept can be pushed.) However, while the stripper's eroticism is indeed unmediated, it remains nonetheless contained, both within the boundaries of the stage area and the imperatives of the act. In the rare instances when the stripper makes physical contact with her audience it is never, in any sense of the term, a sexual advance. Rather, it is almost always in the spirit of the unfulfilled tease. Even when she drapes her legs over the shoulders of someone sitting at the edge of the stage and brings her crotch within inches of his face, the tacit understanding is that her willful, passionate permission, although seemingly written on her face, is withheld. The psychic distance between the stripper (and her consuming sexuality) and the audience is always maintained. The stripper's appeal, beyond her visual pleasure, lies in her *living* personification of the traditional properties of the goddess in extreme proximity to the viewer, without compromising his self-control. The strip club—a male refuge, as defined above—offers a sublime equilibrium between the urge for and the fear of sexual fusion.

But this equilibrium is tenuous at best. The stripper is not a pure form of the goddess. Her roots in burlesque and her freedom of choreography allow for the selective intrusion on the purely erotic components of the show by what has been referred to here as entertainment. The tease and the humor that remain, and the occasional playing of instruments and such, derive from a place much closer to the stripper's passion than does the ersatz eroticism she displays. While they serve to build rapport with the audience and offer them some release of emotional tension, they are disruptive to fantasy. They immediately dissolve the image's property of monolithic sexuality. So do the moods the stripper allows to surface.

One might say that all of the nonsexual components of the show are closer to the stripper's heart than the sexual ones. This serves to explain the disparity between the two lists from the *Spotlight* survey. The men's list reflects their psychic readiness, their predisposition toward receiving the codes of the goddess (monolithic sexuality, in particular) and assimilating her in fantasy. Her entertainment value is secondary, even intrusive; for the goddess resonates with more primitive significance than an entertainer. The men's list is not simply representative of a need for carnal stimulation; it also reflects a need for the resolution of some deep-seated conflicts.

Strippers cannot be expected to know that their main focus is the resolution of anxieties deriving from a man's neonatal scenario. On the other hand, they are aware, through cultural and historical conditioning, of what the established codes of the goddess are. Their answers to the questionnaire reflect their desires to animate the codes with some creativity, some empathy, and some soul.

But it is the business of stripping to push against the allowable limits of exposure. The entertainment has always been its cover, not its draw. The spirit of the goddess image is driven by its quest for the pure form. The ritual of the strip is ever shorter, the moves and gestures more mechanized, the genital exposure and focus more intense. In some areas now the stripper dances to one song, removes her single article of clothing—a body stocking—performs nude to one more song and is replaced by the next one. This progression seeks to discover how refined monolithic sexuality can be in a live format. And so it aims at pure fantasy unencumbered by soul.

7
The Sublime Vision
Part 2: Screen

Nature and art, being two different things, cannot be the same
thing. Through art we express our conception of what nature is
not.

Picasso[1]

Conceptually, the goddess presents the resolution of men's ambivalence about women. Each of the properties of the goddess serves to resolve
a particular aspect of this ambivalence and turn it to pleasure. "Ever available," the goddess delivers herself into male control; she is there whenever desire wants her. "Infinitely gratifying," she satisfies his every wish.
"Monolithically sexual," she is constitutionally devoid of any potential for
contrary moods. (This property may be compromised somewhat for the
goddess-as-wife fantasy, which remains nonetheless gratifying.) "Physically ideal," the goddess equates with extreme value and embodies the
codes for a vehicle of supreme aesthetic and sensual enjoyment.

These are the properties of the goddess as she appears in fantasy. An
image of the goddess, designed for the stimulation of fantasy, embodies as
many of these properties as it can within its medium, but obviously the
fulfillment of her promise can only occur in the imagination. The vitality stripped from natural femininity in its elevation to the status of a goddess image can only be replaced in fantasy.

The stripper is the first commercial live rendition of the nude goddess image. What factors led up to her appearance? How did she evolve
out of the mediated image?

Before we can fully appreciate the history of the nude goddess image,
some concepts particular to images and their apprehension by the mind
will be helpful.

Images present an interface between consciousness and what they

95

refer to. The two interlocking relationships between the image and its viewer and the image and its referred object suggest six areas of inquiry. The first is the realm of fantasy in the viewer (who, for our purposes here, is assumed to be male), that is, the scenario that plays in his mind stimulated by his looking at the image. The second is the particular format of the image, that is, either the statue, painting, photograph, or video. The third is the image itself, the goddess contained by the format. The fourth, the rendition, is the particular way in which the image is presented, indicated by her choreography, her degree of nudity, how explicit she is, and how she is posed. The fifth, the referent, is the (imagined) living replica the image refers to, the real goddess who has given her image to the painting (or statue). Finally, the sixth is that of the model, or the living, breathing woman (or women) who modeled for the image.

The image conveys the properties of the goddess through its rendition (pose, cosmetics, and photographic techniques for the celluloid goddesses, and artistic technique for her painted cousins) and is assisted by the format and, of course, by its intended fantasy, especially for the first and second properties. The goddess's format contributes to the property of the ever available through its inherent implication of her "capture" within it, for instance, within the borders of its photographic representation or within a statue. The format may make an additional contribution to this property by making the image actually available through purchase of the format—as in a photograph, painting, or video—while some formats—such as priceless works of art in museums—remain unattainable. While the rendition of the goddess makes her *appear* infinitely gratifying, she *becomes* so only in the realm of fantasy through the viewer's imaginative reanimation of her. Even where the goddess's format is a video or a strip show—where the image is obviously already animated—she is, nonetheless, reanimated in the viewer's mind to serve his particular desires.

The distinction between the image's model and its referent is important. A *Playboy* centerfold, for instance, refers to the woman who posed for the photograph *and* to a living, breathing replica of the image, that is, a woman who personifies all the properties of the goddess. While the first, the model, is usually a real woman, the second can never be. No living woman can ever live up to the ideals embodied by the image. Such an ideal can only live in a reanimated form in fantasy. The image, therefore, presents a paradox. Although the format may enhance the image's property of availability (as explored above), it may also convey a sense of remoteness or distance. The goddess referred to by the image—infinitely gratifying, monolithically sexual, and physically ideal—is intrinsically unavailable. This paradox is illustrated by the tale of a man who said he used to date a centerfold. "But I'll tell you," he said. "She wasn't that attractive. I'd make love to her and then later I'd pick up her centerfold picture and fantasize about fucking her. And I had just fucked her! It was crazy!" The image resonates with the implication of the unavailability of its referent—even when its model *is* available.

Two aspects of distance are implied by the image: that between its real life model and her rendered appearance in the image, and that between the image and the living goddess to which it alludes. The first, which may be called the "rendered" distance, represents the degree to which cosmetics, dress (or drapery), pose, or facial expression transport the image beyond normal femininity into the realm of the ideal. The second, here called "imagined" distance, is directly proportional to the rendered distance. The more ideal the goddess image appears to be, the greater her degree of remoteness and the greater the desire attached to her. The importance of distance to the image rests on the fact that the more remote the goddess is imagined to be the greater the value of her image. This is borne out by the values placed on paintings of Venus, Diana, Psyche, and others by revered masters such as Botticelli, Titian, and David. The implication of such renditions of the goddess is that their visual manifestation from their inaccessible Olympian realm has been achieved only through the singular genius of their renderers.

We can now proceed with an historical overview of the nude goddess image.

The very first images of women that we know of were nudes. Crafted some 30,000 years ago, they appeared during an age that saw the creation of language, art, religion, and music. They have been called the Venus figurines by modern men who saw in them examples of the first goddesses.

Carved in a variety of materials from limestone and serpentine to ivory and bone, the figurines differ from each other markedly and yet they share some noteworthy characteristics. They all have exaggerated breasts and buttocks, while exhibiting almost no facial detail as though this most dynamic barometer of woman's inner life was unimportant. What did they mean to prehistoric man? What were they used for?

The impact from the invention of representative art must have been felt with the very first doodle that turned into a picture. That a link was forged between him (or her) and the animal—by drawing a bison or a reindeer—must have been inescapable to the primeval artist. It may have seemed as though he had captured what he had drawn in a timeless, motionless world. It may have seemed that the animal had sprung to life before him; perhaps the creation of the animal's image also brought to life something of the animal's spirit; or perhaps the animal could be affected in some way by appealing to the spirit held by the image. By sketching a bison or a reindeer, the artist effectively drew the animal a little closer to him, perhaps close enough to exert some influence over it. By possessing the image he was that much closer to capturing the real thing.

The true meaning of the Venus figurines may never be known, but they have provided archaeologists, anthropologists, and art historians with endless hours of speculation and debate. The power of the image to transport unpredictable living things into inanimate and possessable forms leads one to believe that its initial focus logically would have been the things in the natural world man had the most vital need to control. The record of prehistoric art supports this idea. Consisting almost entirely of images of animals (both game and dangerous carnivores), images that have been interpreted to be carved vulvas and the Venus figurines, the record reflects the vital themes of nourishment, protection, sex, and reproduction. René Huyghe, editor of the *Larousse Encyclopedia of Prehistoric and Ancient Art*, comments as follows:

> Art is primarily an act of taking possession. There seems no doubt that it is a means afforded man for attaching himself to the external world, for lessening the natural difference which separates him from it and the terror he experiences when confronted with it. Even the earliest examples of art show two aspects: in one man attempts to project himself on the universe, to make his mark on it, to put his name on it; in the other to annex it to himself, to make it his own. In both cases there is a struggle for possession, because he wants either to confirm his impress on the universe or to secure it in the form of an image, a carbon copy, which then becomes pliable and submissive. The first is a case of projection, the second of capture. The desire behind both is the same.[2]

In this context the Venuses and the carved vulvas conceivably represent man's attempt to exert some influence on the body of woman, both as the vehicle for the generation of life and the locus of the satisfaction of his sexual desire, in Huyghe's words, to "put his name on it" and "make it his own."

In Una Stannard's view, the male compulsion to commandeer the mechanism of reproduction has not abated throughout history. The various tactics employed, befitting the temper and the knowledge of the times, have involved either exalting the male function in procreation or denying that of the female. Even until relatively recent times, the male role in procreation was assumed to be more prominent, even to the extent that a woman's role was considered to be merely soil for the seed. As late as the mid-nineteenth century it was still widely believed that the mother contributed nothing to the physical characteristics of her children. Now that science has revealed the equality between the genders in creating life, geneticists (mostly male) tinker with the possibility of harnessing procreation in the laboratory.

Stannard makes the cogent point that long before science began to encroach on the supernatural, men must have thought that they were not involved in procreation at all. The connection between intercourse and pregnancy is not knowledge we are born with and the visible facts of pregnancy do not appear until well after conception. "Impregnation was believed to occur at quickening, the moment when the woman feels the fetus move. It was thought that at that moment a spirit had entered the woman, either from the wind, stars, water, moon, ... trees, lizards, birds, food, or whatever happened to be near the woman at quickening."[3]

The early days of mankind reflect the early years of the infant. The male fear of women, engendered by the mother's all-encompassing power over the child, translates in the adult as envy of woman's preeminence in the natural order. "It was only woman who could procreate, which meant that woman was the superior sex, and not merely because it was upon her that mankind depended for its continuance but because it was woman alone in whom the spirits chose to reside."[4]

John Onians, editor of *Art History*, offers the opinion that, rather than aimed at women's reproductive capabilities, the figurines were explicitly sexual. Onians thinks that while the depictions of game animals on cave walls were made for the eyes, the portable three dimensional Venuses—"respond[ing] to the palm of the hand just as would the swelling curves of a real woman"[5]—were primarily extensions of the tactile. While admitting to what may be a "naive notion," Onians ponders that if prehistoric man "ever day-dreamed, it is surely the sight of a nice edible reindeer or the touching of a nice rounded pair of buttocks which must have passed through his mind. If this is so, could he, perhaps, have been led by the strength of such fantasies to scratch silhouettes of animals on pieces of rock and to form stone into the resemblance of female bodies?"[6]

Onians theorizes that the reason facial details were left out is because they contributed nothing to the intended tactility of the figurines. Others believe it was because the magic in such talismans lay in their being representative of a whole species, instead of an individual member.

When the [prehistoric] painter captured the likeness of his model, he never represented a particular animal. From the limitless variety exhibited by individuals within a species, he extracted the common factor which is also an abstraction: the type. The prehistoric artist never produced particular bison, horses or reindeer, but the bison, the horse or the reindeer. The generalisation was required in order to make the magic effective, for it would have been pointless to cast a spell on a specific animal which the hunter would have very little chance of meeting.[7]

Besides being the most visible symbol of individuality, the face also registers the visual evidence of moods. The rendition of women into face-less images in passive postures is therefore also in keeping with the second step in the alchemy of fantasy, that is, the separation of the form from its personality (and hence, from its demonic uncertainties).

The depersonalization of the image served still another purpose: "the law, so essential to man, of the least effort also drives him to seek a type which is formulated once and for all and only needs to be reproduced."[8] Embodying a generic ideal, the image becomes a prototype for the crafting of others. Unimpeded, the image can be expected to evolve through time and culture, absorbing the influences of each, shaped and displayed according to the sophistication of her artisans, and providing historians with endless hours of discussion about her lineage.

But the image is not just a doll; it is also a message. It embodies a belief system—whether it is invested in the divinity of the image, its particular ideal, its deliverance or its capture—and it becomes the focus of some ritual activity, such as worship or fantasy. By uniting many around it, it may also alienate many others who either do not share in the belief or are excluded from it. The image generates opposition as well as reverence. It is thought that the disappearance of the Venus figurine and the scarcity of representative art in general between 20,000 and 14,000 B.C. may "reflect a fairly consistent policy of suppression, possibly as a result of such cults having a disturbing effect."[9]

This hypothesis is grounded in the more recent historical evidence of similar occurrences. The classical goddess, for instance (the image developed in Ancient Greece), was outlawed during the medieval period. The Ancient Greek nude had, however, attained such an incomparable sophistication in the Western mind that when the medieval period drew to a close and artistic freedom was given new license, it was the model to which artists of the Renaissance turned for their inspiration.

The masterpiece that became the definitive exemplar of the classical goddess was crafted by the great sculptor, Praxiteles, in the fourth century, B.C. Sculpted in white marble, the goddess of love stands naked, one hand holding her robe, the other held demurely in front of her crotch, about to step into her bath. The statue was purchased for the city of Cnidus and so has come to be known as the Cnidian Venus (or Aphrodite). It created a sensation and became the prototype for generations of replicas, some of which survive today in museums around the world. Although the original is unfortunately lost to history, the Roman writer, Pliny, saw it 400 years later still standing in the shrine built for it; and wrote that it was "superior to anything, not merely by Praxiteles, but in the whole world."[10]

It is thought that the impact of the Cnidian Venus derived from her innovative union of divine and earthly qualities. Previously, nude renditions of the goddess were symbolic, rather than *actualized* divinity. With the Cnidian, not only did her nudity represent a departure from the Ancient Greek practice of draping images of the goddess (justified here by the bath), but her dangling hand betrayed a very human predilection for modesty. So alluring was this alloy that, according to a story Pliny had heard, a besmitten man, under cover of night, embraced the statue and stained it with his passion. It is noteworthy that Praxiteles' model (and lover), Phryne, became almost as famous as her marble likeness. Statues of her as herself appeared, one of which stood at the sacred site of Delphi, further blurring the distinctions between the celestial and the earthly goddess.

The significance of this effect, in the shadow of the sexual repression that was to come, is delineated by Kenneth Clark as follows: "Perhaps no religion ever again incorporated physical passion as calmly, as sweetly and as naturally so that all who saw her felt that the instincts they shared with beasts they also shared with the gods. It was a triumph for beauty; and to the Greek mind this beauty was not simply created by Praxiteles, but was already present in the person of his model Phryne."[11]

While artistic representations of the sensual goddess did indeed become taboo during the medieval period, the Venus statues had apparently fallen from favor some 300 years before the last Roman emperors (Greece was by now a Roman colony). Few, if any, were made following the second century A.D. In Clark's view, Venus "had passed from religion to entertainment, from entertainment to decoration: and then she had disappeared."[12] But it may also be inferred that the nude goddess had passed on to some other medium, such as the theater. About the time of the demise of the goddess as statue, the Roman emperor Elagabalus is said to have decreed that all female thespians must now appear naked on the stage.

However, any direction the nude goddess might have taken at this time would have been squelched by the Christian church after it became the power in Rome. The classical nude, rhythmic and sensual, could not have survived within an ideology that viewed it with fear and loathing. Nudity in art did not wholly disappear during the Middle Ages, but it was now a symbol of shame. The cult of Eve had replaced the cult of Venus and the nude ceased to represent the capture of an unattainable ideal.

As the Holy Roman Empire began to fragment, its ideology weakened in part by a new spirit of intellectual freedom, artists rediscovered the classical nude. Gradually, cautiously, the nude goddess reemerged into representative art. Of one of the first renditions—the Three Graces in Botticelli's painting *Primavera*—Clark writes, "It is significant that Botticelli should have felt his way back to antiquity through the image of the Graces, for their nudity had been sanctioned, as emblematic of sincerity, by Christian writers who condemned the nakedness of Venus."[13] Once the concept of the nude had acquired some momentum, however, Venus, as its highest symbol, became the inevitable and ultimate test of the artist. Botticelli followed his Graces with *The Birth of Venus* which became one of the most enduring visions of the High Renaissance and one of the most reproduced paintings of all time. Other milestones followed. Giorgione's invention of the reclining Venus established a genre that lasted for 400 years, emulated in works by masters from Titian to Renoir. With his *Venus of Urbino*, Titian is said to have brought the reclining nude indoors, from the idyllic pastoral setting to the sumptuous bed. From Correggio to Rubens to Ingres, the nude goddess appeared in all her guises, each one an alloy of tradition, innovation, and personal style, and rendered in the spirit of some ideal.

It is thought that the great age of the painted nude ended with Renoir, in the bright lights and indistinct boundaries of Impressionism. Renoir's rosy, plump nudes inspired one commentator to write: "For Renoir the precondition of pleasure was the fantasy of a world without edges, without sharpness or conflict, a world that enveloped like a mother's open blouse and breast,"[14] suggesting a resonance with memories of arcadian fusion.

The crafting of the goddess image in representative art begins, by means of the alchemy of fantasy, with a suitable form or model. Since finding examples of artistic ideals in nature is, by definition, impossible, the artist's challenge has always been how to transform natural femininity into a transcendent vision. There were essentially two approaches to this problem. One could assemble the ideal from its constituent parts found in nature (the head from one woman, the torso from another, the breasts from a third, and so on), or one could map it from a grand design or geometric template.

Perhaps the first reference to the assembly method is the Ancient Greek painter Zeuxis, who is said to have had the entire population of young women in the city of Croton paraded before him naked so that he could combine the best of them into one glorious rendition of the goddess Hera.[15] The same spirit is found in a letter of Rodin to Mistinguett, the French music hall sensation of the early 1900s (whose legs were reputedly insured for 500,000 francs): "If I had to personify the Muse of Music Hall, failing the peplum and the Greek profile, I would give her your legs, Mistinguett."[16] A more recent example is a 1990 *Esquire* magazine construction based on opinions supplied by readers. The resultant dream woman had Kim Basinger's hair, Geena Davis's mouth ("until she opens it"), Michelle Pfeiffer's torso, and Jamie Lee Curtis's legs.[17]

The template method was also prevalent in antiquity. Because the Ancient Greeks believed mathematics to be the measure of all things, the classical nude was constructed according to mathematic ratios. One of the "classical canons of proportion," was to use, in Clark's words, "the same unit of measurement for the distance between the breasts, the distance from the lower breast to the navel, and again from the navel to the division of the legs."[18] Another reference to this method is found in the writings of Dürer, who relates how a more senior painter one time showed him "a male and female figure which he had drawn according to a canon of proportions,"[19] but, alas, would not reveal its secret to him.

One might say that the former method appealed to the engineer in the artist and the latter to the mystic. The first aims at a divine construction made of earthly parts, the second at an earthly personification of a divine symmetry. While both result in devitalized images, the assembly method, based on the dismantling of women into their constituent parts, takes no chances.

Beyond the idealized symmetry of her shape, the nude is transported ever upward with careful attention to her facial expression, posture, and nudity-enhancing accessories such as drapery and jewelry. Just as the magic of the prehistoric Venuses lay in their typification, successive renditions of the goddess have followed certain formalisms. Facial expression, for instance, denoting attitude, has usually been rendered within a specific range. The goddess may look controlled, vulnerable, wistful, devoted, rapturous, or asleep, but she must never appear to be angry, arrogant, imperious, supercilious, flippant, or hysterical, to say nothing of analytical. She did not always exude sexual readiness, but she almost never appeared not ready either. Her facial expressions, befitting the morality of the times, the daring of the artist, and the adherence to classical conventions, were generally united by one common element: they all served not to stand in the way of sexual fantasy.

Clark's observations on this subject recall the crafting of the Venus figurines:

> We look first at the face. It is through facial expression that every intimacy begins. This is true even of the classic nude, where the head often seems to be no more than an element in the geometry of the figure, and the expression is reduced to a minimum. In fact, try as we will to expunge all individuality in the interest of the whole, our responses to facial expression are so sensitive that the slightest accent gives a suggestion of mood or inner life. And so with the nude there is a double problem: the face must be subordinate, but it must not go by default, for inevitably it will colour our response to the body. The solution of this problem involves what is called "creating a type"—of all forms of creation the most revealing of an artist's whole being.[20]

Elsewhere, Clark says of one of Botticelli's nudes: "No doubt it is the strength of Venus that her face reveals no thought beyond the present. It is a fruit among fruits, and by excluding the further dimension of thought, it gives to the whole body an equal degree of permanence."[21] Here, "permanent" has the same meaning as monolithic.

To digress for a moment, the point must be made that within the genre of the nude fall many works of art that do not pretend to be "goddesses" as defined here. Manet's *Olympia*, for instance, has often been cited as just such a countertrend because of her haughty, defiant, almost contemptuous look and the way she sits rather than fully reclines, her body possessed of an unusual tenacity or resilience. She traces her lineage directly to Titian's demure *Venus of Urbino*, but her manner is anything but compliant. The insinuation of demonic potentiality is underscored by the presence of the black cat at her feet, which has been interpreted as a symbol of witches and black magic (as well as licentiousness) and is said to have contributed to the painting's negative public reaction.[22]

The nude's posture also follows certain conventions. John Berger, in his critical analysis of the nude, points out how the nude was often positioned to display herself to the viewer of the painting. Commenting on a Venus by Bronzino, rendered in full frontal nudity, he writes as follows:

> Her body is arranged in the way it is, to display it to the man looking at the picture. This picture is made to appeal to *his* sexuality. It has nothing to do with her sexuality. (Here and in the European tradition

generally, the convention of not painting the hair on a woman's body helps towards the same end. Hair is associated with sexual power, with passion. The woman's sexual passion needs to be minimized so that the spectator may feel that he has the monopoly of such passion.) Women are there to feed an appetite, not to have any of their own.[23]

Sometimes a male is painted near the nude, but even here the nude is often rendered looking away from him "out of the picture towards the one who considers himself her true lover—the spectator-owner."[24] Sometimes the convention called for the nude to look at herself in a mirror, which had the effect of making "the woman connive in treating herself as, first and foremost, a sight."[25]

The distance between the ordinary and the ideal rendered in the image is illustrated by the art historian's distinction between naked and nude. Although this distinction has been made by others, Clark has become the usual authoritative reference on the subject.[26] Simply stated, naked is natural and nude is affected. Naked implies nothing beyond "without clothes" and suggests all the things normal people feel in this state, such as embarrassment and vulnerability. Naked also implies the natural individual proportions of the body—its lumps and warts, pimples and blemishes, bones and flab—that remind us of our mortal imperfections. To be naked is to be seen as we really are. Nude is naked projected onto the ideal. The nude is what the naked aspires to be. The nude is the blueprint for bodily perfection.

In art, the nude is hardly ever naked. That is, her naked body is usually partially draped to enhance her nudity. Or she wears jewelry or something in her hair to impress on the viewer the fact of her nudity by contrasting it with some form of dress. The effect the presence of clothing has in a picture of a nude is illustrated by a newspaper commentary on the nineteenth century American painting by Thomas Eakins of William Rush carving a statue of a standing nude model. "What ruins the picture is much less the want of beauty in the nude model (as has been suggested in the public prints), than the presence in the foreground of the clothes of that young woman, cast carelessly over a chair. This gives the shock which makes one think about the nudity—and at once the picture becomes improper!"[27]

At the time many critics of the painting sniped at the woman's figure. One critic wrote: "All we can say about the picture is, that Wm. Rush was no judge of the 'human form divine' when he selected his model, if the model was really as Mr. Eakins presents it."[28] The problem with the image, in these eyes, was that she was not a classical nude. She appeared more naked than nude and so retained her connection with natural femininity and its awesome powers. Perhaps if her body had been more representative of the typical model, more distant, the shock would have been that much less.

Of equal importance to rendered distance are the goddess's surroundings. A mythological setting, for instance, typical of the early Renaissance nude, suggests maximum remoteness. The accessories of the nude—the Roman beds, the regal luxury of velvet and silk, and the attendant Tritons, Nereids, and winged cupids—all contrive to make her otherworldly. The Olympian motif underscores the fact that the goddess belongs to another dimension, that she is the stuff of dreams and reveries.

Hand in hand with the theme of distance is the theme of capture. This is suggested by both the boundaries of the format, which separate the natural world from the image world, and the apparent containment of female eroticism within male-defined parameters. While the nude suggests a supreme eroticism, it is one that can never escape its confines. It has been effectively locked up within a male design. On the wall, in the nobleman's den or living room, the nude has the appearance of a trophy.

Often the subject of a work of art, its story, is about capture. Favorite themes in the rendition of the nude have been the slave market, the harem, women abducted as the spoils of war, mythological rape scenes (Europa, Lucretia, the Sabines, the daughters of Leucippus), and the oft-rendered legends of Danaë and Psyche, imprisoned—nude—in their respective chambers. Hiram Powers, the nineteenth century American sculptor, had an obsession for this theme. The inspiration for his nude statues is said to have come from a recurring childhood dream of a beautiful woman on a pedestal whom he could not reach because of a deep river running between them. He is said to have accepted this vision as a prophecy of his future métier, but perhaps he was simply driven to capture her in a form from which she could never escape. His *Greek Slave*, nude and manacled, and possibly the most popular work of art in its time, conveyed this sense of capture, and yet, ironically, it was to become an icon of inaccessibility.

> Just as Powers had never been able to reach the beautiful but unattainable woman in his recurring dream, so in later years he denied the viewer of his statues a comparable satisfaction. The unique marble surfaces that he carved and finished to textures unparalleled for their sheer sensual appeal drew spectators in unprecedented fervor to examine and touch those tantalizingly fleshlike surfaces. Yet Powers insisted that no one should be permitted to touch the marble because repeated touching would permanently stain the magic surface.[29]

On some level, renderers of the nude, past and present, understand the importance of the interplay between distance and capture in the cultivation of fantasy. The remoteness of the goddess tears at anticipation. Her sexual charge swells in proportion, her value enhanced by her unavailability. She suggests the idea of her capture, yet this idea pulls against her receding distance simultaneously, and the tension between them makes her move in the mind. One of the many poetic visions written in awe of *The Greek Slave* opined that the statue "Glows and sighs, and trembles with the electric / Fire that flashes through each violet vein!"[30]

An inert image of a living thing presented to the senses cannot help but be reanimated in the imagination. This is the tacit agenda of the nude goddess. But the image's implication of a final destination in an erotic mental tableau requires, in an atmosphere of sexual repression, a *stated* agenda of something wholly different. The reemergence of the classical nude at the end of the medieval period was vindicated by its exemplification of artistic mastery, mythology, and allegory. The rendering of the goddess through these motifs serves not only to enhance the image's distance but also to assist the distillation of eros into logos. Clark, appearing before the Longford Committee Investigating Pornography, testified: "In a picture like Correggio's *Danaë* the sexual feelings have been transformed, and although we undoubtedly enjoy it all the more because of its sensuality, we are still in the realm of contemplation."[31] Everything about the image other than its eroticism may be seen as its necessary cover, its justification, the magnitude of which will logically be proportional to the surrounding moral climate. Compare the grand flamboyance of the early Renaissance nudes, for instance, breaking free from 1,000 years of prohibition, with the relative simplicity of the modern centerfold. The complexity of the neoclassical nudes has invited endless speculation on their symbolic meanings, creating a symposium of critical analysis that has served to deflect attention away from their common origin.

Even today, scholarly art criticism rarely focuses on either the nude's erotic appeal or her deeper significance rooted in gender conflict. Instead, discussion of the nude concentrates on her lineage, that is, her derivative influences from previous works, or anecdotal curiosities relating to the work in question, such as who commissioned it and how it was received by the public. But the weight of critical analysis usually falls on the nude's allegory, her symbolic meaning.

For instance, in one historian's view, Botticelli's *Birth of Venus* is an allegory of Beauty, that is, beauty as divine principle. The description of the goddess makes thinking sexual thoughts about her tasteless and uncouth: "And the beauty of Venus, when she finally appears, is unmistakably a beauty that belongs to heaven."[32] Likewise, the figure of Truth in Botti-celli's *Calumny of Apelles*, a replica of his Venus, points to the heavens where we are led to read her significance. But she is laden with irony. A nude—not a naked person—she represents anything but truth. One won-ders whether the historian is aware of his own irony when he writes, "Repentance leads to Truth; and Truth alone can give, in the purity and serenity of her naked figure, the real bliss that never ends."[33]

Titian, considered to be one of the greatest interpreters of the nude, took the story of Diana and Actaeon as the subject of a painting. Actaeon enters the site of Diana's bath and sees her forbidden nakedness. Diana holds up a piece of cloth to veil the top half of her body from his gaze, which gives the shock that enhances her nudity. But it is the allegory that occupies discussion about the painting: "Titian used the encounter between Diana and Actaeon to explore the relationship of fate and for-tune in regard to free will, a primary question for the sixteenth century."[34]

Ingres, a dominant figure in nineteenth-century oil painting and a master of the reclining nude, seems to have been especially drawn to the theme of the odalisque, or Turkish concubine. While most of his rendi-tions are devoted to a single nude, his *Turkish Bath*, a view inside a harem, is a naked sprawl of some 25 figures. Arranged in a variety of poses around one corner of a sunken bath (suggesting three times as many more beyond the borders of the picture), the gathering of flesh appears to be an effort to make the ultimate statement about the nude. What is the insider's opinion on this spectacle? "To the uninitiated it is a hedonistic wallow; but to those who suspend disbelief to discover the artist's intent it is the masterpiece of a lifetime search to create an allegory of the senses wherein the spectator is the living personification of sight."[35]

The scholarly discussion about the nude absolves us all from feeling erotic about her. It constructs a cognitive space or mode of perception from which it is safe to view her. One can always intimate that he is contem-plating her higher meaning, much as one can insist he buys *Playboy* for the articles. In the previous chapter examples were presented to illustrate how the male fear of women is transformed into expressions of resentment and censure (not to mention images of female demons). The contempla-tive aspects of the nude, while intellectually stimulating, represent the cor-responding transformation of desire. Just as the base emotion of fear becomes concealed beneath a cloud of invective, sexual desire is distilled through contemplation. That's because sexual desire is just as vulnerable as fear. To admit to the fantasy is to admit to a need. On the other hand, reverence for aesthetic refinement, technical mastery, or symbolic repre-sentation comes from the same lofty realm as censure, that is, from the realm of judgment. "It is not that I desire her (paraphrasing Karen Horney); it is that she is ideal, a model of perfection, an allegory of Truth."

While the nude's vehicle of art and allegory enhances its elevation and provides its cover, its erotic charge delivers its necessary notoriety. The nude is a symbiotic relationship between aesthetics and indecency, symbol and shock. The conflicting messages of the nude are illustrated by the public reaction to Adolph Wertmüller's painting of *Danaë and the Shower of Gold*, which has been called "undoubtedly the most sensational picture ever shown in America."[36] Naked, except for a string of pearls in her hair, Danaë reclines on a bed in a state of rapture. Zeus falls toward her as a shower of gold particles (presaging the birth of Perseus), while a winged Cupid attends nearby. When the artist exhibited his painting in Philadelphia in 1806 it provoked an uproar: "For the *Danaë* was recognized almost universally as a great and splendid work; yet its style and its subject did offend. To admire the picture was to condone and even to share licentiousness and decadence; yet, to castigate it was to admit to cultural and aesthetic ignorance."[37]

The proportion of contemplative content to erotic content in the nude goddess image has lessened considerably since the Renaissance. Some would even say that the artistic merits of the contemporary goddess, as exemplified by, say, the centerfold, are now nonexistent. The evolution of the goddess is one of a gradual descent earthward, characterized by the progressive abandonment of her mythological trappings and her intimations of allegory and a consequent diminishing of her properties of distance. Clark observes that by the nineteenth century "the female body, with all its sensuous weight, is offered in isolation, as an end in itself."[38] Always seeking the vogue in visual representation, the goddess followed the artistic drift toward realism.

The shift in format from fresco and wood panel to oil colors on canvas during the sixteenth century (which set the stage for the misogynist disparagement, "She's no oil painting") was instrumental in this process. As John Berger describes it, "What distinguishes oil painting from any other form of painting is its special ability to render the tangibility, the texture, the lustre, the solidity of what it depicts. It defines the real as that which you can put your hands on."[39]

Berger's hypothesis comes alive with a careful examination of Clark's pictorial appreciation, *Feminine Beauty*,[40] which contains nearly 200 plates of women, clothed and nude, spanning 3000 years of art. Since they are placed in near chronological order, it is possible to notice significant changes between one era and the next. The advent of oil painting on canvas sees the nudes become more tactile, less celestial; they are more accessible and more attainable. Even the representations of Venus seem more real, more down to earth. They no longer appear to be goddesses in human form, but human forms fashioned toward an ideal. They might easily be real, although rare, people.

The great age of European oil painting is thought to have come to a close around the beginning of the twentieth century. A major influence on what amounted to a dramatic turn of purpose in oil painting was the invention of the camera. The photograph, an apparent mirror image of nature captured in the wink of an eye, presented a serious threat to many painters. The French realist, Paul Delaroche, when he learned of this innovation, supposedly lamented, "From this day, painting is dead!"[41] From the art historian's point of view, the challenge of photography, "historically and technologically, amounted to an expropriation of the realistic image, the property of painting for many centuries. Within three generations or less from the invention of photography, painting was to lose the realistic image to abstraction."[42]

The importance of photography to the image of the goddess was manifold. For one, it presented a means of immediately capturing something as a vision, stripped of its vitality. In addition, the apparent duplication of reality implied by the photographic image meant a fundamental lessening of the goddess's properties of distance. Because the image conveys the impression of zero rendering, the distance between the model and the image disappears and that between the image and its referred goddess reduces to the spatial plane alone, that is, the woman in the photograph is assumed to reside on the earth. The woman in the picture is assumed to be the woman who posed for the camera and is, therefore, at least conceptually, available.

These effects are not absent from the realist genre in art, but a painting can never convey the verisimilitude that a photograph can. With a painted goddess, no matter how real she looks, one can never be sure that there is a sentient someone out there who looks just like her. A painting also has a rather minuscule audience compared with the potential of a photograph. This is probably the most significant factor of the medium to the goddess. Photography promised her endless reproduction and a proliferation that would dwarf the cumulative efforts of all her previous formats. Soon the average male would be able to possess his own personal image of resolution. The nude goddess was about to enter the mass market.

The nude's transition from canvas to film was initially both exotic and disturbing. The novelty of images of real women without their clothes on was of great interest to many men, but, at the same time, with minimal rendering these images fell away from the nude toward the natural and flawed naked. While certainly erotic, they were both less than ideal and devoid of artistic pretension. Echoing these concerns, George Bernard Shaw wrote:

> There is a terrible truthfulness about photography that sometimes makes a thing ridiculous. ... Take the case of the ordinary academician. He gets hold of a pretty model, he puts a dress on her, and he paints her, as well as he can, and calls her "Juliet," and puts a nice verse from Shakespeare underneath, and puts a picture in the Gallery. It is admired beyond measure. The photographer finds the same pretty girl; he dresses her up and photographs her, and calls her "Juliet," but somehow it is no good— it is still Miss Wilkins, the model. It is too true to be Juliet.[43]

Responding to the need for idealized images, but also in keeping with the law of the least effort—that is, the reproduction of established types—photographers of the nude did as much as they could to duplicate the traditional motifs in oil painting. Early photographs thus show nudes standing and reclining in the style of Titian, Ingres, and others, in allegorical settings with Roman beds and fine drapery, posed beside their discarded clothing or holding a mirror. Many of them also appeared with a shaved mons veneris in the classical style. However, the transposition of elements from a medium at its peak of sophistication to one in its unrefined infancy is the essence of travesty, and these early efforts proved to be counterproductive to the nude's purpose.

Much more effective were technological innovations in both the taking of the picture and the printing of the final product as explained by Jorge Lewinski, sharp definition gave way to soft focus effects, fuzziness, and muted contours. Photographs could be made to resemble engravings, charcoal drawings or watercolors. This spirit of impressionism did more to render the nude's idealized distance than mythological motifs, and the latter were soon dropped. More critically, the elevated nude garnered enough aesthetic appeal to ensure her foothold within the medium. At least in Europe, by the end of the nineteenth century "the artistic nude, well disguised in an impressionistic haze and blur, was finally accepted and widely exhibited, but more naturalistic and realistic examples were still forbidden and prosecuted."[44]

From talisman to statue, to fresco, to canvas, and then to celluloid, the goddess has shed her magic, her mythology, her allegory and progressively much of her "art." Her distancing has become more and more foreshortened, suggesting an omega point where it will finally disappear. The quest for the pure form of the goddess anticipates her manifestation

in the flesh, animated by psychic analogues of her sexually gratifying properties. It would appear that the goddess pursues a determined descent
earthward, back to nature, to regain her lost vitality.

Each transition of the goddess image to a new format brought elements with it from the one left behind. Photography took its motifs from
oil painting, turned them to its purpose, and passed them on to film,
video, and television. The innovation of the celluloid branch in the evolution of the nude goddess was eventually to endow the image with a
powerful vitality and a potential access to millions of living rooms. However, some time before the invention of the camera another branch had
developed from representative art in a rudimentary attempt to make the
statue and the oil painting come alive. This was the *tableau vivant* or "living picture"—and the precursor of the stripper.

Tableaux vivants presented live models posed motionless against
appropriate backgrounds in what were often observed to be faithful repro-
ductions of works of art. Commenting on some particularly inspired
tableaux, one reviewer of the period wrote, "The hand directing them is a
master of pictorial reproduction, while the women that appear in them are
trained to a remarkable degree of efficiency, moreover exhibiting in their
plastic versatility an artistic spirit that falls little short of genius."[45]

The genre appears to have originated in Paris in the mid-eighteenth
century, spread to other European capitals in succeeding decades, and
arrived in New York in the early 1830s.[46] While not completely concerned
with the nude, the nude would eventually become the *tableau*'s driving
force. Favorite motifs included Aphrodite, Ariadne, Diana, Psyche, and
the Three Graces. A reviewer's observation that one of the better shows
produced "excellent artistic results by employing shapely girls in place of
the counterfeits of the human form produced by the artists in the original works,"[47] illustrates the public taste for realism at the end of the nineteenth century.

The effect of nudity in the *tableau* was achieved with the use of flesh-
colored tights, which gave birth to the argument about whether simulated
nudity is as indecent as authentic nudity, an argument that would follow
the live branch of the goddess all the way to the stripper. The irony here
is that as the goddess's formats approached realism, they increased their
capacity for illusion. As the art dissolves, as the image approaches nature,
its eroticism swells in proportion and soon enough attracts public disapproval. The *tableau* apparently covered itself by supporting "various charities and social organizations,"[48] and by making the traditional appeal to
its contemplative aspects. A trade publication of the time rhapsodized that
tableaux "stir in youthful minds a latent fondness for artistic beauty, arouse

a taste for history and biography and turn wavering thoughts toward the great world of literature, painting, sculpture, and archeology."[49] Even so, at its peak of popularity "the questions of nudity and morality overshadowed all other commentary about living pictures."[50]

Tableaux vivants were in decline by the turn of the century, displaced in part by the innovation of the motion picture show, but the foundation had been laid for the appearance of the stripper's immediate predecessors. While the *tableau* was still in its ascendance, the modern burlesque era had already begun. The striptease came into its own in the 1930s and by then it was simply a matter of how much could be revealed. The nude goddess, vital, yet still an image, had arrived.

The ever available, infinitely gratifying, monolithically sexual, and physically ideal goddess is first and foremost an idea. It is an idea that arises as a fantastical resolution to male ambivalence about the opposite gender. Images serve to make the idea come alive. The crafting of the image is inspired by the alchemy of sexual fantasy, that is, the refinement of human form separated from its vitality. Once crafted, the image of the goddess acquired a life of its own. Always seeking the path of least resistance and maximum proliferation, she flourished in proportion to the relaxation of sexual repression and the rise of consumerism. Together, these developments obviated the need for her artistic guise and she was able to more fully accentuate her erotic properties. If the driving spirit behind the idea of the goddess is its manifestation in the flesh, à la Galatea, the stripper represents the transitional stage between the most vitalized image and the actual living goddess.

8
The Goddess

Your eyes, your hands, your breasts, your feet, are unparalleled, out of this world. What bliss to see you, multiplied to hear you too, to touch you is ecstatic. You create a god when you yield to your lover.

Rufinus, untitled, from *Jousts of Aphrodite* (p. 92).

According to the dictionary, a goddess can be two very different things: a female deity, and a woman who is adored, worshipped, or idealized. One is spirit; one is flesh. One is a goddess in essence; the other is a goddess bestowed. One is a celestial being glorified by her descent to earth; the other is an earthly mortal exalted by her ascent toward the heavens.

In modern Western culture (at least) the celestial goddess has been stripped of her objective status. Rather than a spiritual being, she is now understood to be the product of myth, fantasy, and imagination. Venus, Diana, Psyche, and the rest have, to turn a phrase, come down to earth. However, while the Olympian goddess has been demythologized, she continues to survive as a powerful concept, and it is the romance connected with this concept that gives the earthly goddess her power. The exclamation, "She's a goddess!" links flesh with immortality. By itself, removed from the concept of transcendent perfection, earthly beauty may remain precious but not priceless. It may inspire aesthetic appreciation but it will fall short of the spiritual. Without her tacit Olympian reference, the earthly beauty is a mere passing fancy.

This is so because behind the goddess's promise of perfect love or perfect sex is the allusion that, by seducing her, a man will become a god. Woman's body, transformed into a vehicle for the divine light, becomes in turn man's vehicle to the stars. The rhapsody of Rufinus, written in the early classical period, is evidence that this is an ancient belief.

Traditionally, the celestial goddess has been the guardian of one dominion (such as home or hearth) or she has personified one particular human faculty or emotion (such as wisdom or love). However, the ancient goddesses, in spite of their divinity, were allowed complex personalities that were not above typical human weaknesses. Aphrodite, the love goddess herself, was capable of vengefulness, jealousy, infidelity, sensitivity to insults, as well as proficient in making mischief. In her more demonic roles she was known as the Goddess of Death-in-Life, the Dark One, the Manslayer and the Goddess of the Tombs.[1] And yet, today Aphrodite survives in the collective social consciousness solely as the personification of love, beauty, or desire. In other words, she is now apprehended monolithically.

Perhaps it was *because* the Olympian goddesses were understood to be truly superhuman that they could enjoy humanoid personalities without detracting from their powers or their veneration. It is one of the ironies of the goddess that on high she is allowed the luxury of human personality, while as a creature of the earth she must be seen to be perfect, unblemished by human foibles and demonic urges. The earthly goddess can never be angry, sad, sick, tired, idiotic, awkward, flatulent, malicious, rude, or petty. She never menstruates, or suffers with PMS, headaches or sudden emotional changes. All these are eclipsed by the ideal she represents.

The Earthly goddess also never writes poetry. When people found out that Adah Isaacs Menken, who had presented one of the earliest illusions of nudity in motion on the American stage (in 1861), wrote very sensitive poetry, they were taken aback. The public reaction was substantial enough to warrant a story in the *New York Times* that opined, "People were really astonished to learn that the most notorious representative of the 'nude drama,' a woman who in her own person had cast aside all the conventionalities and most of the moralities of society, had moments of serious thought, of poignant mental suffering, of regret, of yearning after better things, of aspirations for a higher life."[2]

The modern goddess is worshipped for her single-mindedness, for her simplicity. The streamlining of her body is mirrored by the distillation of her mind. Simplicity confers on her predictability, controllability, and agreeability. It also facilitates her assimilation into fantasy. Just as the most vivid mirages appear on the clean face of the desert, fantasy projects itself best onto purified screens.

The supreme goddess then is neither the celestial ghost who can't be procured in the flesh, nor the earthly beauty whose temperament is too complex; she is the sublime alloy of the two. A man's ultimate dream is to be loved by the perfect earthly form animated by a heavenly life force.

In one of his papers Carl Jung brings to light an old arrangement of goddesses in which Eve, Helen of Troy, the Virgin Mary, and Sophia represent the developmental stages of erotic attraction.[3]

In the first stage, Eros is nothing more than a biological drive, genitally focused and devoid of conscience. The value of the "other" is tied solely to her satisfaction of a self-serving compulsion. Eve is the target of raw sexuality.

In the second stage, a more refined eros has begun to appreciate aesthetics. The focus here includes those physical attributes that superficially tie in to character, such as poise and gesture. Helen symbolizes physical beauty.

In the third stage, Eros becomes spiritualized. The focus has shifted from the body as an instrument of sexual satisfaction to sentience and intimacy. Eros has learned the value of devotion and surrender.

Beyond even this, the fourth stage represents an egoless state where all the absolutes of purity and enlightenment converge. Sophia personifies the transcendence of ambivalence, conflict, pain, and fear. She is harmonious fusion.

This scheme duplicates many others that recognize and attempt to reconcile the implacable drive of the libido with the controlling, civilizing faculty of the rational mind. The path from Eve to Sophia (mirrored in the Kundalini) is the path from the genitals to the brain, from the physical to the metaphysical, from the outer to the inner, and from the sensational to the substantial. The scheme recognizes that, for men, femininity is a fragmented concept, made whole only by way of an intense odyssey.[4] Mary and Sophia are the goddesses of a mature, developed man, a man who has moved beyond his attachments to sensation and beauty. It would follow then that the bulk of humanity at any one time is mired between Helen and Eve.

The significance of Eve and Helen as benchmarks is that they represent the two extremes of the spectrum of goddess images under the present discussion. On the one side we have the goddesses whose domain is completely sexual, and on the other we have those goddesses who tend toward a more aesthetic, less explicitly erotic appeal. For instance, place the self-possessed stance of the Ancient Greek statues of Aphrodite beside the orgasmic sprawl of the modern skin-book Venus. Compare the current cover girl with the stripper. Though they are all, in their respective ways, embodiments of an ideal, each stimulates in the viewer a different blend of aesthetic and erotic appeal. Each stratifies in the mind according to its resolution of the opposing pulls toward Eve and Helen. The classical Venuses and the neoclassical Venuses of Botticelli, Titian, and others are perhaps the loftiest of such images, because of their exemplification of artistic mastery and their relative modesty. They gravitate toward Helen. On the other hand, the centerfold, the stripper, and the porn queen fall much more within the camp of Eve. They appeal much more to the libido than to aesthetic appreciation.

Among all the images of the goddess, the stripper is the only one to combine nudity and dancing in a live format. And her unmediated presence in close proximity to her viewers makes her a very different sort of image indeed. The submerged presence of a living breathing woman, embodying all the properties goddess images seek to disown, creates a confusion of concepts.

Objectively, the stripper's image derives from a model rendered toward an ideal and refers to an imagined distant replica of herself, just like a painting or a photograph. The stripper's model is the real woman beneath the cosmetics, the costume and the act—which are components of the image—and the referent is the woman animated in the viewer's fantasy of the image. But here's the difference. *Subjectively*, that is from the perspective of the viewer, the model, the image, and the referent are all fused in the one figure. The viewer sees no image; he assumes that what he sees is real. The stripper is not apprehended as *representing* transcendent femininity but as *being* so. She seems to be a model, but one that miraculously embodies the requisite properties of the goddess.

Because the image appears to be fused with the model and the referent, the stripper implies no distance, either rendered or imagined. Distance is a crucial factor in goddess images, not only because it tends to raise the value of the goddess, but also because it signifies the remoteness of the demon. The rendering of natural femininity into an ideal form (per the alchemy of fantasy) leaves behind the woman's sentient self, her personality.

Consider the stripper's demonic potential as an outsider in the men's private club of image appreciation. The men are bonded in their common focus, in the catalytic resolution of their gender conflicts, and in their fantasies, but there is a woman present—a witness—and one who enjoys a measure of power over them. The stripper implies a center of moral judgment that is other than male. The men cannot gaze at this image with abandon. Up front, at or near the edge of the stage, many men are able to look at the genitals the stripper shows them only when she is looking at someone else.

MELISSA WOLF: The big thing that I like to play on them is to do a gigantic spread and then look them right in the eyes. None of them can look at my crotch. They all look straight at my eyes. If I catch them

looking at it, they get really embarrassed, like, "Oh my God! She thinks
I'm a pervert!" to the point where they have to get up and leave before
my next show.

   It's a challenge to see if I can beat them at their own game. I kind of
turn away, I just turn my head away for a second, then I look back and
I catch them!

In addition to desire, fear, hope, and control, the stripper brings up
a measure of guilt.

   By embodying the traditional codes of the goddess image, the stripper suggests—just like a photograph—her possession, her purchase. The
submerged message of an image is that its possession makes up for the
absence of its referent. However, the live image, while implying the availability of the referred goddess, is paradoxically unavailable *as an image.* In
a live rendition the distance disappears (apparently), but the ability to possess the image dissolves with it. According to Sarita, "I've talked to many
men and they all tell me the same thing: 'God, these girls. They put it in
your face and then they take it away from you. They put it out there like
they want it and then they reject you when you respond to it.'"

   One could conceivably rent the image, by paying for a private performance, but one cannot own it. One could conceivably kidnap the stripper, but in such an alarming situation the stripper's act would give way to
her real feelings. One is left with the hope of a relationship with the stripper, but this hope rests on the confusion between the role and the person
playing it. One can't have a relationship with the stripper. One can have
a relationship with the person but it would be a far cry from the fantasy
of a relationship with the image. Out of context, removed from her format,
the stripper's gratifying eroticism soon disintegrates. Thus her remoteness
as an image is greater than all her predecessors, even though—ironically—
she brings the fantasy object much closer to her viewers than ever before.

   While the stripper implies no distance, nonetheless, that distance
is there, even though it is minimal compared to that of a photograph. It
is represented by the disparity between the stripper's appearance (her rendition) and her real self. The stage (a workable if sometimes inelegant
pedestal) and its effects combine to elevate and idealize the stripper's
human dimensions. Somehow she looks taller, her bouffant more galac-
tic, her breasts more prominent, and her skin more resplendent. Her exotic
name and costume, the bizarre ritual of her strip, her seductive poses and
facial expressions, her flamboyant flaunting of feminine indiscretion,
and her makeup, together with the lighting, all contribute a sense of
otherworldliness to her image. (How is it possible that a woman can bare

herself in public so resolutely, so shamelessly?) The stripper invokes the
dream of "the girl from somewhere else"—the girl from out of town, the
gypsy, the mermaid, the space girl—the woman who is long on possibilities and maddening to fantasize about.

The stripper's contextual remoteness must also be considered. The
term "strip show" implies a view of the exotic, the freaky, the aberrant, and
the lawless. It is considered to be antagonistic to family values and community standards: the building blocks of culture. It is a lodestone for strange
elements and a fuel for depraved appetites. The strip joint transports the
viewer not only into fantasy but into the shadow world beyond the pale.

The stripper raises herself above the overtly genital, sex for sex's sake
(sex without intimacy), with her dancing. Dancing, within its context of
performance, is the aesthetic component of the image, the pretext of legit-
imacy and the cover for indecency. Dancing is the stripper's vindication.
On the sexual side, the stripper is more explicit (where legal) than the
Playboy centerfold, but is much less so than the porn queen. Strippers
usually do not fake orgasms and most stop short of vaginal insertions. As
a rule, they stay well within their legal limits and look down upon other
strippers who do not. Those strippers who "show pink" are disparaged with
the epithet "spreader." ("She's a spreader.") However, when one considers
that the art that was burlesque has all but vanished, the trend is clearly a
slow march toward the ever more revealing.

Although the stripper does achieve some artistic buoyancy, it is not
enough to make her respectable. As distance decreases and eros increases,
the model comes closer to the image and can be blamed for it. The animosity accruing to the image—from moralists, feminists, those who see
it (her) as antagonistic to family values or community standards, and those
who view her with pleasure while referring to her as a slut—accrues to a
living person. Sexual explicitness in a live format tars the person with the
actions of the image. Nudity in a photograph does not have the same
association with shame as does a public display. To illustrate this point,
would the effect have been the same if Burt Reynolds had appeared nude,
not in *Cosmopolitan* (as he did several years ago), but on a stage before a
live audience?

The stripper is a low-level sex goddess. She is less idealized than the
cover girl, the beauty queen or the centerfold. She inhabits the gray area
between explicit sexuality and posed nudity, between inexorable remoteness and gratuitous availability, between idealized flesh and a vitalized
image. We sometimes think of her as a *Penthouse* pet come to life and
sometimes as a hooker who advertises by stripping.

Nevertheless, the stripper's dynamism transcends that of other images of the goddess. Her ersatz sexuality is more animated, less mediated, more available, less procurable, more mutable, and less monolithic. The multi-faceted aggregate of image and person presents an oscillation between the anticipation of the ideal and the apprehension of the real. By invoking the interlocking motifs of desire, fear, and control, the stripper's stimulation of fantasy—her charge—may be expected to have more impact than any of her mediated versions. There is some danger involved in viewing her.

The tension between the exalted, idolized, and fantastical, and the ominous, unpredictable, and disparaged is the mainspring of the stripper's effect, both on her audience and in the society in which she operates. She presents a dual image in conjunction with a real self and it confounds the public mind.

The stripper is also the first commercial nude goddess image who can speak to us. She is the first one to be able to report what it is like to look through the eyes of the image and see her viewers looking back. How does *she* see herself as a goddess?

FLAME: It's powerful when I'm onstage. It's a rush. To hear people applaud and cheer and scream, it really gets to you.

SHADOW FIRE: It's sweaty. I don't really see myself so much as a goddess as an entertainer. I would never assume that a man could not see the flaws in a person onstage. On a stage everything is magnified a hundred-fold. A dancer is only human, regardless. She'll still trip, or her Spandex will get stuck, or something will happen to make her mortal again. To me, the concept of a goddess is not someone yelling at you, "Hey, show me some pink!"

JAY JAY: [Thinking and chuckling] I like it. I do. I like the attention. I've always liked that. Even when I go out with a bunch of people I like to be in the middle of everything that's going on.

KARIN WEST: I don't think of it as being a goddess. I think of it as being a fantasy. I feel that I am a vehicle for some man to project his fantasies on. Some men view you as a goddess. Other men don't. You don't appeal to all types at all times. It's such a theatrical thing that if you forget it's an act, you can get caught up in it. There are girls in the business who never stop thinking of themselves as being some kind of super sexy sensational beautiful girl 24 hours a day.

CHELSEA: I get embarrassed about things like that, about admiration. Like last night I made a big dinner and invited this friend and my boyfriend and they were complimenting me on this roast and la da da and I was getting quite embarrassed. You know, like, come on! Okay, you said it was good, and that's great. It was only like, you know, 20 minutes or an hour to make dinner. It's no big deal. Stop it!

EMERY: Well, I'm pretty much a realist as far as that's concerned. I do what I do as well as I can so that I enjoy it. I don't really think I go into any fantasy world. Attention is great for anyone. So that part of it is nice. But when you get into trying to put more into it than there actually is, I think that's where people go wrong. You are not a goddess. You are not this unattainable object. You are an exotic dancer, a girl, generally a young girl with very little life experience. And if you're seeing it for more than what it is, then it's an unrealistic view of what you're doing.

LUSCIOUS LONA: It's a head rush. I love it.
I can take a week off work and it doesn't matter how busy I've been or how much running around I've done or how much exercise I've gotten, it's not the same. I need that fix. And it's just like drugs. There is no drug in this world like a crowd that screams like that for me.
It's gotten to the point now—I've snowballed in the last few months—where I'll work a bar for five weeks, the next week I'll be working another one and I'll get this phone call: "Lona! Listen to this!" and it's the DJ at the last place. He holds the phone out of his booth and they're going [chanting]: "Lo-*na*! Lo-*na*!" And I'm not even there!
After going through so many years of thinking that I wasn't attractive and would never accomplish anything or be successful, I've turned it around and now I'm proud of myself. I think I look really good and I have a huge ego [laughing]. I think I've learned that too.

JANE JONES: There's a technique in stimulating that response [adoration], but just because you get that response doesn't mean that you can walk on water. Some dancers strive to get that attention so much in their lives that they become untouchable. That's why a lot of people think they're snobs and unapproachable. They don't want to associate with real people. When they put themselves on an artificial pedestal, they make themselves stagnant. It takes away their desire to develop themselves.

If strippers do not necessarily see themselves as goddesses, do they recognize the power they have?

SNOW WHITE: Yes, definitely. I like that. You get up there and you are the center of attention; you have control over all those people out there and you can do whatever the hell you want.

BROOKE: Oh, I don't think that, ever. Never, ever, ever. I have no power. If anybody has power, it's the audience. Sometimes I feel really inferior to them. And I don't know why that is. Supposedly the audience, from what I've heard, looks up to dancers; they think we are something extraordinary. Yet when I'm up there, I sometimes get really nervous, like I wonder what they're thinking of me. Maybe if I was very secure I would have a different outlook.

CASSIE: Most of the time I really couldn't give a shit. I'd rather have them all leave. The only time I have a sense of power is when there are men that interest me in the bar. Because I know that I can get 'em if I want. And If I work it right, sometimes it's fun. It's a game. It's a challenge.

KALI: It was a real trick of mine to make the men involved. Usually it was just the guys around the stage. I'd look in their eyes and they felt involved; and that makes them feel like a million bucks. It's not like I love that man and he's real important to me. He's real important to my show. And it's important to me to make him feel that way. You can make them feel happy or you can make them feel real interested or caught up. So it's a real powerful feeling. It's a great feeling. But that's onstage. The minute I get off, like I say, it's over.

That was the real enjoyable part about it—feeling powerful. And that carries off into your other life too. You know, you learn how to be more powerful and more directing.

LUSCIOUS LONA: It can be really frustrating. Sometimes I get a bad crowd or an off day and I start feeling like the hotel owner is going to be mad at me because they're not yelling and screaming. It's really hard. Some places, they're really good to you on Monday and Tuesday, then Wednesday and Thursday, they're so quiet, it's like pulling teeth. You have to go out there and you have to pump and work and yell and scream and jump up and down. And sometimes you feel like, "What is it going to take to get these guys going?" I did half of this on Monday and they were electric. You think, "They're bored with you. They're sick of you. Oh no! The hotel owner's going to scream about how much he's paying you!" And you try everything in the book and it only upsets you. I feel like I'm being inadequate and I don't like that feeling. The head rush can go both ways. A lot of girls break under the pressure.

TERI STARR: I think that's wonderful. I really think it's the most exciting thing. I really feel good about that, especially being able to talk into the mike and talk to people and have people going with you. It doesn't always happen. There are people who want you to get off the stage as soon as possible so they can see the next girl who does all the beaver shots. But still, it's such a wonderful thing to know that some people are there to see you. They want to hear you talk. You make them feel good. And because you make them feel good about being there, they don't have to feel like, "Oh God, what am I doing in a place like this?" They love it and so therefore it comes back to you.

One of the neatest things that happened to me was when I first started. I walked into a little club which used to be called The Gay Nineties. Because I was the last girl going on, I came in late, so the show was already going on. It was a small club and we had to kind of go through the audience to get to the dressing rooms. As I came through, there was a girl onstage and as I came even with the stage people started clapping, so I looked at the stage. I didn't see her do anything particularly exciting but I thought, "Gosh! Neat little audience here!" So I was still watching her and still walking and then the people started standing up, so I stopped to watch the stage. And she never did do too much. I was right beside the band then and I asked one of the band members what happened. And he said, *"You walked in!* Turn around." So I had to turn around and take a bow in the middle of her act. Because of my naiveness, a lot of times I really missed the excitement of the moment.

GIO: I regard what I do as performing and as theater. And that statement can be qualified by saying that it is the theater of the absurd. It is totally absurd that I'm up there taking my clothes off and all these people are happy and they're paying me lots of money for it. As a creative expression it has given me so much freedom to enjoy the performing aspect of it. What I'm doing is creating a fantasy up there. I want them to fantasize that I'm obviously the best woman that they could possibly ever have in bed.

I like to make them think it almost could be a reality. The closer the audience is, the better it is for me. I can wrap my legs around some guy's neck, with or without a G-string—it doesn't matter—and it's so funny to see somebody's nose this far from your cunt. I've got him in a headlock. He ain't goin' nowhere! And the rest of the audience is falling out of their chairs.

There's nothing wrong with that fantasy. It's when it becomes a reality that you're in trouble. This is the argument I have with girls who hook on the side. It's also the argument that I have with people who confuse strippers with hookers. It's very upsetting to me.

9
The Demon

The stripper presents a conflict. First of all, she brings up emotions that cannot be freely expressed in public without garnering social disapproval. Sexual desire, for instance, clashes with self-control. Secondly, these emotions are in conflict with each other. Desire clashes with fear and hope collides with guilt. The stripper radiates the codes of the traditional sex goddess but her vitality is rooted in a center of natural feminine sentience. The viewer is not free to pursue his desire for the stripper while she performs and pursuing her offstage brings up the real—and unpredictable—woman in her. By simultaneously resolving and reinvoking man's primeval fears about woman's ambivalence and her power over him, she literally tears him apart. The goddess she presents masks the deeper motive of manipulation and rejection. So the stripper is really a demon.

The view from the audience does not coincide with the cultural perspective on the stripper, but here too she is seen to be a demon, if for somewhat different reasons. The general public impression of strippers is that they are women of low character, low intelligence, and low moral standards. Stripping is not a vocation one joyously anticipates for one's daughters. Observed Allen Smith, a reporter for the now defunct *World Telegram,* in an article on the burlesquers Margie Hart and Sally Rand: "It is a rare thing, indeed, to find a stripper who has more intelligence than a backing-off lathe. If they have any sense before they come into the trade it goes away. Generally speaking, these girls are hard, tough-talking babes, with the social consciousness of the black widow spider."[1]

It is also assumed that strippers move within the underbelly of the city where crime, drugs, and prostitution thrive. College students, surveyed for their opinions on strippers, described them typically as "dumb," "stupid," "uneducated," "lower class," "oversexed," "immoral," "hard women," "prostitutes," and unable "to do anything else for a living."[2] (It is noteworthy that such associations are, for the most part, assumptions about the nature and character of the *person* based on the actions of the role she plays—something like tarring Boris Karloff with congenital malevolence for all the evil characters he played.) In another survey stripping was ranked lower in status than the occupations of sales clerk, janitor, artist model, and professional gambler.[3] The cultural view conflicts with the pleasurable side of the audience's view and supports the negative side. The viewer's desire for someone designated a social deviant may bring up some guilt in him and it may also generate some rebellious excitement. The stripper is bad in that colloquial sense that makes her deliciously good. But when fear, anxiety, and then anger surface, and the emotions are objectified into verbal abuse of the woman playing the role, the viewer falls in line with the cultural attitude that is similarly rooted in fear and anxiety. The cultural disposition supports abuse of the stripper. That's why strippers often don't call the police when they have been assaulted.

Western culture, as we have seen, has been especially supportive of depictions of the ever available, infinitely gratifying, monolithically sexual, and physically ideal goddess image, at least since the Renaissance. For instance, Western culture invented the Miss Universe pageant and tolerates the dissemination of photographic erotica more than any other culture. However, there is a fine line between Helen and Eve, a crossing of which Western culture will not sanction. That is, although millions of magazines along the lines of *Playboy* and *Penthouse* are sold every month, they are not, for the most part, read in public (for instance, on the bus), nor do they grace the reading tables in doctors' or dentists' offices. They are (at least marginally) socially disapproved. This is because their genital exposure has exceeded their aesthetic content, shifting them more toward Eve than our culture will presently embrace. Compared with photographic nudes nestled among articles on politics and short stories by respected authors, the stripper has little to counterbalance her fall toward Eve.

Social disapproval of the stripper is not only rooted in her genital exposure, it is also a reaction to her aliveness, her eroticism, her dancing, her symbolism, and her secondary effects. Based on the landmark 1991 U.S. Supreme Court ruling upholding the state's right to ban nude dancing, these properties are so dangerous that, for the most part, each one by itself is sufficient to warrant official regulation.

The aliveness of this image is the source of most of its controversy because its transgressions can be pinned on a person. The distance between the image in a photograph and the person who modeled for it somewhat removes that person from the consequences of the image. In addition, on some level we comprehend the mediation and the mediator (film and photographer) that stand between the person and the final product. The stripper, with no mediation, can never fully distance herself from the role she plays. In comparison, an actor can because an actor is assumed to be in character onstage. Even if we suspend disbelief for a moment, we always know on some level that there is an act going on. We apprehend the actor's image; with the stripper we don't. The stripper takes her image home with her.

Nudity and eroticism make a potent combination, but harnessed to the dance their effect is intensified, both on the pleasurable side for the viewer and in the general cultural view. As Supreme Court Justice David Souter observed in his opinion on the nude dancing question, "When nudity is combined with expressive activity, its stimulative and attractive value certainly can enhance the force of expression."[4] American culture still carries with it relics of medieval Christian fears about dancing, especially free-form dancing. This goes back to the Christian attempt to clean up Roman sin and pagan waywardness as celebrated in both the theater and the folk festival. Dancing is anathema to both pious reflection and rational control. It is a thing of the body, not the mind, and is, therefore, like the passions, closer to both the devil and recklessness than to either God or decorum. And it can easily lead to sex. Letting go of rational control opens the door to all kinds of demons. Nevertheless, the frenzy with which pagans danced their way through the Middle Ages has earned it a place in the historical record. It is difficult to know how much is fact and how much is Christian bias in the various accounts of dance epidemics during the Middle Ages. But it is clear that the reporters, clergymen all, thought that scores of people had suffered some kind of possession. Of the epidemic of 1374, a Dutch monk wrote: "Persons of both sexes were so tormented by the devil that in markets and churches, as well as in their own homes, they danced, held each others' hands and leaped high in the air. While they danced their minds were no longer clear, and they paid no heed to modesty though bystanders looked on."[5] Another account reads as follows: "They indulged in disgraceful immodesty, for many women, during this shameless dance and the mock-bridal singing, bared their bosoms, while others of their own accord offered their virtue."[6]

Five hundred years later a similar account appeared in the *New York Times:*

> An epidemic, which the Board of Health is powerless to arrest, has seized upon New York and infects it in every part, counting its victims by the tens of thousands.... [It is marked by] a tendency in the patients to dispossess themselves of their clothing, and it requires the greatest exertion to keep anything on them; then follow a series of piercing

screams called comic singing, distorted and incoherent ravings called puns, and finally, strong convulsions, denominated breakdowns and walk-arounds. Exhaustion supervenes after a fit of two or three hours each night. The remedy for this serious visitation has not yet been revealed.[7]

Here the epidemic referred to was the proliferation of burlesque shows precipitated by the arrival in 1868 of Lydia Thompson and the British Blondes. Although the report was written tongue in cheek, it is an echo of an ancient chain of associations linking dancing with hysteria, madness, contagion, and the primitive impulsiveness of the common folk. In the United States the chain runs from Cotton Mather, the seventeenth-century Puritan, who declared that "A dance is a work of Satan ... which all baptized persons are under vows to renounce,"[8] to modern Southern Baptists, many of whom still view dancing as a sin. Even beyond a religious context, dancing in its wilder forms makes many people uncomfortable as it so graphically conflicts with the orderly public presence to which one becomes accustomed. Dancing to rock and roll has the appearance of a regressive, primitive, and irrational catharsis and can only inflate erotic content.

But it is the stripper's nudity that causes the most trouble. Dancing erotically while fully clothed is not nearly so threatening to American culture as a public display of nudity, even without motion or erotic intent. This distinction became the basis for the 1991 U.S. Supreme Court decision that states have the right to prohibit nude dancing in public venues in the interest of protecting "morals and public order." Upholding Indiana's right to enforce the wearing of pasties and a G-string in strip acts, the Court ruled in a 5–4 decision that, while the erotic content of the stripper's performance was entitled to a measure of First Amendment protection as expressive behavior, her appearing fully naked was not. Writing the majority opinion, Chief Justice William Rehnquist articulated the difference as follows:

> We do not think that when Indiana applies its statute to the nude dancing in these nightclubs it is proscribing nudity because of the erotic message conveyed by the dancers. Presumably numerous other erotic performances are presented at these establishments and similar clubs without any interference from the state, so long as the performers wear a scant amount of clothing. Likewise, the requirement that the dancers don pasties and a G-string does not deprive the dance of whatever erotic message it conveys; it simply makes the message slightly less graphic. The perceived evil that Indiana seeks to address is not erotic dancing, but public nudity. The appearance of people of all shapes, sizes and ages in

the nude at a beach, for example, would convey little if any erotic message, yet the state still seeks to prevent it. Public nudity is the evil the state seeks to prevent, whether or not it is combined with expressive activity.[9]

Rehnquist seems to think that the naked body beyond certain parameters of shape, size, and age is not visually erotic. The eclectic gathering on a nude beach thus provides him with an example of public nakedness that has little, if any erotic content, and that nevertheless must be banned in the interest of the common good. However, as Justice Byron White points out in his dissenting opinion, the Indiana statute was not aimed at the nudity in stage productions such as *Salome* or *Hair:* "Neither is there any evidence that the State has attempted to apply the statute to nudity in performances such as plays, ballets or operas." Since the statute in question is not "a general prohibition," White concludes that "the burden [is] on the State to justify the distinctions it has made." Declaring the majority opinion "transparently erroneous," White also intimates that its hidden agenda is in fact the regulation of erotic and sensual feelings.

If, for the sake of argument, we accept that erotic stimulation is not the evil in nude dancing, what is the evil in public nakedness? Most people would agree that naked people strolling about city streets and parks in this day and age would be a disturbing spectacle and ought to be legally prohibited. But many people of sound mind also would allow that areas set aside for consenting adults to be naked together, such as nudist colonies or nude beaches, or for naked people to be consensually viewed by a clothed audience, as in a strip show or a Miss Nude World pageant, do not present a threat to social order. Justice White, for example, commented: "The purpose of forbidding people from appearing nude in parks, beaches, hot dog stands, and like public places is to protect others from offense. But that could not possibly be the purpose of preventing nude dancing in theaters and barrooms since the viewers are exclusively consenting adults who pay money to see these dances."

The issue is, and has always been, the extent to which some people can prevent the consensual and private actions of others. On this point, Justice Antonin Scalia, concurring with the majority opinion of the Court, wrote as follows:

> Perhaps the dissenters believe that "offense to others" ought to be the only reason for restricting nudity in public places generally, but there is no basis for thinking that our society has ever shared that Thoreauvian "you-may-do-what-you-like-so-long-as-it-does-not-injure-someone-else"

beau ideal—much less for thinking that it was written into the Constitution. The purpose of Indiana's nudity law would be violated, I think, if 60,000 fully consenting adults crowded into the Hoosier Dome to display their genitals to one another, even if there were not an offended innocent in the crowd. Our society prohibits, and all human societies have prohibited, certain activities not because they harm others but because they are considered, in the traditional phrase, "contra bonos mores," i.e., immoral. In American society, such prohibitions have included, for example, sadomasochism, cockfighting, bestiality, suicide, drug use, prostitution, and sodomy. ... The purpose of the Indiana statute, as both its text and the manner of its enforcement demonstrate, is to enforce the traditional moral belief that people should not expose their private parts indiscriminately, regardless of whether those who see them are disedified. Since that is so, the dissent has no basis for positing that, where only thoroughly edified adults are present, the purpose must be repression of communication.

The focus on nakedness as evil is akin to the objectification of woman as evil. What is obscured by the analysis and debate is the underlying fear. Discussion of the issue hardly ever centers on the rationality of the fear, but rather occupies itself with judgments about the fear's object. Public nakedness is held to be immoral and therefore subject to legal prohibition. But how many naked people does it take—and in which venues—before the private act becomes *too* public? One individual in a bar? A handful in a play or ballet? One hundred on a beach? Sixty thousand in an arena? The inability to know where to draw the line fuels the fear. The suspicion that if it remains unchecked it will spread is tied to the psychological mechanism in each individual through which his or her own internalized controls on public nakedness and sexuality are maintained. The overthrow in others of their internalized controls sends a seditious message to our own repressed urges. This is not to suggest that we consciously struggle with a deep-seated drive to get naked; only that where more and more people join a movement the more we become concerned that general social approval will become tied to doing as they do. The fear is that, if it spreads, it will eventually infect us, like a plague or an epidemic of dancing. The dread aroused by the specter of public nakedness is that of contagion and contamination.

The trial of Mitzi Dupree, "The Ping-Pong Queen," is instructive. Dupree, a stripper from Los Angeles, attracted a lot of attention with some unusual stunts. She played a tin flute, signed autographs, and blew out flames, all with the use of her vagina, but her tour de force (as her lawyer put it) was firing ping pong balls into the audience. She was arrested and tried in Calgary in 1984 for having participated in "an immoral, indecent or obscene performance."[10]

The original complaint was filed by a self-described feminist who was "disturbed" and "very, very sad that Miss Dupree ... use[d] her body in such a way that was degrading to women."

In his summation to the jury, Dupree's lawyer articulated the predictable defense that her performance was artistic and entertaining; as well, he attempted to highlight its athletic values.

> You might ask yourself: Has she done anything of redeeming social value? It's a matter of some importance in cases of this kind. She put on an artistic show, it had artistic merit. Maybe it was more of an athletic contest ... than an erotic dance. It was very interesting yesterday listening to her evidence talking about the way that she propelled the ping pong balls around the room, apparently to the great enjoyment of the audience; how she played "Mary Had a Little Lamb" on the flute and followed it with the encore of "Frere Jacques"; and then we heard about "Jingle Bells." Is that an obscene performance, ladies and gentlemen, or is she just providing entertainment and amusement?

The prosecutor countered with an appeal to the jury's sense of social values, emphasizing the point that their personal opinions had to be subordinated to their sense of what the view was from the point of community standards.

> You are not to apply just your own opinion because if that were the case then every case would turn on the individual thinking of the particular judge or jury....You have to try to be objective about this and try to impose the standard that you believe exists throughout the community, the community standard of tolerance that my friend has referred to.

That is, the jury's own opinions were not authoritative, but their guesstimates of the consensus opinion were. The prosecutor then invoked the cancer metaphor:

> The question for you really is: Do we want this sort of thing in the community, in our community? Is this a cancer that is growing in our community, or is it something that I can just ignore because it's behind closed doors? In determining these questions, let's think about whether this is something that has absolutely any merit to it at all. Again my friend calls his witness nice, athletic, really impressed with her professionalism. They try to make her out as some sort of Nadia Comaneci of the vagina for goodness sakes.

For emphasis, the prosecutor returned to the cancer metaphor again and then he raised the specter of its inevitable epidemiology:

> Your neighbor would say: we don't want that, that is a sickness, that is a cancer in our community, get it out, we don't want it.
> We are on a very slippery slope here with this. Again you people, Albertans, probably most of you have been in Alberta for awhile, five years ago [there] wasn't anything like this here. There was maybe one or two topless bars. These things really accelerate. We are on a very, very slippery slope. It's time to draw the line. It's time to put on the brakes and say: "Enough. Wait a minute, we have had it. We don't need that. Get it out."

The jury found Dupree guilty and fined her $1,000 on each of two counts.

"Secondary" effects refer to various social problems that are assumed to be incidental to strip joints, such as prostitution, rape, drug dealing, assaults, and general disturbance of the peace. Some property owners and merchants also blame neighboring strip joints for declining property values and profits. Judge Souter based his concurring opinion on Indiana's right to ban nude dancing solely on the state's interest "in preventing prostitution, sexual assault and other criminal activity." Souter's opinion rested on a previous case that found that "a concentration of 'adult' movie theaters causes the area to deteriorate and become a focus of crime," and on two other cases that found prostitution to be "associated with nude dancing establishment[s]."

What is curious about Souter's opinion is that the question of whether nude dancing *causes* an increase in criminal activity is not the issue. "It is possible," he allows, "that the higher incidence of prostitution and sexual assault in the vicinity of adult entertainment locations results from the concentration of crowds of men predisposed to such activities, or from the simple viewing of nude bodies regardless of whether those bodies are engaged in expression or not. In neither case would the chain of causation run through the persuasive effect of the expressive component of nude dancing." In Souter's opinion it is sufficient that there is a correlation.

But similar correlations can be found elsewhere. Prostitutes have been known to seek out isolated gangs of oil workers and highway construction crews, sometimes setting up shop in nearby gravel pits.[11] They also frequent the lounges of hotels known to cater to the traveling businessman. Sydney Biddle Barrows—dubbed the Mayflower Madam—who operated New York City's most renowned escort service, claims in her autobiography that every October, when the UN General Assembly opened, business doubled. Delegates and lobbyists alike, she writes, "called us for their own pleasure, ... to sweeten a deal, repay a favor, or arrange for several girls to accompany a group of clients to a fancy restaurant or a nightclub."[12] If a simple correlation with prostitution is sufficient to warrant state regulation, then the oil business, the hotel business and the United Nations ought to be regulated as well. If this notion seems ludicrous, then the discriminating factors that make the business of stripping a special case must be determined. Nowhere in Souter's opinion are these factors discussed.

On a final note, Indiana's petition to the Supreme Court was based not on the right to close down strip joints, but simply on the right to enforce the wearing of pasties and G-strings. How this simple restriction might make a difference in incidents of prostitution or other criminal activity, Souter does not divulge.

The implication of character deficiency places strippers among the many social groupings who, for one reason or another, are labeled deviants. These include criminals, homosexuals, prostitutes, political radicals, drug addicts, perverts, and Bohemians. Being outside the norm and not exemplifying its refinement (like the wealthy, the athletic, or the saintly) infers some kind of pathology.

However, social scientists who specialize in the study of deviance no longer view it as rooted in pathology. Although deviants are endemic to all cultures, their respective tolerance varies from culture to culture, from person to person within a culture, and according to the times. The inherent subjectivity of what constitutes deviance suggests that the concept originates with those who cast the stone and not with those who are its targets. Howard Becker, the author of a seminal work on the subject, writes: "*Social groups create deviance by making the rules whose infraction constitutes deviance*, and by applying those rules to particular people and labeling them as outsiders."[13]

That is, "deviance is *not* a quality of the act the person commits, but rather a consequence of the application by others of rules and sanctions to an 'offender.'"[14]

Edwin Schur, professor of sociology at New York University, who has written many books on the subject of deviance, observes that "the very process of deviance-defining seems to serve some important overall functions for a social system."[15] The most important of these is the reinforcement of conformity, the glue that binds a society within a common ideology, a common purpose. The norm sets the boundaries of order, sanity, health, morality, and security. The social order that supports and sustains the power structures also conveys a sense of predictability to its adherents. Conformity to the norm implies a social consensus ("we the people") and establishes the rules for power sharing. "Although economic, legal and direct political power may sometimes be involved, what is most essentially at stake ... is the power or resource of moral standing or acceptability."[16] Those who cast the stone place themselves in a superior social ranking by virtue of their monopoly on moral uprightness, mental health, dignity, order, and progress. The quickest means of elevating the self is to debase others. To have an in group requires the creation (and maintenance) of an out group. Outsiders serve to underscore the limits of the acceptable, to set in relief the zone of privilege.

A society needs its outsiders (or will always have them) because its norms solidify in relation to them. As Schur says: "Deviance-defining is now recognized to be central to the maintenance of social structures."[17]

Outsiders exist in a state of internal exile. The barriers that hinder their access to the zone of privilege may be attitudinal—that is, public disapproval, suspicion, or exclusion—and they may also take the form of physical boundaries, sanctioning or sequestering certain activities to specific areas such as red light districts. As long as outsiders remain within their own boundaries they can usually avoid active persecution. When they step out of bounds and become visible to insiders they risk increasing public scrutiny, legal arrest, and sometimes physical attack.

For instance, a neighborhood pub suddenly begins featuring strippers, a stripper makes the evening news by going beyond the usual exposure, or it is discovered that the woman on the arm of the best man at a debutante's wedding strips for a living. By making such appearances, the stripper not only invades hallowed ground but she intrudes on the psychic space where community standards or traditional values are enshrined.

The rationale for the creation of Boston's tenderloin district was containment of a potential epidemic. Dubbed the Combat Zone, its chief sponsor in government shrugged, "We must deal with the world as it is. If we don't contain it, it is likely to spread into residential areas."[18]

In the unconscious, where symbolic equations are catalogued, deviance is to the social body what cancer is to the physical body. The specter of an alien presence incubating and expanding from within is one of the most profound of human fears and one of the most insidious threats to order. To staunch conformers, deviants are alien, intrusive, contaminating, subversive and potentially ruinous.

Broadly speaking, strippers do not entertain or fall within what most people consider to be family values. Clearly, strippers break some fundamental rules of comportment, especially female comportment. They turn the private public and they make the sacred profane. They take the hard won gains of civilization to sanctify sexuality with love, flesh with intimacy, and biology with poetry—and in a flourish, turn them carnal again.

By appearing to be available on a grand scale, strippers symbolize freedom from social control. Public female nudity, flaunted and enjoyed, cannot help but suggest to more rigorous conformers (such as fundamentalists) the seed of something perilous to social order. Its immediate implications are the unfettering of male lust, the contamination of commerce with sex (and vice versa), and the unsettling of family values. The stripper personifies the exotic and dangerous outsider, like Blanche Dubois in *A Streetcar Named Desire,* the woman whose sexual aura creates havoc everywhere she goes.

How does the collective definition of deviance impinge on strippers themselves? What do they think about it and how do they cope with it?

VENUS DE LIGHT: Burlesque is the toilet of entertainment. Nobody respects it. It doesn't matter if you go out there swallowing swords or spitting fire. All they see is: "Oh! She's stripping! She must have no talent." They figure you're a social outcast, that you've sold your soul. That's why I earn my money. If I have to live with what everybody thinks about me, even though I know different, then why shouldn't I get paid?

LAVA NORTH: A dancer is considered easy, no good, and probably unintelligent. She's just there to be used and abused. If you go to a party and people find out you're a dancer, the conversation changes right away.

DYNASTY LAYNE: Some people look down on us. It's understandable because there are a few dancers who give the rest a bad name: the coke heads, the ones who spend everything and go in debt, the ones who get drunk and bomb out onstage or fall off the stage, the ones who turn tricks on the side.

PEARL IDAHO: I tend to agree with people about dancers. There are a lot of air-head dancers and a lot of looney tune broads in this business.

CHELSEA: When I became a dancer I lost some people in my life. They regarded me as garbage for wanting to be a dancer. One girlfriend was getting married at the time I started dancing and Mike and I were going to their wedding together. But after she found out I'd been dancing, she told Mike: "You can bring anybody you want to the wedding, but don't bring the stripper."

SARITA: My first show was over with. I had a three hour break so I took my daughter in to the hotel buffet to have lunch. I walked in dressed very nicely. I always dressed very conservatively at my jobs, with hardly any makeup. I never pranced around looking like a stripper. And I had my daughter with me dressed in a nice dress. We looked like we came out of church. I'm not joking. We went in there to have lunch and apparently the owner of the hotel was sitting there having Easter lunch with his family. And he stood up and he ran over to us and he said, "What the hell are you doing in here?"

And I said, "Having lunch."

He said, "You get your ass out of here! You don't belong in here. This is for decent people."

I said, "Well, I am a decent person and I am dressed appropriately and this is my daughter." And my daughter started crying. The whole place went quiet. I was freaked out, humiliated. We left.

KYRA: In the small towns everyone knows everyone else and they all know you're the stripper. Now if you go to a party there, you're, like, the freak. As soon as you walk in the door you have to become an actress. You're going to get every rude remark from the guys and all the girls are going to be jealous. Sometimes there's girls that are really trying to make friends with you and sometimes there's people that are trying to understand you. You know what I'm saying? Everyone sits around and they're so fascinated. And a lot of people are rude. A lot of people instantly don't like me or a lot of people instantly fall in love with me. They either really hate me or really love me.

In one place, the week before I arrived, the dancer got run out of town by a protest group. I had no idea that happened. I was in a store, and there was a little girl looking at candy and I said, "Do you want some candy?" And I said to the man behind the counter, "Isn't she cute? I'll buy her whatever she wants." And her mother was standing behind her and I'm telling you, man, she grabbed her kid like this and just yanked her out the door. And I looked at the man and I said, "What the hell did that woman do that to that kid for?" The kid was screaming and crying by the time it got to the door.

The man looked at me and said, "You're the stripper over at the hotel, aren't yuh?" And I said, "Yeah." He said, "We don't like your kind around here. That woman there is a devout Mormon."

And I thought, "Oh. Lovely. Lucky kid. That woman thinks she's better than me?" Just grabbed her kid like that?

DELILAH: I was in Huntsville, Alabama, in '72 or '73. I was in the back room waiting to go onstage and I heard footsteps out the back. Because, like I said, when you're on the road you'd better be alert, like all ears, eyes and whatnot. So I heard these footsteps and a lot of pulling, dragging— funny kind of noises. And I thought, "What are they doing?" And then I heard like splashing water. So I thought, "Well, maybe they're taking a leak or something."

Then, all of a sudden, I see smoke coming through the door. The dumb sons of bitches put gasoline all over the building and set it on fire.

I had a fur rug at the time. I grabbed that and I grabbed my suitcase and I had a big fancy gold rhinestone gown on with a hairpiece. I'm solidly dressed for the stage and I'm running through the building, yelling, "Fire! Fire!"

And they all looked at me like, "What? Is she nuts, or something?"

So I'm running out of the place and the owner says, "Hey. Come back. You've got to do a show!"

I got out of the building and the whole building was on fire. Of course, needless to say, it was the last night I worked because the next day the building was burned down.

Some people in the town didn't like topless.

Since the stripper's deviance is her behavior within an occupational context and not something that need be apparent to the straight world when she is out and about, her path of least resistance would be to keep her job a secret. This defense may become part of an elaborate scheme to maintain dual identities. Many strippers have kept their parents in the dark for years, and there is often a good reason not to tell the boyfriend's parents. A few don't even tell their boyfriends.

LAVA NORTH: My parents think I'm a waitress. It's a double life. When they visit I have to hide all my costumes and all my jewelry. I scan the place to see if there's anything that can give it away. But they've not been that inquisitive as to what I do with my time. They've never asked to come and visit me or eat where I work. I've been really lucky because I've named places where I supposedly work. I'm always preparing myself for the day when one of my parents' friends might see me dancing some- where. But I'm a big girl and I don't have to worry about it. It's just that my parents wouldn't be able to handle it.

RAUNCHY RITA: I don't always tell people what I do. It depends on where I am and who I'm being introduced to. Like say, for example, my boyfriend's family: they think I'm a model. Or I tell a lot of people that I'm a singer. For the last two years my parents thought I was singing in a band. It wasn't until about two months ago they finally found out I was dancing when I got arrested and landed in jail.

I was in Edmonton and I was doing a duo with another girl. We were billed as "An Act Too Hot for Vancouver." We were really explicit. The vice squad came down and arrested us. So there I was in jail for four days and I needed bail money. The hotel wouldn't pay us what they owed us. They held back our paycheck because they thought they were going to be fined and they wanted our money to cover it. So I finally broke down and told my boyfriend to phone my mom. She was shocked, but she accepted it and bailed me out.

BRANDI WEST: My parents are very religious, very strict Baptists. It seemed to me that when I was younger anything that was fun was a sin in their eyes. Consequently, I grew up doing anything that was negative to them because I thought, well, that's where the fun lies. But I eventually mellowed out. To this day, they don't know what I'm doing. They live in Dallas. I don't worry about it because they would never go to bars and that. But I didn't do a layout for a magazine because of it.

They think I'm a waitress and even that's a sin because you're serving alcohol. Once I tried to tell them about the drugs I'd done. I got to pot and acid and my mother was sitting in this rocking chair just crying hysterically so I stopped at that point. I've tried to be honest, but I finally realized that it's easier if I just stick to the waitress story rather than hurt them.

They visited me in October which was a really traumatic experience. I had to move everything out of the apartment and I took the week off work. I drove them by a night club and told them I worked there. They don't drink so they didn't want to go inside.

I moved out a truckload of stuff, costumes, pictures, and stuff, anything that had Brandi on it. But my friends ended up calling me Brandi a couple of times. I said, "It's just a nickname." I kept thinking, some time I'm going to be downtown shopping with them and someone's going to come up and say, "Brandi West! I haven't seen you since you danced out at... ."

My Dad found some of the matches from the club out on the roof, so I think he thinks maybe I waitress at a strip club, but he's pretty cool. He didn't say anything about it.

The sex goddess's public esteem derives from the equilibrium she maintains between art and explicitness. She rises by virtue of her aesthetic value and she falls in accordance with her genital exposure. At a critical point the veneer of artful pretensions wears a little thin and the image becomes overwhelmed by its licentiousness. The weight of moral opprobrium carried by the nether goddesses pulls them earthward and below, into the underworld and the shadow of their most visible and most notorious matriarch, the prostitute.

The stripper is often confused with the prostitute.[19] Both are live images who appear to be advertising the availability of their bodies without concern for the status or personality of the buyer. Both are symbols of sexuality beyond the pale of the family unit. Both represent women whose sexual life transcends traditional values. In both, the conflicting realms of sex and work converge, contaminating each one in the bargain. The stripper and the prostitute also often share the same area of town, the "tenderloin," and it is easy to think that they are after the same market, the lonely horny male. The door between the stripper's realm and that of the hooker appears to be a revolving one. Nevertheless, the stripper is not synonymous with the prostitute. As images, they remain mutually exclusive. This is so because each is defined by the boundaries of her format. If the stripper were to sell herself to someone, she would, at that instant, cease to be a stripper and become a prostitute. The question properly phrased is this: Do women who strip also sell themselves for sex?

This question ultimately hinges on economics, personal morality, and market capability. Strippers are themselves stratified by pay scales according to their shapeliness, their showmanship and their dedication. The top earners have no need and little time for moonlighting of any kind. As well, in recognition of their status within the profession, most of this elite are concerned about their public image. For them, the artistic and entertainment aspects of their métier are never in doubt; stripping is a noble profession on a level not even close to that of prostitution: to be a hooker is to prostitute not only the self but the industry as a whole.

Nevertheless, the Faustian temptations at this level can be substantial. Having artfully raised the libido of the wealthier patrons, strippers may be offered sizable sums of money. It must have been said somewhere that the only thing standing between a prostitute and the rest of us is that our prices are higher.

At the lower levels of the industry—the B rooms and the C rooms, where the atmosphere is seedier, the show is less sophisticated, and the wages are much lower—the stripper's self-esteem may easily be tested. The stripper, after all, has removed the visual barriers to her private self. Her nakedness in front of strangers becomes almost gratuitous. Changing unabashedly in front of other dancers' male friends in the dressing room is not an uncommon occurrence. Money in troubled times may be just enough for some of the lesser paid strippers to go all the way with a stranger. One stripper who worked the B rooms confided: "You've got to understand. There isn't one of us who hasn't hooked once."

CRYSTAL ROSE: Very few strippers hook. However, in the titty bars, I don't know.[20] I've seen some of the girls, where some guy'll offer them drugs—they'll have coke or something—and all of a sudden, they don't feel well and go home; and he leaves two minutes later. So I don't know if you'd call that prostitution.

Some of the girls are either not attractive enough or they just can't seem to cut a living out of that kind of an environment. Hookers are basically lazy. I wouldn't spend so much money on coordination, music, pictures, contracts, agents, or travel if I was a hooker. I'd go to Frederick's and buy something real skimpy and hit the street. Especially here in Nevada where they can drive right outside of town and go to a brothel.

CHELSEA: Oh, I've had lots of people offer me money. Shit, I've had people offer me their credit cards. I don't like to insult anybody. And I don't think it's a real big insult for someone to offer me money. Because I think that's the way some people think. I just make it clear in the beginning: "No, I don't accept money for sex."

BRANDI WEST: I was in a town once where the girl who had been there before me had been turning tricks. This guy there bugged me all day and I kept saying, "I don't work! I don't work!" So all night he shoved money and notes under my door. I finally had to phone the desk to tell them to come and get the guy. That made me angry. I can't stand people who don't take no for an answer. I don't blame anybody for asking, but when you give them the answer, what's all this, "Are you sure?"

Seems to me there's nothing wrong with prostitution. I have nothing against it and I have friends who are prostitutes. I have no qualms about it. It's just that it's not for me. I think it's two separate things. It makes it difficult to work in a place after someone or with someone who does. I just think it's two entirely different things. Either dance or hook. It just makes it difficult because everyone figures, "Well, this one does, so that one does, too."

Everybody has a price. I will say that that is probably true. I mean, I can't say that if someone offered me a vast sum of money I wouldn't do it. I'm just saying that for the amount of money they usually offer I wouldn't do it.

JENNIE: I was sitting with these guys having this intellectual conversation about pollution and this old guy—there's always gotta be one, right?—kept whispering in my ear: "How much?" And I'd say to him, "Get out of here!" And we'd go back to our conversation. Then: "How much?" So after about 15 times I stood up and I said to him [in a booming voice]: "I've told you once, I've told you 15 times! Leave me alone!

I'm not going with you tonight or any other night for that matter, for any amount of money!" This guy just shriveled up and I suddenly realized the music had stopped and everybody had heard everything I had said. And the place was jammed! I got a standing ovation for that one, too.

FARRAH GOLD: The most I ever got offered was $1,000. At that time I *did* go out. That was the only time I've ever done that. I won't do that anymore. I'm engaged… Well, for many reasons. That was years ago before AIDS and everything. I couldn't even think of doing that now.

MARLO (1): I had this one guy who was going to give me $7,000 to go to bed with me once. He was an old man. I laughed when he first asked me. Everybody in the town knew he was a rich man. He was about 83 years old. He had rotten looking teeth. He asked me to go to bed with him for $200. I just laughed at him. "Okay. $400." I said, "Look. Don't push your luck. I'll pretend I didn't hear you."

So the next day he came back and he said he was going to give me $3,000 to go to bed with him. He said, "I know you probably have your values, but money's money." I said, "Fuck off!" So he took out his check book and started writing. He said, "I'll give you $7,000. You can even cash this before you come over to my house." And I said, "You're fucking serious! You're really serious about this! I could never sleep with someone like you! You think your money can buy everything?"

DEE DEE SPECIAL: I remember a man came over to me and offered me $50,000 to marry his son. He came down; the check was done. I never saw his son. His son was about 25. I was about twenty-two. He brought me his picture. From what I could remember he was a good-looking man. I guess he must have been pretty shy if at 25 he couldn't find a girlfriend. I didn't believe in those things. But I thought about it.

HEAVENLY LACE: I have hooked before. I had to do that when I was 15 years old. I was on my own when I was 15 and I was living with this girl and she was hooking. One day she brought this trick home and said, "You better start earning your way around here." That was a really heavy trip.

She was my best friend at the time. She brings this guy home and sends him in the room with me. And he says how he wants her in it, too. I was only 15 years old. I was barely getting into sex, let alone with tricks, 'cause I was not into it. So I didn't want to do it and he just hauled off and hit me a good one. I saw stars. So I said, "All right. All right." And the next thing this chick comes in and starts fondling me and shit and going, "Oh. Isn't she beautiful?" I felt like ripping her face off. I did punch her out later on.

Ever since then, I've done it off and on. You just don't think about it too much. You just think about the money. I would just go out and have a few drinks after and think, "Well, at least I'm not broke."

I started going to the Holiday Inns and Skylines and places like that. I'd dress up and go buy myself a drink, sit there, and they'd come along and say, "Can I buy you a drink?" And I'd say, "Well, I'm working. If you're interested, fine. Sit down. And if not..." I was like, 100 bucks an hour and we'd spend most of it just talking. They're just lonely business men, a lot of them. They travel a lot. They've got expense accounts they don't know what to do with. They just want company, most of them. The sexual part would be only 10 or 15 minutes at the most, more like 5.

What would strippers like people to understand about them?

EMANUELLE: Well, first of all, we're not for sale. And not all of us do drugs. And not all of us are going to be here for the rest of our lives, you know; we do have career ambitions just like everybody else. I mean, it sounds like we're an alien nation.

REBECCA: Some people think that since we're up there taking off our clothes that we want to go out with people and stuff. A lot of us are married and have kids. This is a job. We're regular people. Some of the girls are wild. They party a lot. But a lot of us are our own people.

BROOKE: We're human and we have feelings.

10
Scenes from the Sushi Bar

A look from her creates a storm.

From a poem written for Brittany Fox

The appeal of mediated erotica is tied to the private visual appreciation of an infinitely gratifying, monolithically sexual and physically ideal woman who is devoid of sentience. Stripped of her vitality, the photographic image of the sex goddess comes alive in the mind as an extension of her viewer's particular fantasies. The image is devoid of intention; she (it) has no real feelings for her viewer, but she possesses no contrary intentions either. She is frozen into a mindless sexual arabesque. The image is also devoid of judgment; what the viewer does with her is witnessed by no one. He can lose himself completely to the fantasy without compromising his autonomy.

The stripper, however, being a live image, retains her sentience and displays herself within the context of a public gathering. There is a real person looking through the eyes of the image. It is crucial, therefore, to the integrity of the image that the stripper's sentience appear to be in line with her performance. Sophia Loren recalls that when she prepared to do the strip scene in the movie, *Yesterday, Today and Tomorrow*, her coach, hired from Le Crazy Horse nightclub in Paris, gave her a seminal piece of advice:

> He said that a girl cannot undress with style and be convincing if she does not look straight into the eyes of a man, *one* man, casually selected among the audience. I experienced the truth of such an expedient. I was very embarrassed and uncomfortable during the shooting of that scene. There was a moment when I thought to drop the strip sequence and beg for something else. Now I can be positive of one thing: if I was able to do successfully the scene, it was because I picked one person and I performed only for him, looking straight into his eyes.[1]

Loren's coach instructed her in the art of the pure form. It is based on the understanding that the stripper's purpose is to appear to be an extension of her viewer's desires. Looking the man in the eyes conveys an air of confidence and self-esteem and commitment to the effect. It implies agreement between intention and behavior. It also implies approval for the viewer and his fantasy of her. Meeting the man's gaze with unabashed sensuality soothes him into a state of suspended disbelief.

But the magic seems to work even without the stripper's intention:

> SARITA: You have no idea how many men in the audience believe, that really believe, that you're dancing and looking at them. I've had so many men come up to me and say, "I saw the way you were looking at me, the way you singled me out." And I'd be going, "I don't know what you're talking about, man. I don't know you from Adam." They have delusions that you're telling them that you want them. That only tells me I did my job well.

Even an inadvertent meeting of the eyes can enflame a man's desire and trigger his hope. But the stripper's eyes may convey other ostensible elements of her psyche besides interest. As the opposite gender, the stripper is an outsider to the men. As an object of desire, she is imbued with power. But as a person, she necessarily implies a locus of moral judgment. The stripper thus personifies an external point of view that may easily acquire the stern perspective of a judge upon whom is projected the men's moral conscience: their link with family values.

Thus, enjoyment of the living image must be attended by a degree of defensiveness. To express the naked truth would be to invoke the vulnerability that mediated images of the goddess serve to resolve. Few men show their desire in the strip joint. And none show fear or guilt. What the stripper sees is a diverse display of fortified egos.

While the stripper does sometimes slip into her own link with community values and judge the men from a moral standpoint, the inherent contradiction in this view is unavoidable. As Toni says: "It's easy for me to look at that guy, fully dressed with his buddy, drinking a beer, spending money, and think, 'What a jerk. He watches strippers.' But where does that leave me?"

How the stripper ultimately judges her audience is more a reflection of their emotional response to her.

> CRYSTAL BLUE: There's the Orientals who wouldn't know what to do if it slammed them in the face. They don't even know how to clap. Half of them don't even smile.

Then you get the young guys who are all "Tee hee hee hee." Those are the ones you tease the most, the ones you get a big kick out of.

Then you get the dudes who think they're the greatest. They think they know everything. They'll wait 'til you get off stage and then they'll send vibes to you like, "Hey, Baby. Look at me." Instead of them looking at you, they want you to look at them! You can pick them out really fast.

Then you get the dudes who are the regulars in the bar who are there every day, every week. They've seen every one of your shows.

Then there's the guys who just hang out at the pool table and look over every once in a while: "Oh, floor show! Stop playing!"

CRYSTAL ROSE: Well, you got your lonely hearts. Then you got your guys—I don't know how to describe them—they would really love to have a dancer as a girlfriend. They don't come on. They are truly afraid of women, so they end up being kind of buddies to the dancers. Those are your real regulars. They don't spend a lot of money in the clubs. If your car breaks down, they might try to help you fix it.

Then there's your cock-of-the-walk who thinks every woman should be in love with him.

A lot of the guys are looking for something, some kind of acceptance from a beautiful woman, to be treated a little special. If they're married, it's because they don't get it at home, their wives bore them. I've met older men whose wives are deceased. They have nobody. They've worked all their lives and there's really nothing else in their lives. Their kids have moved and have their own families somewhere else. They're misplaced souls.

Then your younger guys all think that all the dancers are hookers and we're just waiting for them to walk in the door. For some reason, a lot of men, especially young men, have it in their heads that it's more of a conquest to get a dancer and it's kind of scummy to go get a hooker. And I think it's because they see you onstage and if you're sexy and sensuous it's like, "Boy! She really knows men!" And my ex-husbands will tell you I'm very naive [laughing].

DEVLIN DEVINE: Some men are women haters and they go there just to think about how disgusting we are. They sit right in Gyno Row. They won't look us in the eye. And if you bend down to look at them, there's this feeling of aggression and hatred oozing from them. Those guys are so weird. I don't know what they're doing there. Just getting all twisted up in their heads.

Women in the audience are a special category.

JAY JAY: Whenever I get a compliment from a woman, that's when I take it as a real compliment. A woman is the best critic. If she says, "I enjoyed your show," she obviously wasn't looking at my "lolo" or whatever.

If the strip show remained true to the pure form, there would be much less to write about. Its intrigue lies in its edges and anomalies, and its lapses into the authentic. The lack of training or the benefit of a professional coach, the infrequency of controls on the performance, the remnants of burlesque brattiness that remain in the genre, the disagreement about what the show is all about, and the unpredictability of the audience mean that the stripper's personality may easily filter into the act. The price of an image that appears to back up its sexual promise with genuine intention is that at any moment its intention may change. At any moment the stripper's monolithic sexuality, her promise of infinite gratification, may become infused with something contrary.

As long as the stripper stays in character the viewer can dissociate from his suspicions about what she might be thinking of him. But the stripper's indwelling judge is not as threatening to the viewer as her resident brat. The danger is that she might suddenly lapse into some form of manipulation, spurring his defenses and jarring his fantasy; she might embarrass him. This possibility increases with the viewer's proximity to the stage. The closer he is to the stripper, the more she is able to interfere with his defenses. Some strippers, usually veterans, have raised the art of the tease to humiliating proportions.

Gio, for instance, employs a unique device. At the end of her routine—a repertoire of motion and arabesque with myriad variables—she positions herself in the nude on her back with her head resting on the edge of the stage. She bends her knees, bringing her feet close in to her buttocks. She beckons a viewer to come closer. As he obligingly approaches the stage, she raises her torso toward him and, poised on her shoulders and feet, she ignites her abdominals in a rippling, mesmerizing flourish. Entranced, the man bends forward, as though drawn in by her vibrations, and places himself within range. With the deadly accuracy of a chameleon's tongue, she snaps her feet up and over trapping his head between them. Then with quick, piston-like motions, she pulls his head in toward her crotch and then out again, faster and faster, until it looks like the man may lose consciousness. When he reflexively gropes for some support, which brings his hands around his captor's buttocks, she immediately releases him and springs to her feet. Disoriented, somewhat sheepish, but with a glimmer of uneasy pride, the man returns to his seat amid resounding applause. One of Gio's favorite stunts, she calls it the Man Trap.

The possible motivations for toying with the men's internal conflict are many. For one, it is fun. It turns a mindless routine into a creative social interaction. For another, it contributes to the entertainment. Making a fool of one man always makes everyone else laugh. And some men really appear to enjoy being duped by the stripper, thrilled to have made some genuine connection with her and become part of the show. On the dark side, there may be some evil intention. The stripper has an extraordinary opportunity to reverse the gender inequalities she experiences in the real world. From a generally safe place she can make a room full of men grovel.

But refusing to play the game has another function. It affords a means of not losing oneself to the role. As we have seen again and again in their narratives, many strippers have a conflict with what they do. On some level they may recognize that the man is the true point of reference in the show. The role of the infinitely gratifying, monolithically sexual woman is a projection from his consciousness, not an expression that originates in the stripper's mind. She may rebel at the idea that as a stripper she has become an extension of the man's desires. She may intuit that the pure form is antagonistic to her *own* autonomy. By turning the seductive into manipulation or defiance, she retains a measure of power. Gwendolyn, a 15-year veteran of the business, explains it this way:

> I've been confronting the audiences in strip clubs for years. I don't allow myself to be a screen to project their fantasy on. They have to be able to look me in the eye. Can you look at my pussy and keep talking? Carry on a conversation? So I've got a reputation for being "that girl Gwendolyn—she's a bit challenging or threatening."
>
> It's just not as easy to get a hard on with somebody who's trying to engage you. When a guy says just shut up and bend over—well, I'm not the gal for you; I'm here too. That's probably why I've been able to stay so long—because that keeps me from going through the motions. I'm still engaged, involved.[2]

At close range, the stripper ceases to be a strictly visual happening; she acquires some tactility. Less distance, in this sense, means greater intimacy, and intimacy is the least of what this show is about. Intimacy is an image destroyer. It presents a major threat both to the integrity of the image and to the adult male's personal sense of autonomy. When the stripper spreads her legs right in front of the viewer and stares at him for a response, where does he look? If he gazes at her vulva, he will feel her eyes burning on the peripheries of his consciousness. But if he looks into her eyes, she will see through his cool. She will see the desire that he loathes to show. She will see his discomfort and his guilt, his trouble and his need. But more than this, the man's eyes are the channel to his fantasies. By looking into his eyes, the stripper may see what he is doing with her in there.

Only three types of viewer will unabashedly follow the vision: the very young, the very bold, and the very drunk. The younger men in the audience—the college boys who exist on a perpetual threshold of discovery and adventure—can't help but express their wonder. And the seasoned occupants of Gyno Row will try to follow their vision wherever it goes in a mutual dance of cervical contortions, their necks mirroring the articulations of the stripper's torso as she conceals and then reveals what they want to see. The inebriated may simply gaze blankly, with a numbed conscience.

When the stripper looks at the man looking at her private parts, her point of view is "human." To the viewer, this is the least valuable part of her, and the most frightening. But suppose the man gets a chance to spend some time with the stripper between her shows. They have a drink together. They talk. Unless she is the type who plays the vamp consistently, the man will discover her selfhood. He will discover that she is much less of a goddess, less purely sexual, more complex, more earthbound, more sensitive than her stage presence had him believe. She will have transcended the merely visual. She will have touched him. After that, his fantasy of her will be much harder to sustain because her personality will be that much more difficult to erase. After that, he may not be able to sit up front anymore when she is onstage. And she may find it somewhat more difficult to sustain her act in front of him. This is one reason why agents often counsel their strippers to remain aloof from the audience. This is confirmed by Thistle Downs: "If you go and have a drink with one of them, he won't sit in Gyno Row after that. And *I* can't look at somebody after I've talked to them."

The front-row seats, often arranged right along the edge of the stage, are collectively known as Gynecology Row or, more informally, as Gyno Row. In a bygone era the term was "ringside," and perhaps there is some significance to the transition from a boxing metaphor to a medical one. Some strippers have coined their own pet names for this perimeter of their existence, such as Pervert Row or the sniff seats. Holly Carroll refers to it with the expression "drinkin' pink." Sheri Champagne calls it the Sushi Bar.

The temperature is noticeably warmer in these seats, in some measure because of the stage lights, but the heat is more a reflection of the intensity of interaction with the dancer there. She is sweaty and vital. She is charged with the exhilaration of her dance. Sometimes her naked body towers over her viewers. Sometimes she graciously sits down and displays herself within inches of them, but at any moment she may interact with their ego defenses and make public spectacles of them. Gyno Row is the domain of the demon.

TRACY TSAR: Nobody I ever knew liked the men in the front row. They were usually pretty slimy and rude people.

LUSCIOUS LONA: Most of the men who sit in Gyno Row are very quiet. They watch, but they're trying to be cool. I look them in the eye and they're trying not to sweat: "I'm not going to let this lady know that I'm getting excited." A long time ago, I found that if I look right into their eyes, I can practically sit on the edge of the stage with nothing on, with my legs spread, and they're not going to look at my crotch. They're going to look at my eyes because they're too embarrassed to look down. Or they'll not be able to look at me at all. They'll turn away. It's a test.

Sometimes I'll be on the floor and it'll be like, "Show us over here! Don't forget about us!" It's like "Hey. Look. Time out here. If you can hold on for two minutes you're going to see more pussy than you can handle anyway. So just relax!"

JOCELYNE: I like looking at a guy who's staring at me in ecstasy and all of a sudden I make a funny face or cross my eyes and he just, like, snaps back into reality and realizes that I'm actually a human being with a personality. "Oh my God! It's alive!" I just crack up laughing.

A lot of times I play a staring game where I just stare at somebody right in the eye with a look like I'd want to be with him sexually at that moment in time. And he's just looking at me like, "Oh my God! She's looking at *me*! Oh my God! She's moving closer!" And I can almost see him about to have a heart attack or faint or something. Sometimes I even get nervous as to what's going to happen, because I can see his eyes dilating. I like it when they react like that. It's a really big compliment to me when the guy really gets freaked out.

VENUS DE LIGHT: Part of what I do is embarrassing one guy to make the rest of the audience laugh. A good one that always surprises me is after I get out of the champagne glass, I put bubbles right here in my crotch and I go like this [motioning with her finger to stand up] and every time, they'll stand up. I don't know what they think is going to happen, but it works every time. They stand up. I go, "Closer, closer..." They get real close and then I go "*Poof*" in their faces and get them covered with bubbles. And they fall for it every time! I don't know why they keep coming back. Just to have fun, maybe, to be part of the show and to have the performer acknowledge that person. If I use them during my show, they'll come back later and talk to me. And I can see that they feel they know me and that I know them.

MICKEY: I think the guys in Gyno Row are a riot. I'm like a comedian on stage: if I didn't have any hecklers, my show would be lost. If they're sitting in the front row, they're there because they want to be close to the action. So I give 'em action. I try to put a smile on their face.

I've pulled a banana out of my G-string and fed it to the guys, you know, get it real close to their mouth and then pull it away just as they're about to bite. It just embarrasses the shit out of them. But they don't care. They just love it. They line up for that stuff.

But there's times when me and my quick mouth just aren't in the mood. At those times, I'll look darts at 'em ... *heavy* darts.

DEVLIN DEVINE: One night, there were these two lesbians sitting in Gyno Row and I couldn't see them. The lights were turned up so they were shining right on my body and in my face. And I was right there in front of them [making all kinds of seductive gestures]. I didn't know they were lesbians. One was really, really butch. After my show she came up to me and started coming on to me. I didn't even know she was a girl [laughing].

While the men in the audience, for the most part, shy away from expressing desire as they watch the stripper (with the exception of the young boys), they may communicate a token of their affection directly to her when she is offstage. Many of them write poems to their favorite dancers:

Sheri: "Lady of the Lights"
From town to town, bar after bar,
So close to all, but yet so far...
Baring her lovely body, for all to see.
The real lady dancing amongst the
Changing lights, dances alone...

No one! No one! is supposed to see...
The little girl in her dances

Alone in a meadow.
She is beautiful and grave and
Never wants to be old.
When she dances, her toes are
Filled with delight.
Her hair hangs down, her arms float
Like weed in a lazy stream, like a mermaid's
Tresses.

The little girl dances ... alone in the
meadows of life.
She is beautiful and grave, and never
wants to be old.
She dances alone...
No one! No one! is supposed to see
her dance.
(For she dances as a broken grass
dances in the wind, or as a bird
fluttering to reach the tree tops.)
Written for Sheri Champagne, by Frank

she, before his eyes has grown
as one by one the days have flown
from girl to woman sure and strong
with limbs so supple, lean and long
she moves with such an easy grace
and often joy will light her face
as she flows across a circle raised
and deservingly is highly praised;
perfection in the female form
a look from her creates a storm
within the breast of he who waits
to open wide the iron gates
that strain to hold the love within
while seeking one heart's matching kin
For Brittany Fox, by David

Senorita Carmalita

Tanned and lovely with big brown eyes
ˋYou are a beauty, such a delight
Long firm legs, so cute an ass
Your movements my heart excite
Oh Carmalita you dance so good
Your full breasts they sway

Oh Carmalita dance for me
Carmalita be mine someday
     Unsigned

Some men, smitten with a particular stripper, may follow her from club to club and even from town to town. They often make fools of themselves, or become pests. They take any sign of friendship on the part of the stripper as a prelude to romance. Once in a while a miraculously heavenly arrangement results, but more often than not the man's hopes are dashed.

AMBER FLASHING: Guys will send you flowers. Guys will send you drinks. I have had guys buy me bottles of French brandy. Things like that are nice, but it's something you don't want too often. I had this one guy doing it all the time. He'd drive me home from work and we'd stop for a bite to eat sometimes. Then he started to fall in love with me. When I told him there was nothing there, the guy really flipped out. He started crying in the bar and raising a scene. I didn't realize his emotions had gone that far. I felt confused. I didn't provoke him or anything. It just happened. I wasn't single at the time and he knew that. I mean, he had plans to marry me, to sweep me off my feet, or something.

BILLIE JO: One guy came right up the side of the hotel. I do not know how he got up six floors. I sleep with my window open because I like fresh air. I was lying in bed, trying to get to sleep. Somehow, I felt something was wrong, so I got up and went over to the window. I looked out the window and I couldn't see anybody. Meanwhile, the guy was on the side all the time. I almost had a heart attack because, just as I looked to the side, he came flying through the window. I stood back and, with a reflex action, grabbed the phone and hit him with it. It didn't even faze him. This was a *big* lumberjack.

I told him with authority: "You're in the wrong room. Get out!" I sort of stunned him, I guess, because I wasn't screaming or freaked out. I stayed pretty calm. I said, "Instead of going back out that way, you can use the door." And he did. He walked right through the door—didn't open it—walked right through the door!

The desk clerk came up. He'd heard the bang. I said, "You ain't gonna believe this, but…" I was standing there with my window wide open and no door to my room.

BRANDI WEST: In the state of Pennsylvania it is illegal to talk to a stripper. A customer had to ask the bartender to ask the dancer if she wanted a drink. You could sit beside him, but in order to converse you had to talk through the bartender. I met an interesting man there. He was an older man and he restored works of art. He asked the bartender to ask me if I would like to have lunch with him. Well, why not? I was going home in two weeks and you've got to get out. I'd been cooped up in a hotel room for too long. I was nervous about going to lunch with him. He picked me up in a Mercedes and he had a bottle of champagne. We went for a drive to a great restaurant up on a mountain, and we came out of the restaurant and he opened up another bottle of champagne. And then he said, "I can't find my cocaine." This guy was like, 65. So he found it and we did all these lines and he took me on a tour of Pittsburgh and we drank some more champagne and he dropped me off at work. That was a neat thing that happened. A gentleman.

TERI STARR: This lasted a long, long time. In California.

This old man—I shouldn't say old man because he was probably about ten years older than me, but I *lie* about *my* age, so—he painted his car with my name. He had a big Cadillac convertible. A stripper who helped me in the beginning told me I needed a tag line with my name because when people hear your name they also remember the little tag line. Just a gimmicky kind of thing. So she said, "Teri Starr, the Heavenly Body." I felt stupid using that for a while, but pretty soon you get used to anything. So all over this stupid car was "Teri Starr, the Heavenly Body."

He always wore a suit, like a lightweight summer suit, but it looked like it had just been through the washing machine. He was an artist, so he had all kinds of pamphlets and portfolios and things that he used to bring into the clubs. He'd say, "I have some artwork for Miss Starr and I need to see her about it." He was blackballed from every club, eighty-sixed from every club I worked in. He never did anything really, really bad; he just drove you crazy. He followed me from club to club. He followed me to my home. He would do things like, when I was onstage, he'd stand up and say, "Teri, you changed the curtains in your bedroom. I really like what you did." And I knew he had been there. That particular time I had changed the curtains to Austrian sheers. So then it made me get a little bit nervous. After he did this to me three different times, I said, "Well, did you notice the trophies I have for sharpshooting?" And I do. I have two.

And he said, "No. I didn't see those."

And I said, "Well, they were sitting right there." (Which they weren't. They were in the closet.) And I thought that ought to end it, but it did not.

One day, the housekeeper told me she came home and this guy was sitting on the couch in the living room. We lived in a small area in West Covina in California. Nobody ever locked their doors. This was 20 years ago. And she said, "What are you doing here?"

And he said, "Well, I wanted to see Teri."

That went on for eight years or more. Finally, I called the cops and had him arrested. When they were taking him away, he just kept saying, "But I love her. And she loves me!"

I don't know what happened to that man. He was still around in '76 when I left and came to Las Vegas with that same old car painted with all those names and things.

The club masturbator is a special kind of fan:

> TRACY TSAR: I never wore my glasses onstage, so they were just vague shapes out there. I'd smile at vague faces. One time I was smiling encouragingly at a man who was sitting right up front. Later, I was sitting at the staff table and all the girls kept coming over, saying, "Did you see that asshole?" He had been masturbating during everyone's show.

> CRYSTAL ROSE: I remember one time in San Francisco a guy was masturbating and when he climaxed it hit the top of the head of the guy sitting in front of him. We were all grossed out. All the girls went, "Aaagh!! Gross!" We all ran. It was embarrassing. The guy who was masturbating got up and split.

For some men, it goes beyond infatuation with one stripper to an addiction to the whole concept.

> SARITA: Somewhere deep down inside we know there's a lie happening. But some people lose that objectivity completely and they get sucked into it. They get crazy. There are some men who are literally addicted to watching naked girls. Like I said, I don't believe there's anything wrong with that, but there's something strange about an obsession with watching a naked girl get up there and do her manipulation on you for money.
>
> The men who I have known who watch dancers consistently are sexually impotent. I know this for a fact because some of them have become friends. They have performance anxiety to the max. They're afraid of women.

> KYRA: It was my fourth week of dancing. I took off my G-string and the whole bar burst out laughing. I didn't know what was going on. I was so embarrassed. I got offstage and this guy came up to me and said, "We weren't laughing at you. Didn't you see the guy in the front row with the magnifying glass?"
>
> "What guy?"

"The Oriental man."

I had noticed the guy and he was writing things in a book when I started. I thought he was an agent and I avoided looking at him through my whole show.

My very best friend came down onstage after me and I told her about him. She said, "You watch that guy!"

So I sat by the bar and sure enough, as soon as she took off her G-string, he took out his magnifying glass. He was in Gyno Row and he was like, this close to her. She threw her cover-up on top of his head.

Later, I was talking to one of the waitresses about the guy and she told me that he was always in there. He would order draft, four at a time, and he would put these little black covers over the glasses to keep the draft from going flat. Then, just as we were laughing about him, I hear, "Excuse me."

I turned around and looked at him and I said, "Yes?"

He handed me this big folder and I opened it up and looked at it. I didn't know what it was. I kept looking at it. There were all these lines with names and there were pieces of tape, full of this stuff. And then I noticed something was different and I put my hand on it.

Oh, I just about died. I took this thing and I just threw it in his face. It was a collection of pubic hair, one from each dancer, taped in the book with her name.

If adoration can become obsessive, frustrated desire can become violent. In spite of the advice of agents and some veterans of the business, strippers often mitigate the loneliness of the circuit and the routine of the job by talking to people in the bar between shows. The individual stripper *thinks* she has become a good judge of character (after all, she's met so many!), and the interesting ones she meets—the eccentrics, the musicians, the dealers, the polite young men—are an effective panacea for boredom. But she might easily misread someone's veiled purpose as friendship. And he might easily misread her friendliness as sexual attraction. When he makes his move and loses, he might get angry. The latent demons in the men are far more dangerous to the stripper than the other way around.

SARITA: Strippers press buttons and they enjoy that kind of power. What they don't realize is that there's a price to be paid. It could backfire. They could get raped. They could get killed. Women play that game and they end up there.

Now, all men are not rapists. It's like a sickness that can be aggravated or brought to a boiling point. You have to be respectful of this. You're dealing with elements you cannot control and you cannot understand and that element is subconscious and it lies within the murky waters of a psycho mentality. When you're dealing with things you don't understand, you are always vulnerable.

AFRODITE: My sister said it. She was a dancer for ten years. The men that hang around strip joints are *desperate!* They're *desperate* men! They've got nothing. They've got to go hang out in the bar to get laid. They manipulate you to get things. You know, it's like there's something that you want, but you can't quite have it. You know, when you want it more just 'cause you can't quite snafu it, you know what I mean? You know how men manipulate, right? You know, na na na and then they get a little bit more out of you and, you know, they turn their back and then you give them more, right? And you think that this guy's not so great. How come he doesn't like me? And meanwhile the guy'd probably fuckin' kill his mother for you. But you know, he has to play his cards right. You know, he's a loser.

JOCELYNE: I always forget the name of this place, probably because I want to. It was Monday and I had just done my show and this big biker walked up to me and said, "That guy over there wants you as his birthday present. It's his birthday tonight and you're coming."
I said, "Are you out of your mind? Forget it."
The guy sat me down and tried to talk me into it, but I kept refusing. So he grabbed me and bit my cheek. He growled, "Now you get upstairs and you change and you get right back down here. Don't worry. We'll give you drugs so you won't mind being his birthday present. Get going!"
I ran upstairs and ran right out the door into a cab. I took another hotel room somewhere else for the night. I went back the next day for my first show around lunch time. I walked in and they told me at the front desk to go straight to the office. The owner was sitting there with my full pay for the week, which was really kind, a plane ticket, and a ride to the airport. After I had left, the bikers broke down every single door in the hotel looking for me and they beat the shit out of the other dancer.

JANUS: Some guy tried to kill me once. I came down to the bar after work one night and I was talking to some of the waitresses. This guy kept on coming up to me and asking me to dance, over and over again. I kept saying, "No and no and no." Finally, after about the twelfth time, I said, "Don't you get the hint? I don't want to dance." He was all mad and stuff.
The next day, while I was doing my floor show, I noticed him coming toward the stage. The waitress grabbed him and told him to get out of the bar. He had one of those hooks that you put fishing lines together with and he told the waitress he was going to kill me with it. She told him she was going to call the cops, so he left.
The same week, somebody tried to kick down my door. I don't know

who it was. I screamed my face off. I dialed downstairs and it rang and rang and all the while I was screaming. Luckily, the band was just down the hall. They came running and the guy took off.

ANGEL CARTER: The most frightening experience I've had was when I was at the Body Shop. It was my birthday and someone sent me a box. Inside was a leather coat with a fox collar and a diamond necklace. I asked who it was from and they said, "Oh, some guy just dropped it off." Well, I wanted to give it back. I didn't know who it was from. So I just left it at the club in my dressing room.

The next day, I came to work and I got this message: this gentleman wanted to say hello to me. So I went downstairs. And he said , "Did you get your present?"

I said, "Yes. I like it very much, but I'm sorry, I can't accept it because I don't know you."

He said, "I'm just an admirer. I enjoy your show and I think you're beautiful. I'd like to take you out for dinner."

"I'm sorry, but I don't know you. I don't go out with people just like that. I've got the gifts upstairs and I'll give them back to you."

"No. No. That's okay. You can keep them. No strings attached."

That night, I went out for breakfast with a couple of girls. I ordered breakfast and I turned around and there was that guy, sitting right across from me. I was now getting this very funny vibration. I was feeling very uncomfortable. I told the manager what was happening and he moved us downstairs. Sure enough, he followed us down. The manager tried to stop him and an argument broke out, so we left.

I went home—I was staying at a friend's place—and went upstairs. I know I saw a car, but I'm not sure if it was his. Now I'm *really* nervous. I was by myself in this big penthouse and my friend was out of town. I got undressed and got cleaned up. A few minutes later I hear someone knocking on the door. There was no peep hole in the door. I said, "Who is it?" No answer.

I ran to the kitchen and locked the other door. There were two entrances and I bolt locked that one, too. I was pretty panicked. He knocked again. I said, "Who is it?" and he said his name. I said, "I'm sorry. You can't come in. I have a boyfriend here."

He said, "Bullshit. You don't have a boyfriend."

I said, "I'm sorry, but I have my boyfriend here. Let me go get him."

I went and grabbed the phone and I called my private detective friend. Fortunately, I caught him. Whew! He was there in ten minutes. Meanwhile this guy tried to break down the door. He was about six foot five. My detective friend arrived, the police came, and they took him away.

RAUNCHY RITA: I've got a gun. I don't carry it with me, but I've got my mace with me and that's enough. And I can run. The reason I got the gun and the mace was because of a psycho. The first night I auditioned at the club he waited for me to leave and followed me in his car. I was walking down the street and I was mad. He asked me if I needed a ride and I was, like, "No." I just kept on walking. He pulled into the parking lot and I'm like, "Oh, great." He gets out of the car and kind of like trots up to me, not run, not walk. He grabs me, and this is like a stranger doing this to me. I couldn't really do anything. He was from New York.

And I was curious. I like tough guys. I like their masculinity. The way they carry themselves. I mean, I'm not talking about Stallone; I mean, *Schwarzenegger*, because I like muscles. And I like big "dings." I like cocks.

But he was a jerk. I mean, he had a nice body too, but, you know, that was about it. We just went out for drinks, just for talking and stuff like that. I said, "Okay. Fine." If this is the only way I can get rid of this guy, fine. I'll just have a cup of coffee, or whatever. We went out, like three times, just to see if it would work or not and it didn't work and we both agreed on the third date that if it didn't work, don't call me.

Because my hair is cut short, the guy gets intimidated or his ego gets hurt. He says, "Oh, you're a dyke!" Tough guys, or macho—that's what he called himself: the macho man. And I'm like, "Aw Jesus!" And I figured, maybe it'll stop. But it didn't stop and it got worse and I almost went to the cops for a restraining order.

And he was always putting me down for stripping. He'd say, "You're not going anywhere" and this and that. And I'd say, "Okay. Whatever." 'Cause he doesn't know me. He said, "When I saw you onstage—you've got such a body—I *had* to go out with you." He always told me how gorgeous I was and how nice, and stuff like that, but he'd treat me like shit. It was like the modes that most of the girls get into, you know, like supporting the guys, and the boyfriend is abusive mentally as well as physically. And I saw that coming. And I said to myself, "No way. It's not happening. Not to me, it won't." And then I thought about it and if it had been a little bit less abrasive I probably would have still seen him, maybe. But it was overbearing.

I said, "Please don't call. Don't come by. Don't even talk to me." He did not get the message. And then, after that, he just wouldn't leave me alone.

So I bought a gun because he began calling me up and threatening to get me and stuff. He said, "Well, now that I can't get you, I'm gonna *get* you!" And then he said, "And then again, I may just wait for you." He called me a dyke-bitch and he'd say, "I'm gonna marry your fuckin' ass" and shit like that. I'm like, this guy's off his rocker. So I went out and bought a gun.

GIO: I was raped once by a guy who was supposed to give me a ride to the subway station. I was working in Long Island and there was no train at three o'clock in the morning. The guy drove me to a deserted beach, pulled a gun on me and said, "Okay, start sucking, Baby." He was supposed to be a friend of the owner. What do you do? You can't go to the police. They'll laugh. They'll say, "Well, you took a ride from this guy and you've been dancing naked in front of him all night. What do you expect?"

11
Being Supported and Getting Crushed

One might expect long term relationships to be problematic for strippers. Typical of the entertainment field in general, the late hours and extensive travel mean frequent separation from one's lover and an irregular home life. But just meeting a compatible partner is difficult, given the circumstances of the stripper's job. While she attracts a stable of potential suitors far in excess of the average woman, usually she considers them ineligible both from personal observation and as a general principal. This is one of the ironies of working in an occupation where one's sexual attractiveness has been exaggerated way out of proportion to the totality of one's real self. The man in the audience wants a relationship with "the stripper" while the stripper's resident "I" only wants a relationship that transcends her role. The incompatibility of these two points of view would appear to doom them both to disappointment.

The stripper knows that the men in her audience want her for only one thing. At her most cynical, she thinks of them as degenerates or perverts. Beyond the abuse, beyond even the danger the men present to her, her real concern may be that they are just a low form of life. In the stripper's mind it is the men who are the unstable ones.

CARMALITA: I like the men outside the club, but a lot of the men who come in to watch your show are goons. The men who do come in to watch those shows usually are really strange perves.

MELISSA WOLF: Sometimes I think they really suck. Some of them are really classless. Some of these guys come in in really nice three piece suits and their mouths are just... Nice suit! Too bad your asshole's showing, buddy!

I may be an exotic dancer, but that doesn't mean I'm trash. That doesn't mean I talk like trash. That doesn't mean I've got the IQ of beer temperature.

AMBER FLASHING: They're all animals. More or less. Especially when they're with the boys in the bar. They're all trying to outdo each other with grossness. But deep down I don't think they're like that. When they're alone with a woman, they're not like that. They're totally different. They're all sucks and babies.

CLAIRE LOVE: I don't know. I think the majority of men are scum. That's my saying, by the way. You're gonna hear that a lot. I started the saying "Men are scum." I also started the black hair dying craze, too.
Basically, it's their mother's fault because men are raised by mothers and they go out looking for mothers. I think a lot of men do because a lot of mothers baby their man and give him everything. But then again, I meet some men who are really open-minded. I think it all depends on the individual and the experiences he's encountered in his life and how open-minded he is. I mean, if you live in a small town all your life and work in the mill and you were raised by a mill worker and your friends are mill workers, I think you're gonna have a very small, narrow space of mind because it hasn't been broadened in any aspect. And that's not their fault. It's conditioning.

BRANDI WEST: Many dancers go through a period of hating men. I went through a period like that. Like, if you work on the road a lot in these small towns and you deal with jerks a lot, you do. For a little while I really started to hate men [announcing]: "*Men are all creeps!*" But then you realize you're getting a very limited view of men as a whole by what comes in the bar.

Many strippers have an unwritten rule not to go out with anyone who has seen them perform. On the other hand, most strippers cannot help but hope that Mr. Wonderful will one day chance to walk into the club, a man whose aura, whose strength, and whose sensitivity will make him stand out among the rabble. She might scan the audience with regularity in this quest, all the while knowing that it is a long shot.

Some club-wise men take advantage of this scenario by playing on the stripper's hopes. They understand her loneliness, her emotional vulnerability, and her need to relate to someone as a human being. They come across as very different from the rest of the men. They don't buy into her sexual allure. They appear to like her for other reasons than her body. They treat her like a person. But it is all a skillful facade designed to add another notch to their list of conquests. Known in the trade as "stripper-fuckers," they are an enduring occupational hazard, especially to the novice. When someone gets branded as a stripper-fucker, most strippers will avoid him like the plague.

THISTLE DOWNS: Men are undoubtedly led by their dicks. That's for sure. I mean, that's for sure, for sure. Some guys you meet are really stupid. They just don't know. Some guys are cool. They know the business. Some guys are goofs. They're stripper-fuckers. You just stay away from them, right? You don't want anything to do with them because ten to one they've got something you don't want.

The men who are somewhat in sync with the stripper's lifestyle and her consciousness—the musician and the male exotic dancer—make convenient short-term affairs when their respective paths cross on the road, but neither one of them is noted for his stability.

RAUNCHY RITA: There's a thing between dancers and bands. Musicians think that dancers were made to screw them alone, that dancers were put on earth to screw bands. I've seen dancers with band guys fucking in the hallways. I've seen a dancer with five band guys in her bed. She said, "I'll get as many skinny musicians in my bed as I can." They're skinny and small, right? Like, you can sit a whole band in your bed.

Without someone to travel with her, the stripper can get very lonely, especially in the small towns where residents tend to view her as a suspicious intruder, if not an alien from a depraved planet. The need for affection rises with the miles and the weeks away from home. Meanwhile, back home, her lover may be well on his way toward drink or madness thinking about what might be going on out there. His racked imagination and his own rising urges make a powerful conspiracy for being unfaithful before she is unfaithful to him.

This scenario meshes conveniently with another one. Because the stripper must be wary of the vast majority of men she meets, the safest ones—indeed, the most attractive ones in some cases—are her coworkers' boyfriends. If the boyfriend happens to be going with a stripper who is also a competitive threat, then seducing him while she is out of town becomes an especially tantalizing prospect. In light of this enduring possibility, the boyfriend-fucker is considered to be an even lower form of life than the stripper-fucker.

In some rare situations the stripper's boyfriend or husband travels with her as her manager, light man, or cameraman. (Some strippers supplement their income from the stage by selling Polaroids of themselves posed with members of the audience between shows.) But this arrangement hardly draws enough revenue to make his participation profitable. Alternatively, a stripper may elect never to go out on the circuit, but as Venus De Light says, "If you want to make this a career, you have to travel. There's no two ways about it." The stripper's choices are often very painful. A frequent resolution to all these contentious forces is to support an unemployed musician.

The man in the relationship has to deal with some formidable stresses of his own. In the beginning there may be a heady exhilaration, not the least of which is tied to the fact that he's won the attraction of the goddess. Sitting in the audience, the thought is inescapable that all the rest of the men's fantasies are his reality. If she dances just for him, à la Sophia Loren, he gets the added boost that the others now know it. A stripper's boyfriend, who frequently traveled with her, explains it this way: "This one day a friend of mine came with me and he'd never seen my girlfriend dance, eh? And she's giving me the most sensual looks in the world, especially when she's doing her floor show. He looked at me and said, 'You must be in your prime now 'cause every guy in here is giving you a dirty look.' And I'll just sit there with this big smile on my face and think, 'Too bad, suckers!' And that makes me feel good."

However, as time goes by, he may begin to notice that the audience is really an intrusion on his private and intimate space. He may become jealous of the attention his lover pays to them; he may seethe at their abuse of her; and he may become increasingly disturbed by their visual consumption of her body. Then again, he may find that the audience intrudes even when they are alone together. A veteran light man from Las Vegas, who worked eight years in the business and lived with a stripper during that time, articulates what this last concern meant to him.

> For all performers there exists a triangle. We speak of triangles in love affairs. In this case the personal relationship is one side of the triangle and the second is between the stripper and the audience. They have, in effect a relationship with both, this personal relationship with a mate, or a lover, and a relationship with the audience. And it is a love relationship—oftentimes a love-hate relationship with the audience—I think there's both. Just as in a three *person* triangle, this triangle may or may not be compatible. The reason that it becomes a triangle is because sometimes the personal relationship can be at odds with the need for the audience relationship. And I think that that is one thing that puts pressure on relationships in the entertainment industry at large. For an individual, it is similar to the division between career and mate, or career and family.

They come home. Do they say, "I'm glad to see you; I need love"? No. They say, "This guy did this and this guy did that." And for two hours, all you hear about is this audience. Well, you might as well be listening to them talk about a lover. Because, all of a sudden, it's like you're not even present. Then you realize you're not enough. Your affirmation, your love, your caring for them isn't enough to overcome any deficiency in this other relationship.

Being married to the job is not unique to stripping. Anyone who lives with a career-oriented person or a workaholic will likely experience occasional jealousy of the other's job. But *this* particular job threatens the intimate foundations of the relationship. The man can't help but wonder what is going on when he is not there. If *he* met her in the club, isn't it highly likely that someone else could, too? Even though he may have moved beyond attraction to her image to love of her person, he can't help slipping back into the viewer's suspension of disbelief. The illusion the stripper creates onstage can convince even her lover. Kyra explains this in one interview, "My girlfriend got beat up by her boyfriend because she was teasing some guy in Gyno Row. Another girlfriend had a fight with her boyfriend because some guy gave her his phone number. I know guys who sit in the audience and, if she smiles too much or if she teases too much, she's in shit."

One man, who married a stripper, saw her retire from the business, and raised children with her, remembers the anguish:

> I found it really hard to deal with. I'd think, "She doesn't ever look at me like that or smile at me like that." Let's face it, we've all got egos. So I'd come home and bug her about it. And she wouldn't want to be bugged about it because it was an act. She'd say, "Tom, when I get offstage, I don't remember flirting with that guy."
> It's really hard to handle. I mean, she was a dancer before I met her. I should have known better. It's tough when your wife or girlfriend is up there taking her clothes off in front of a bunch of guys and they're all hooting and hollering and making comments like most guys do in bars.
> Debbie Sue [not her real name] used to do an oil show, a very sexy, sensuous oil show. One day, I sat in the bar waiting for her to finish her show. This guy was sitting beside me by himself and his buddy comes out. And this other fellow sits down with this other guy and he says to his friend, "Where yuh been?"
> He says, "Oh, I just came from the lobby. You know that Debbie Sue? She gives oil rubs in her room between shows."
> And I was sitting there—you know, we weren't married yet, we were just dating—and I mentioned it to her, and I even kind of questioned

her with that tone like, "You don't, do yuh?" I mean, I should have known, but you hear stuff like that. It can be rough on a relationship.

What happens all too often is that the stripper's boyfriend eventually starts pressuring her to quit.

With so many factors working against long-term, committed relationships, it is no wonder that strippers' lore is generally pessimistic about fairy tale romances. All too often, they end up in disappointment. The individual may decide to eschew relationships altogether. In one letter, a stripper confided to another as follows:

> I am beginning to think of myself as a little bit Queen Elizabethish, finding it highly advantageous, in a strategic way, not to be noticeably involved with anyone. My ideas of love are too ideal, I'm afraid. It seems to me that love in the real world is a colossal waste of energy unless it's near perfect, and near perfect love affairs just don't present themselves every day! Oh well, I should never have gotten onto this subject—it makes my blood boil and my blood is already boiling for other reasons.

The stripper's own fantasy—if not the rich dude who will take her away from all this—is simply a guy who will love her for herself and support her in her vocation. And once in a while the magic does happen, in spite of the odds.

TONI: I would say very few dancers have solid relationships. Of the girls who have relationships that aren't solid, I would say the problem there tends to be lack of judgment, letting yourself get involved with a man who's met you in a strip joint, which occasionally can work out. But only occasionally. I think that a man who goes to a strip joint once in a blue moon isn't about to want to meet one of the strippers in there. I feel that it's only the guys who are more used to the strip joints who feel comfortable enough to even come on to the stripper. And those are the ones you're going to meet. And those are the ones you wouldn't want to get involved with.

DAYNA: Why is it that so many dancers get involved with some of the most horrible men? All the men I've gone out with have been really wonderful people. Well, most of them—not the casual ones [laughing]. But with some dancers, it's like: "Hi! You beat up women? All right! I like *you*! Are you gonna spend all my money and get me on real hardcore drugs? All right!"

MICKEY: That irks me to no end. That's from sitting in the bar after your show thinking you've got to talk to all those guys and sit and drink with them. A lot of girls have drinking problems. A lot of girls have cocaine problems. They have the money and it's affluent. They can't get enough for some stupid reason. And you're going to get some smart guy who's going to come along and say, "Hey, Baby. That's okay. I'll look after you. Here, have some more drugs and here, have another drink." The girl is disillusioned into thinking that's love, that's caring. A lot of the girls are quite young and may not have had many relationships. If all they've had is crushes, then they're going to get crushed because they don't have that stamina to fight for their individuality and their independence.

RAUNCHY RITA: Ninety percent of dancers are supporting guys like poor broke musicians that got nothing. When you're a dancer the most lecherous leeches come out from the fuckin' rocks and caves, you know, because you're a dancer, right? You could say between 75 and 80 percent of dancers have some poor fuckin' bastard they're supporting. They never get anywhere because they're supporting some lecherous leech. You know, you see a lot of dancers that go on the road with these young guys that got no money, they got no future. They're supporting them, buying drugs for them, feeding them. The majority of dancers get suckered in by that.

JOCELYNE: A lot of men, not all men, but three quarters of the men that I encounter have a really bad habit of flirting with their girlfriends' girlfriends. It's very, very hard to find a man who will not flirt with other beautiful women and just be their friend. Especially among dancers because everything's focused so much on physicalness that it's nice to meet a man who's focusing on the mind and the person rather than physical beauty. It's like, if all of a sudden, they seem equally infatuated with your girlfriend because she's beautiful too, it's all gone. We always run into men on the circuit who have girlfriends as dancers and there's maybe one in five who does not flirt with us while she's out working somewhere else. One in five.

GIO: For the longest time I was an emotional masochist. I allowed men to play their power trips on me. I'd get really hung up on them. I was married for three years and discovered that the guy was scamming me. I've always had a difficult time with relationships in my life. But I don't blame it on my work. I think it has much more to do with the fact that I am a very independent thinker.

I was mentally abused the whole three years I was married. And I liked it. I'd come back to our loft in New York City from working in New Jersey totally bedraggled from doing go-go for eight hours, a half hour on, a half hour off. I'd come back with $400 in ones and he'd say things like, "Who'd you blow in the bathroom?"

I cried out for love and this guy was giving me a lot of love. The possessiveness and jealousy in his nature didn't start out being abusive but as he gained an upper hand... I've never had as much attention or as much love from any one individual in my whole life and the more I became dependent on that, the more abusive he became. It took me a year to wake up and realize what he was doing to me.

I'd never been able to be possessive before. I have a fairly possessive nature as far as emotionally wanting to own somebody, to have a boyfriend. The first boyfriend that I ever lived with decided that he was gay and there was no way I could compete with that.

ROBBIE: In this business it's so hard to find someone who actually likes you for you. Guys just take you on trips. Some girls come into this business and they're really naive. I know I was. Guys just fill your head with compliments and put you on a pedestal and tell you how wonderful you are a hundred times over. And you think, "Wow! This guy really likes me." But it's not because he likes you. It's because he wants something from you. As soon as he's got it, you can hit the road.

Men are shallow, cold, superficial. They don't think we're people. They think we're robots. They don't understand that we get tired. They don't understand that we get sick. They just think that our lives are perfect because we make such good money.

MUSIDORA: I met him in a bar. I was attracted to his eyes. He had very beautiful eyes. He was very handsome. I supported him for six months. He went on the road with me. It was just awful. I vowed I would never, ever, ever go out with a guy who didn't have a job. It was a threat to his manhood. He more or less bit the hand that fed him. So I escaped.

He would make me angry. He exhausted every emotion I had and then he'd laugh and say, "You know what I just did to you, eh?" And then he'd explain it to me.

He got violent with me. He picked me up and threw me against the wall. He stole $700 from me.

I took $500, my costumes, and some of my clothes and I was gone. I was history. Goodbye.

But that relationship wasn't all bad. See, he taught me something. He taught me everything about how conning men can be.

In the end when he tried to get me back, I looked at him and laughed and said, "You can't con a con" [laughing].

MAZIE GODIVA: I'm attracted to a certain look. I like dark skin, not really dark, but dark, smooth skin ... and a sort of wild look, but not really wild. It's the wrong look to be attracted to because most guys who have this look are usually quite good looking and they've been spoiled by women. They're spoiled guys.

I had a really bad experience with a guy last year. He took me for a lot of money. A lot—$4,000. He had me believe that I was in love with him.

He'd wake me up in the morning and say, "You know what you told me while you were sleeping? You told me that you loved me." He made me believe all these things. I guess I really did fall in love with him. Madly, passionately I was in love with this guy. He was having trouble with the police at the time.

He was a mulatto guy. He was gorgeous and sweet and had a great sense of humor. There were a lot of nice things about him. So I said, "Take $2,000 and set us up in San Francisco." I wanted to go back to San Francisco anyways. We had already been together for a while and he never took anything from me. That very same night, he went and blew all the money on cocaine.

I didn't forgive him at first. But then I realized how sick he was. He said it was the first time he ever did that, that when you start, you can't stop. He was only going to do a $100 worth... That was the night before his birthday, so, you know, I kind of understood.

Two months later, he was in jail and I paid for his bail fees and some of his lawyer fees. Then he got out and was supposed to go back to court and he never did, so I lost all the bail money. Then when I saw him, I realized I didn't care about him anymore. It was all an illusion.

Then, to top it off, I found out he had been pimping all along.

BRANDI WEST: My husband hated me dancing. He was a musician. The reason we split up the first time was because he was in prison. When he got out we got back together and he started performing in lounges and that, and I was already dancing. Musicians think that stripping is not a form of entertainment, you know, *they're* talented but we're just doing something... He tried but he didn't really like it.

We did a show together for a while: " Young and West." He would be onstage playing guitar and I would be a waitress and I'd start singing off key and he'd say, "Would you mind not doing that?" And we'd have this little dialogue, right? And he'd say, "All right. That's it. No matter what you do, I'm going to ignore you." So I'd come up and rip his clothes off and I'd take mine off. He would continue playing throughout. He'd never miss a note.

But it's difficult, you know. It's two different worlds. Even though he was in the entertainment business and I was in the entertainment business, he had a different type of crowd and he went different places. It ended up that we had two separate sets of friends. You grow apart. You can't share it. We tried to share it but he couldn't handle this. He hated it. He hated taking his clothes off. That was degrading to him.

JOCELYNE: I have a best friend right now and he's never let me down. We trust each other more than we've ever trusted anyone—ever, ever, ever. It's a very special, strong friendship, relationship, if you want to call it that. And if he ever, you know, broke that trust, I don't know if I could fully trust anybody ever again.

That was the problem I had with men. I totally lost all my trust for men, because I trusted and turned around and got shit on. I find, now that I'm with men, I can love them now and I can be happy and everything can be just hunky-dory. But there's this teeny-weeny little section of me that is not going to be entered. He will never do that. What I have to do is not let that space be noticeable.

And I hate it. I wish it didn't have to be there. I wish that I could just let it go. But I've been proven so wrong every time I've let it go, that I feel that I have to leave it there. Because so many people that I've loved have let me down.

CRYSTAL BLUE: We met at the club where I was working. I mean, the taboo is that when you're a dancer, you're not supposed to go out with anybody in the bar, because they've seen you. They've seen you perform. They've seen your body. They think that they know you, they know this person onstage and they want the person onstage. So the thing is, in this business, is not to go out with the people who are in the bar. You try to keep that part out.

But I figured he was nice. He was polite. I liked his accent [chuckling]. So I let him drive me home. He was down every night that week. I went home with him every night that week and then it just got bigger. That was cool.

JENNIE: The songs I used usually expressed something about the relationship I had. The relationship was what made me grow and face life, more than the dancing.

He was quite a strong man. I was with him for ten years. He was always making me face things that I probably didn't want to face in life. And it was very painful for me a lot of times. In a lot of ways, he really taught me…

He liked me dancing. He had problems when I quit dancing. He always thought I should dance. He'd say, "You're good at it. You're lucky you have an opportunity to work in a field where you can creatively express your innermost feelings when a lot of other people don't have that opportunity."

That was a good point. Actually, now that I look back, I think he was more secure when I danced. I think he knew that as long as I was dancing, I wasn't doing anything. When I was waitressing I had more time to talk with men. I think he had trouble with that.

HOLLY CARROLL: I'm usually wary of men. I don't ever leave the club with them. If I go to dinner with them, it's in the dining room of the hotel where I'm working. I never get in a car with anybody. My woman's instincts told me that it was okay this time.

I met him the first two days in this small town and he asked me if I liked venison steak and I said, "Yes." Then he asked me if I wanted to come over to his place and he would cook me a venison dinner with all the trimmings. And I said, "Well, I don't know. Where is your place?"

And he said, "Not very far."

But when we started driving away from town and he turned down a road going towards the woods, I immediately grabbed a hold of the door handle and thought, "Oh, no! This is it!"

He noticed I was nervous, so he stopped the car, put his hand on my hand, looked me in the eye and said, "Look. If you want me to take you back, I will, but I'm really not going to harm you. I really like you and wouldn't hurt you for anything. I just want to cook you dinner 'cause I thought you might like some home cooking. And you'll like my place. It's real cute."

When we got there, he was so nice that I kinda relaxed as he busily fixed the dinner, which was excellent. After dinner, he brought me back to the hotel and continued to treat me to dinners in town the rest of the week. I'm going with that fellow now and he is one of the nicest men I've ever met in my life.

He said, "Anything that's worthwhile is worth waiting for."

About my profession, he said that if I couldn't be onstage, it would be like sticking a flower in a closet and shutting the door: it would wither and die. "And I don't want you to wither and die. I want you to bloom like you do when you're onstage." I thought that any man who has that much foresight has got to be mine.

12
Family

Strippers are involved in in a common lore. They all cope with similar occupational problems; they endure the same abuse from men; and they experience the same rushes of approval; they are all linked in a common discourse.

But they compete with each other, too. Those rushes of approval, measured in applause, are presumed to be a limited resource. The younger ones have the benefit of youth—its resonance and its contours—but the older ones have the experience, the grace, and the confidence. The younger ones, entering the business on the wave of a more permissive era, can get serious approval simply by being more explicit than their elders. To the older ones, earning the precious appreciation with genital exposure and lewdness more than with theatrics is to corrupt the business as a whole. It's akin to lip-synch in the music world. It signifies the distillation of the genre down to its raw essentials: beneath skill, creativity, and learning. But the view from the high ground may have more than a little jealousy mixed with it. To the veteran stripper approaching her late twenties, the younger ones represent what is rapidly dissipating from her, slowing her down, shortening the applause, and foreshadowing the end of her career.

Most of the time the competition is friendly and only taken *really* seriously by the few. Often as not, the more experienced dancer will take the novice under her wing and pass on the benefit of her knowledge. Often the younger woman is also looking for a mother figure to confide in. Indeed, strippers' best friends are frequently other strippers. Holly Carroll has a saying: "Dancers are the most giving people on earth."

A major source of intrigue in this experience is one's interaction with the other women. So many diverse egos! So many angles! So many games! The stripper plays in a league where the rules are made up as events unfold.

CARMALITA: When you work as a stripper, everyone is really close. They all go through the same things that you do and they feel what you do and they can really understand and relate. The girls you work with become a close family and it's like you have five or six mothers. I've never really been able to get along with women too well. I've always felt very different than ordinary women. If I go into a nightclub, I immediately feel down. They're all dressed up like peacocks and really plastic and harsh. Strippers are really different people. They can really express their feelings. They can say anything they want and it's not bizarre or strange. When you talk to other women they are often horrified by some things you say just because you're being honest. But most dancers have seen a lot of life. I find them a lot closer. I like them. It's a big happy family.

TRACY TSAR: When I was dancing there was an incredible closeness among the women. It was like girls' school. Everyone was quite supportive. Everyone had gotten up onstage and felt powerful and incredibly high. Everyone had gotten up and felt like dying. There were no jealousies or backbiting; the competition just didn't seem to be there.

There was a wide variety of women working there. Students, single mothers, girls who seemed to have it all together. One girl I remember came in and from the start she worked double shifts, first dance to the last of the day, six days a week. She was saving for a trip to South America or Asia or somewhere. She came, she worked, she saved, and she left. There were space cadets, aimless women—the mélange was incredible.

TONI: The other dancers are competing with you. There's a dancer who will rip off her G-string three bars [of a song] sooner so she can have the extra little attention. The competition is getting ruder and cruder. And they're willing to work for less and less.

Have you heard of Felicity [not her real name]? I watched her show and she completely blew my mind. I thought it was disgusting. I thought she was a pig. As a person, she is fine. We've gone out together and we're friends, but I can't relate to her onstage. I have to have a clean act. But Felicity doesn't. Felicity likes that feeling of a man wanting to fuck her. That makes her feel better as a human being. You don't think of anything but sex when you watch her. Then the girls started following her because she was the popular one. She was the one who made the money and got the standing ovations.

Lots of girls in this business are incredibly insecure. They're so insecure, it blows me away. Along come the new 18-year-olds who are convinced by the agent that this is the way to go. They're so naive and so out of it and so thrilled by the business, they go for it. Now, all of a sudden, there's a new breed of 18 and 19-year-olds who have no pubic hair, who know how to do back flips and stay in that position for 20 minutes— I don't know how they do it—and it's spread from here to kingdom come. To me, it's disgusting.

LUSCIOUS LONA: I don't like watching a dancer with no class. I don't like working with them. I've had a couple of girls fired from my shift because I told the hotel owner, "It's them or me." They had a very poor presentation. I hold nothing against a girl who shows a lot of pussy, a lot of pink, but it's the way you show it. You can show any part of your body with taste and you can also show any part of your body without taste. There's girls who I've worked with who have no taste at all but show very little. But they still have no class onstage. They look like they're empty-headed no-minds who are stoned out of their faces on drugs and I abhor working with them.

CITY LIGHTS: Some girls have this thing that they want to sleep with your boyfriend. This girl I was best friends with, turned around and slept with my boyfriend. I said to her, "Why the hell did you do that?"

She said, "Well, if I didn't do it, someone else would have."

We worked together some time later. She's very competitive. She used to say things like, "Oh! The crowd was great!" And I'd go down there and wonder why they just sucked! I couldn't figure out why they hated me so much. Then I went down there while she was dancing and they were no better for her than they were for me. She said that to make me feel insecure.

She'd keep telling me I was overweight to the point of making me go down to, like, 102 pounds. Meanwhile, everybody was saying [in a whisper], "You're too skinny." And I'd say, "No. I'm heavy. Felicia [not her real name] says I'm heavy." I trusted her judgment. When she said something didn't look good on me I wouldn't wear it. Or if she told me I looked heavy, I lost weight. I really looked up to her. I believed everything she said until I found out she was doing it because [a stripper's competition] was coming up and she wanted to win it. She figured that was a good way to do it, to make me insecure, make me worry and get really nervous. It didn't work. I won the title anyway.

DEE DEE SPECIAL: Sometimes I've had costumes stolen. Sometimes the girl won't take the whole outfit, but she will take either a bra or a bikini just to ruin the whole outfit.

DELILAH: The only problem I had with another dancer was in Nashville. Usually, a club had one feature and one cofeature. They had hired a big black girl out of Detroit or somewhere as the headliner. And I came out from California as a headliner. But what happened was she had the same name I had—Delilah. Personally, at that time and at that particular place I didn't care as long as I got my money. But this girl was so jealous of me that she threatened to blow my car up with my dogs in it. Naturally I called the police and I'm lucky I got out of it alive. How

I don't know, but that was one of the few incidents where I had a problem with a girl.

GIO: Just this past year, a girl attacked me onstage. She was a table dancer. She was jealous of me. I had just finished my act and was putting my stuff in my bag and she jumped me from behind. I didn't even see her coming. She pummeled me like crazy for about 30 seconds until people realized it wasn't part of the show. They pulled her off me.

MARNIER: One time one of the dancers was borrowing this other girl's stereo and they asked me to take it downstairs 'cause I was the last girl dancing. So I said sure, why not. So I took it down there and the next day her stereo went missing. She accused me of stealing her stereo. She and her fat friend came up to my room and started threatening me. She started pushing me and I blew up at her. I picked her up, rolled her across my back, and I smacked her right across the chair—broke the chair right in half. She went at me. She went to punch me in the face and I stopped her hand and I just smoked her in the gut.

The next day she phoned me and said, "My stereo's back. I don't know if you brought it back, but thanks anyway."

PEARL IDAHO: I put a girl in the hospital a little while ago. She kicked my door in while I was on my last show and went in there and seized all my clothes and jewelry and stuff. I ran into her again at another bar. I was just going to do my show when she came in and I just fuckin' killed her. That was probably the worst I ever beat anybody up, dancers anyway.

THISTLE DOWNS: Some girls are extremely unreliable and always end up fucking you up somehow. Either by not being responsible at work or getting really drunk by their second show and putting all the pressure on the other girls. Some of the girls drink heavily during work and by the end of the night they're pissed. So you have to try to keep them in a good mood because while getting pissed they're going, "Oh, fucking *guys*..." and ranting and raving. You have to keep them in a good mood because if one's in a bad mood, it's going to go right around the circle and it's going to be a shitty night.

TERI STARR: They're like a bunch of cats backstage, just tearing each other's hair out for some reason or other. But because I am, and always was, a kind of shy, quiet person, I hardly ever talked to anybody. I stayed by myself. I never got involved with anybody else's business. And I traveled almost always alone. When I went into a new club and there was a dancer there, as far as I was concerned, I was the headliner for a week, she was there all the time. There was no need for me to step on her toes. That's her home. That's her territory. So I didn't have an awful lot of problems with that, or if I did I was so naive that they just kind of went over my head.

LAVA NORTH: I find that when I'm away from the business I don't swear as much, I'm not as cruel. There's something that happens to you when you're in that atmosphere. The more you hang around with those types of people—and I'm one of them, so I can say that—the nastier you get. That's why I work only three weeks and then take a week off after. I find that by the time I get home at night, if I'm working a night shift, I can just about tell everybody to fuck off. The swearing just comes out because that's what you've been listening to all night.

But when you don't socialize with the other girls, they turn on you. They think you think you're better than them, which is not true. You just don't have to go and be a pothead or a cokehead or a drunkard and be burnt out at 25.

DENISE BRESSETTE: Gossip. "This person makes this much and this person has fake this and fake that and did you know what so-and-so did last week and this is why she got fired…"

The question I get the most—I inherited my breasts from my grandmother (they passed right by my mother)—is, "Do you have silicon boobs?"

One day a dancer came up to me and said, "So-and-so told me that you borrowed $3,000 from her friend to buy your title [Miss Nude World 1985/86]."

I was working this one club with a girl who was a sex change. All the other girls were sitting there watching her and talking back and forth: "Did you know that she's a sex change?" Telling all the bloody customers! What kind of a person would do that? That's the girl's own secret.

I find so many of these girls are so caught up in this and that and "I'm so beautiful with my fake boobs and my fake hair," they forget what life is all about.

FLAME: I'm really into karma. What you give is what you get. Stephen King quoted this perfectly in the book, *Pet Sematary*. He said, "What you buy, you own, and what you own, belongs to you, and what belongs to you comes back to you all the time." A person plants what he wants and tends it, and it grows and he owns it, and it's his and he got to keep it. That rings true in everything you do in your life. If you do real bad dirt to somebody, then something really bad is gonna happen to you, because that's yours, that's your bad dirt, that's not that person's, that's yours. Like, I've heard a lot of people talk about me behind my back. This girl I didn't know, another dancer, stood in front of me and told me all about myself. She told me all these dreaded things about me, none of which were true. Then she asked me what my stage name was and I said, "Desire." I didn't want to say Flame and have her drop into a puddle on the floor.

LIPS LOGAN: One time I met the best looking guy I've ever seen in my life. Like, Oh wow! So nice. He wined and dined me, took me to his hotel, you know, spent a lot of money on me. I fell totally in lust with the guy.

Later, I was in town and I met this dancer and she goes, "Did you run into a guy who looks like this ... black hair, blue eyes...?"

And I go, "No. No. I don't know what you're talking about."

And she goes, "Well he ripped me off for about 800 bucks."

And I'm thinking, "Holy fuck! He spent it all on me" [laughing hysterically].

ANGEL CARTER: Quite a few things have touched me in this business, but especially Sally Rand, the late Sally Rand. She's a legend. She was a top dancer and the woman was 67 years old! When she passed away, it just tore me apart. She told me, "You've got it, girl. You just keep it up and you hang in there. You're gonna go a long way. You're gonna make it." It was nice for a lady to adore me like that. You know, just like a grandmother. What a sweet, sweet lady.

EMANUELLE: It's more fun when you have the support of the other girls, when there's no real jealous people there. If they're accepting you and admiring you and saying, "I wish I could do that. Would you teach me something?" That's great. That's flattering. It's nice. Everybody likes to hear that.

Rumors of lesbian behavior among strippers abound. A recurrent joke among bar staff who go out with strippers is said to be this: "I never have to worry about the old lady on the road because her nearest fuck is the dancer across the hall." One might easily think that in light of strippers' difficulties in securing stable relationships with men, that their path of least resistance would be toward other strippers. This, in part, was the conclusion of the sociologists, Charles McCaghy and James Skipper, Jr., who considered this question in their research in the late 1960s on strippers. In their estimation, the rigors of the job—the hours, the travel, the distrust, if not disdain, of the majority of men in the audience, and the loneliness—"promote the homosexual aspect by generating caution and skepticism where relationships with males are concerned."[1] They quote one stripper from their sample as saying, "When you are lonely enough you will try anything." While cautioning that the unavailability of reliable statistics means that there is no way of knowing whether the incidence of lesbian behavior among strippers is greater than for other groups (such as tennis players or schoolteachers) or the general population, they conclude that in the business of stripping, "an opportunity for a warm, intimate relationship unaccompanied by masculine hazards becomes increasingly attractive."

JOCELYNE: Women have a tendency—especially women, because it's not that shameful these days for women to be with women, especially around the dressing room—and they don't really mean it, when they get really upset with men, when they've been really hurt and stuff, to say: "Fuck men. I'm turning gay." It's usually in a joking or resentful way they're saying it, but every now and then you get some woman who's just gone through so much bullshit that she means it. And I got to the point where I said it and I really meant it. And my dream was to find a woman to be with, to hug me and hold me and not to lie to me and sweet talk me and all that kind of stuff.

But, see, I think because I'm not hormonally imbalanced from day one as being gay and preferring women, because I'm very healthy and have always been with men and loved men and they just hurt me and screwed me up so much that I did eventually become a little bit bisexual; and it was just something to run away from my problems and just go to women.

That was fine for six months and then reality hit when I started thinking about children. Something started feeling empty and I didn't know what it was and then I just realized it felt like I was with my girlfriend all the time and not with a boyfriend. That empty space was needing a man there.

13

Circuit Lore: Images, Oddities, Drugs, Death

The business of stripping has its own internal discourse, a lore made up of the events that stand out from the routine. It is trade talk, insider talk; each story circulates among agents, light men, and DJs, as well as strippers, fueled by the energy of intrigue. Generally, circuit lore divides between the unusual and the dangerous. (Danger survived intact is, of course, intriguing.) While the stories represent rare occurrences, collectively they place in bold relief the potentialities for gut-wrenching humor, bizarre interactions, uncommon adventures, extreme vulnerability, and sometimes death. They spark the emotions and they fascinate the mind.

As with any lore, rumors abound. And like all rumors, they tend to manufacture their own authenticity.

MAGENTA MOON: There is a rumor (and it has a thousand variations) that an old burlesque stripper was shot onstage while she was wearing yellow. I didn't know this and I wore this yellow costume for years. One day this dancer told me about it. I just looked at her. I said, "Why did you tell me that? I don't want to know that."

The next time I wore that costume I bashed my hand on a light fixture and it oozed blood all over me while I danced. I haven't worn it since.

A yellow dress splattered with blood, moving seductively under the lights—colorful images with discordant tones are the essence of the lore. Colorful discordance is, of course, the stripper's specialty. Unavailable to the crowd that craves her and incorrigible to those who loathe her, the stripper could not be harmonious if she tried. Indeed, her apparent disposition, erotic and willing, is at odds with her inner self. But these are all by-products of the form. In fact, discordant as they are, they are nevertheless routine. They are either expected or they remain unnoticed. It is when the routine unexpectedly cracks up that the lore of stripping is fed.

177

On the road, for instance, the stripper expects that her accommodations will be less than ideal. Nevertheless, every stripper has a story of a dive or a dump, a place so terrible that she will never be able to erase it from her mind, nor refrain from talking about it whenever she gets the chance. Having a dump story is the circuit stripper's pedigree.

No matter how much approval she gets in the bar, no matter how much her ego gets stroked, she has to return to that room and once again come to terms with its mold. The room tells her that she is human. The room reminds her that she is a heavenly body but not a star, more like a meteorite that dazzles for a moment before it falls to earth.

LAVA NORTH: I took my bags up the stairs—rickety old stairs—and it smelled already. The whole hallway was lined up with green garbage bags that had obviously been fermenting for days, and a little mangy cat and kitty litter that had never been changed.

Then they showed me what was supposed to be my room. I couldn't believe it. A jail cell would have been better. There was a rustic old spring bed and the mattress looked like it came from a garbage dump. There was a sink on the side of the wall all wrapped up with a garbage bag with a rope tied around it. The shower was one of those white shower stalls with this mold growing all the way down the sides and the floor was half rotted away. It was right out of a horror story.

Then they took me down to show me the stage which consisted of two pieces of plywood that were stuck together on the floor.

You wouldn't let your dog live in some of the places you are expected to stay for an entire week. One time I opened up the closet to put my costumes away and there was dog shit all over the floor of the closet—from a dancer's dog which had been there over a month before.

Most of the perceived "shit" in and out of the business is metaphorical. It represents what happens below a certain line of tolerability. Audience abuse, manipulation, and exploitation by agents and club owners, scorn from townsfolk, drug overdoses, ripoffs, trouble with the boyfriend, and obsessive and violent people: all these represent the dark side of the lore. As Sheri Champagne says, "You could be hanging out by yourself with nothing going on and then, all of a sudden, out of nowhere, shit happens." (The phone will ring, someone will come to the door, she'll get the munchies and have to go out, and another complication will begin to take shape.) For that reason, sometimes what stands out in the stripper's memory are the truly interpersonal moments, like the time someone reached through her erotic armor and touched her heart.

TRACY TSAR: There was this old Indian carver sitting up front who just loved my show and he was yelling, "Yeah!" and screaming, and I just started laughing. It got to the point where I couldn't dance. I was down on my knees and laughing and he was laughing and smiling and the whole bar was picking up on this and becoming very amused and we were all having a good time. He asked me to sit with him when I was done and I did and we had a great time together, talked for quite some time.

Then, on my last night there, I'd done my last set and was sitting with some people I met and another man came up and started complimenting me and it was sort of like, oh yeah, here we go again, but then he said, "There's one thing I want to say to you. I saw you here the other day with Tom, the Indian, and I just thought that was the nicest thing that anyone has ever done, just sat down and gave an old Indian some time for nothing." Then he looked me in the eye and said, "You mean something to this community," shook my hand and walked away.

Nice things like that would come out of nowhere and make all the shit worthwhile.

Interactions with the audience usually remain within the framework of the show, that is, true to the assigned roles of goddess and adorer. But the rustic formalism of the show allows for all kinds of glitches and anomalies to occur that tend to dissolve the roles. In an instant the stripper becomes human and the audience is transported out of its collective fantasy into something else, like raucous laughter or wide-eyed astonishment.

Sometimes one is left with the lasting memory of a vivid image. Like a black high-heel shoe spinning and glistening under the lights, reflecting a panorama of wide-eyed faces as it seeks out a suitable landing spot. Jennie related this story: "I was dancing onstage and did a really high kick. It was a beautiful kick. My shoe fell off, did a perfect spin and landed in a guy's beer mug just as he was about to put it to his lips. It was perfect. I got a standing ovation."

Most glitches in the stripper's routine are predictable. That is, problems with costume removal, slipping or tripping onstage, and the like are not extraordinary. A glitch that defies predictability is a meta-glitch, something so unusual that it has to occur first before it con be conceptualized. When meta-glitches happen, the stripper may find that she has put more of herself into the performance than she had intended—or imagined.

CASSIE: I was doing heavy-duty sets. I was killing myself, actually, but I didn't realize it at the time. I used to work up such a sweat that I'd pass out onstage from heat exhaustion.

When I did spins, sweat would fly out into the audience. I have chronic bronchitis, too, and I get lots of phlegm and stuff. I began to notice that when I did a lot of spins toward the end of my third song, snot would fly out of my nose. But usually nobody would notice.

My cold was quite bad and I was doing these spins round and around the stage and then I came closer and closer to this guy in Pervert Row and then I stopped. And when I stopped, this long string of snot, about a foot long, came out of my nose and continued to spin toward this guy. And I'm looking at him looking at me looking at the snot! His eyes were getting bigger and bigger and bigger, and this thing was coming toward him and he didn't know what to do.

And all of a sudden, it went splat on his shoulder. He looked at it and he went like this [eyes wide and mouth open]. He took it off and looked at it and showed it to his friend who was just killing himself laughing. So then he got up and went to the bar to try to get a Kleenex from the bartender, but he didn't have one, so he took it to the waitress, but she didn't have one, so finally he went into the bathroom.

GIDGET: The most memorable thing I can tell you about is this stripper who used to dance in Las Vegas named Monica Kennedy. I was working the lights at the time. She was a real classic act at the time. She always went out there bouncy, bubbly and laughing and everybody loved her. She always did the thing with the whipped cream on her nipples and down there and everything, and she had heavy buns. She sat down on top of this guy's head one time and stood back up and she had this guy's toupee stuck in her... All of a sudden, she realized what she had done so she took it and tried to put it back on the guy's head without being too obvious, and patted it back on his head—and I was dying. I was laughing so hard I almost fell out of the light booth. That was probably the funniest thing that ever happened. The audience was dying. They were just dying.

The strip joint attracts all kinds. Mostly, they all blur together into a faceless mob. But sometimes people drop in who are out of place and the possibilities for intrigue begin to soar. When middle-class couples sidle into the stripper's arena, the incongruousness of their presence creates a tension in the place that, when skillfully handled, can create an inspired release.

GIO: Saturday night, my last show was about midnight. Earlier that evening, from about six o'clock until the beer ran out, they'd had this social at a church just down the street from the bar. Everybody in town had been there. Then they all came to the bar—all husbands and wives. The room was half full of women.

Because I knew there were a lot of ladies in the audience I decided to do a really pretty show—my Oriental show. I come out with long brass finger nails from Thailand. I have Chinese robes on, my hair's up, and I've got Chinese makeup on. I've got two huge yellow fans and I do a fan dance with the fans going and the parasol going around—a very artistic and pretty show.

I got to the part where I had to take my G-string off. So I slid the G-string down my legs and this woman who was sitting close to the stage let out this gasp, like "*Ooooooouuuuh.*" You could tell the whole room was poised to see what would happen next.

I turned to her and said, "Lady, I'm a stripper. You expected to see some cunt, didn't you?"

The whole place fell out of their chairs. They just died laughing. I got this huge round of applause. They insisted on an encore and everybody wanted to buy me a drink. And the lady said I just had to come and sit next to her.

Strippers create an illusion. It is the illusion of femininity crafted from men's fantasies, the illusion of spontaneous eroticism. The audience is taken in by it. They are mesmerized. When the show is built around an S and M theme, the illusion may go beyond the realm of the sexual. Someone may want to put a stop to it. Someone else may want to join in.

BILLIE JO: Pain and Passion was an S and M show I did with Jay Jay. It's about a 37-year-old housewife whose husband's off to work and the kids are off to school. She does the whole first song, "The Ballad of Lucy Jordan" [Marianne Faithful] by herself. As the song goes on, it talks about her going into a fantasy. Her fantasy is a woman decked out in leather with whips, an image of bondage. She's all in white, like an angel, floating around the stage.

The second song, "Working Class Hero" [Marianne Faithful], is my cue. I come out all in black leather with whips and chains—quite a contrast. I chase her around the stage a bit. I grab her, pull her back by the hair and throw her across the stage and start going into the hard stuff where I show her this is what she wants. I show her I'm in charge.

When the third song comes on, "Grande Finale" [Alice Cooper], I hypnotize her and make her walk over to where the chains are hanging and I handcuff and shackle her to the chains. Then I snap my fingers and she comes out of it and sees she's all tied up. She starts to scream and tries to get away. As she does I take the whip and show the audience that it's really going to hurt. Then I go up to her and slowly show it to her and then start using it on her. Halfway through that, when it looks like I'm going to finish with her, I lay the whip down in front of her and go get two torches and light them. Now she's really freaking out. I do this fire show for the audience and then I use them on her. It looks like I'm going to set her on fire. Then I put out the fire. It's time for the love scene.

She thinks she's going to get more torture; instead I let her out of the handcuffs and I carry her across the stage and lay her down, take off the ankle shackles, take a bottle of baby oil and rub it all over her, soothing her burns and whip marks, and then we do a very sensuous love scene to Rick James' "Make Love to Me."

People would hear rumors that I was goosing her with the whip and beating her so hard she bled onstage. So this woman came down to see the show with her son. We went into our act and I started beating Jay Jay and she was screaming and trying to get away from the whip and out of the chains. (I guess we really put on a good show because we had a full house.) So this woman came right up onstage, grabbed my whip, and said if I hit her one more time she was going to kill me.

I said, "Hey, calm down, lady! It's just a show! Go sit down." So I chased her off the stage and continued with the show. I lit up the fire and the woman started screaming. She had heard about me goosing her with the whip which was during the love scene at the end, but she did not know about all this torture that the girl goes through first. She left disgusted.

But then a couple of days later she came back and she came up to Jay Jay after the show and asked her if she could look at her body. Of course, there wasn't a mark on her from the fire or the whip. She said, "That's incredible! I could have sworn that girl was killing you up there!"

She told me she had brought her son because he was into that. He had handcuffs and stuff in his room.

BILLIE JO: One time a big biker bent over the stage, lifted up his shirt, and asked me to whip him and I did. He had two brothers, nicknamed Sasquatch and Tiny, two humongous lumberjacks. He came back the next day with his brothers. His brother had on one of those flannel checked shirts and as I was doing my show, he came up and bent over, teasing me. I had Passion up in the handcuffs by this time. I was just about to whip her, but I turned around and whipped him across the back, ripping his shirt right off his back. You could see the welts come out. I was too close, so I really did hit him. And all he did was let out like a bear yell: "I like it!"

It freaked me right out. He and his brother came back every night and came up to the stage to be whipped, but I stopped because I knew they liked it so much.

If one conceives of all the ways in which one's expectations might be confounded in the strip joint, one possibility might not come to mind, possibly because it calls into question the entire nature of the illusion and one's fantasy: that the sex toy onstage isn't really a woman.

> GIO: Summertime in New York gets really gritty. You can't breathe and there's crowds and everything. So I got this gig up in the country across the street from a race track in Monticello, New York. I checked into the hotel—it was an old age home, bed and breakfast; there were people walking around with those guard rail things and people sitting on the porch in rocking chairs—and the lady at the front desk said, "The girl you're working with is across the street at the diner. Why don't you go say hello to her?"
>
> So I went over and I saw this girl sitting in the corner with a blue jean cap on and long hair. And I said, "You must be the other dancer."
>
> And she said [in a deep voice]: "Yeah. I am. There's something I gotta tell yuh before we can work together."
>
> I sat down. "Yeah. Well, I'm really nervous because I've never worked without my G-string before."
>
> And she said, "Oh, no problem. The guys are so used to it they just look at it, then turn around and keep drinking their beer. But I've got a problem. I had my balls off last year but I still got my dink. Wanna see how I tape it up?"
>
> She actually turned it inside out and tucked it up inside of her.

Obviously, the strip joint attracts voyeur types, but exhibitionists may be drawn to the medium too. Many folks may wonder what it would be like to get up in front of a crowd and strip. The idea is intriguing. Imagine the exhilaration. While, for most of us, the idea remains an idea, once in a while someone will fortify the courage with alcohol and try to steal the show.

> SHADOW FIRE: The other dancer just got offstage. This guy, a fairly good looking man, about 30, got up there and he started taking his clothes off. And the crowd began to cheer him on. Then he climbed into the shower and he showered himself. Then he came out and he dried himself off and then he put his clothes back on. Then he discovered he'd put them on inside out. So he put them on the right way. Then he went and sat down. Meanwhile, they had called the cops. He sat there for a while and then he grabbed a towel and went back up there and started drying off where he left wet spots on the floor. I was overwhelmed because he at least had the responsibility to think, "What if somebody trips on the water spot I left." The police came and took him out.

When the stripper goes out on the circuit, she never knows what will happen. Her expectations can be confounded in a variety of ways. A sort of culture shock may set in. Naked boys onstage dressed in black socks, for instance. The veteran stripper often survives on her sense of humor alone.

DELILAH: In '77, I was in Canada. I went on the French Canadian side because they paid more money but I didn't know they were lewder, or ruder, than the English side. There was a little town—Trois Rivières—I was the stripper there. Now all the night clubs were downstairs, underground, so you had all the pipes above you. And they had go-go boys there. They were totally nude with black socks on. I never forgot that. They wore black socks because they didn't want to get splinters in their feet. And they were dead serious. But I could never take it serious. I always laughed, so I had to leave the room. Any time I saw it, I had to laugh because to me, to look at a naked man is hilarious. Especially when he is trying to bounce up and down. I was sitting at the bar. Now here was this one blond little, cute curly haired guy doing some gymnastics in the nude. He grabbed one of the overhead pipes and he pulled his feet up between his arms. Now you can imagine my view. I see the A-hole with the two balls hanging down. I started to laugh. Everybody looked at me and they asked me to leave because I thought I was going to roll off the chair. It was the funniest sight I think I've seen in my life.

Stripping can be a dangerous business. Danger arrives unexpectedly. The survival technique is to use whatever is handy to ward it off. Imagine a woman, naked and screaming, running through the bar with a frying pan in her hand. What events could have led up to such a scene?

MELISSA WOLF: Luscious Lona and I were dancing in the same place. We were partying it up there together. We decided we were going to go out and just tie one on 'cause we didn't have to work 'til noon. You could party 'til three in the morning and still get enough sleep and be up and ready for work. But I wasn't feeling well. I had bronchitis and I was taking a prescription. We got in about three o'clock in the morning and I set my alarm for about four-thirty or five to take my penicillin. We were lying in bed together—we slept together because we didn't like to sleep alone, and because we could sit up and gab about each other's boyfriend. I was asleep and I just happened to wake up and see this guy hanging down from the skylight over the bed, just getting ready to let go and drop down.

It was obvious he was going to murder or rape us or something. The only way out of the room was the door. There was no window and it was impossible to go back through the skylight once he had dropped down. So I started screaming at the top of my lungs. Lona sat up and did absolutely nothing, with her mouth hanging open to the floor. The guy in the skylight told me to shut up and calm down. (Oh, right. Sure. No problem. Just come on in!)

Anyway, I was screaming to her, "Grab a frying pan! I'll grab his legs and you bang him over the head."

Finally, someone came to the door. The guy climbed back onto the roof and got away.

The next day we were in our room and out in the hallway some guy tried to screw Murray, the guy who chased the intruder away through the skylight, from behind. He banged on the door and we let him in and he said, "Some guy tried to screw me!"

So I got the frying pan and I said, "You open the door, you grab him, and I'll hit him over the head." We figured the guy must be touched, right? It might have been the same guy from the night before.

We went out to get him and he was gone. So Murray went running down one way and I went the other way. I was stark naked, running through the bar with a frying pan, screaming.

Anyway, they caught the guy and just beat the crap out of him. But it wasn't our intruder. They caught *him* jacking off on top of the skylight. They beat him up and threw him off the roof.

The stripper has an ambiguous relationship with the police. On the job they watch that she doesn't stray too far from the law onstage and off. They are often not very sympathetic to her complaints about abusive men or rapists. Off the job, of course, they may unwind in a strip club just like stock brokers, lawyers, and accountants. A stripper at a police convention, therefore, is a little like a debutante at a biker rally; she is out of place, and she is the focus of a collective and possibly uncontrollable desire.

MARLO (1): I was working in Canada when they had an RCMP conference or something in town. It was the weirdest thing to dance for 500 policemen. I became really good friends with a lot of them during the week. They were the first policemen I've seen who loved pussy so much. They got down, lying back with their heads on the stage, with $1 bills and $5 bills in their mouths. I tried to kneel down and get the money between my legs. Some of them would try to stick their tongue up while I was taking the money.

Anyway, this one asked me if I wanted to marry him. Oh, I loved this one who asked me, "Suppose I tell you I'm an RCMP; will you sleep with me?"

"Fuck off!" I said. "I don't give a damn what you are!" The funny thing about this one was he didn't drink at all.

I did a 12:15 show and a two o'clock show and I had a three-hour break after that. And he wanted to go for a swim. He said, "Boy, would I ever like to dress up like you."

So I said, "Well, I've got a bathing suit that would fit you perfectly!"

So he decided I should wear his shorts and his shirt and he would wear my bathing suit, my pink and black bathing suit. And we walked to his hotel like that in broad daylight! I thought it was hilarious. Everyone that went by looked and laughed. When we got to his hotel, this girl who he worked with and who knew his wife, quickly took our picture. When he realized she was about to take another, he hung her a moon. I never did know what happened with that, but she said she was going to blackmail him with it.

He was a good one, but he tried to go to bed with me. So I taught him a lesson I hope he never forgets. I let him try and try and try and then I said, "Did you ever stop to think I could have herpes or AIDS? You've only known me for a week; I could have any kind of disease. You'd screw me, go home to your wife and sleep with her. Your kid wouldn't have a father because you slept with someone you didn't know."

He knew I didn't have anything, but then he looked at me and said, "I can't believe you."

The next night, he asked me to do a stag for them. I said sure and I went over there. While I did my show, there were two police girls cheering me on. So I did my show and then another group came in and they wanted a show, too. So I said, "Okay. $150." Then another group came in and I did one more and said, "Forget it. That's enough!" And I got dressed.

I'm the kind of girl who, in the summertime, wears these little dresses with an open back and no panties on. I've always dressed like that in the summer time. You get fresh air...

So I had this favorite dress on and no panties and sticking out my back, you could see my ass, easily. Furthermore you could drop down, lie on the floor, and look straight up. One of the cops did that. He was lying down right in front of me, looking underneath my dress. So I closed my legs.

And they kept saying, "Don't go. Do another show."

And I said, "No."

So one of them grabbed me and tried to pull me back and my dress ripped a little bit. When he heard my dress rip, he began pulling more and guys were coming from all over the place, grabbing me. Soon, I was naked.

I said to them, "You guys are not men. You are pigs! You are animals! You are fucking assholes and jerks! You touch me again, I'm going to make your life fucking miserable! I'm going to sue every one of you, your mother and your father and everyone I can find!" I started getting really mad.

So the guy that was trying to screw me came out of a room and said, "This is fucking bullshit! What the fuck do you think you're doing?" He had to take me out the back way.

About 200 of them had a pizza fight in the dining room of the hotel, one night. This is a very elegant hotel. This place is a classy place. You couldn't tell the room from the pizza. The ceiling was covered with it, pizza, pizza sauce... On the second floor they pulled out all the fire hoses as far as they could go and left them there.

One afternoon I saw this one coming down the hall so drunk he probably couldn't remember his mother's name. His shirt was tied around his waist and his pecker was hanging out, covered with the wrapping from a bar of soap. He was bouncing from wall to wall, and singing.

The stripper is commonly linked with drug taking. Within public rumors and innuendos about strippers, the links run through child abuse, parental alcoholism, running away from home, prostitution, organized crime, and possibly jail. The worst is assumed about strippers. And every so often, a story will unfurl that will confirm our suspicions. It is, however, true that strippers enjoy their intoxicants. Most of them got onstage that first time fortified in some way against the trauma. Since there is a common bond around drug taking for many of them, drug stories abound in the stripper's lore.

JAY JAY: It was a 12 to 12 shift. I was sitting with this guy who kept buying me special coffees. I was slipping away. I didn't think anything of it. I didn't realize there were four ounces of alcohol in each one. I had about four or five of them and then, all of a sudden, I was gone. I remember Billie Jo trying to straighten me out: "You've got to do a show!"

She took me upstairs and got me dressed in this really nice Marilyn Monroe–type dress with garters and everything. She got me onstage, the music came on, and I danced. No problem. Then it got to the last song and I had all my clothes on. I forgot to take my clothes off.

And Billie Jo's going from the side [whispered emphasis]: "Take your clothes off!" I could see her making all these signs and I was waving away at her.

Finally, "Oh! My clothes!" So I got out of my dress and I got out of this and this and I was right down to my nylons and I was just going to do a roll to take my G-string off and I rolled right off the stage and landed on my bum. I put my hand up: "Taxi!" I don't think I did get my G-string off.

CRYSTAL ROSE: The funniest thing I remember is a roommate of mine, a gal who was a dancer. She had exactly my body except she was short. She had gone to the dentist and he had given her some pain pills. And she was up onstage and she was doing her pillow show. She would do these sensuous movements with a pillow in her floor show, kind of like making love to the pillow. And she was moving her butt and all of a sudden, she stopped moving. And I was standing with the club owner at the time and we were going, "What the hell is going on?" She had fallen asleep onstage [laughing]. We had to go and wake her up.

AMBER FLASHING: When I came back from Canada and I went through customs, I had a small bag of marijuana on me. They asked me what my occupation was and I told them. They said, "Well, I think we should search you."

So I threw open my coat, put my leg forward and said, "Great! Got any good music?"

They let me through.

MARY: One night there was a bunch of us working together and, for some reason, all the girls clicked. I came in one night and they said, "Mary, here! Do some mushrooms!"

I said, "Nah, nah, nah."

They said, "Come on! Here!"

I looked at them and thought, "It's now or never."

So we all did these mushrooms. And we had this overabundance of energy coming out of us. Especially dancing. I remember my girlfriend walking around—she was a black girl, a beautiful girl, just beautiful—and I'd look at her and we'd just break into scads of laughter.

I went onstage and all these boys came in and sat down. I was dancing to the Rolling Stones—I had just seen them play Seattle. I danced my little heart out. I got offstage to a standing ovation. They were banging on the tables, yelling and whistling. The owner had to cancel the last two girls because he was afraid there was going to be a riot.

LIPS LOGAN: I've got this friend who's a scientist at the power company. One day he arrived at the back of the hotel with this tank of laughing gas in the back seat of his car. So in between my shows I'd go out there and we'd have a gas [laughing]. We'd sit there ripped and laughing and having a great time and then I'd go back onstage, do my show, run back out and do it again. So my girlfriend's there with us and I was telling her how to do it. "You can't take it all in. You can't do that. You've got to take it with air—*whiff*—like that, because if you get it all in your system, you can die, right? It cuts you right off—you're dead."

So she had to be a pig, right? She sucked on the hose and she went—*pooh*—like, out. Like fucking dead!

I was going, "What are we gonna do?" I thought she was dead. I was freaking out, fucking panicking, smacking her face: "Wake up!" It was about two or three minutes before she finally came to.

Well, my friend and I decided to do it together, to see how much we could take all in one hit. That did it. Both of us—*pooh*—out. My soul left my body. I was standing looking and I could see him and me lying on the ground. No kidding! I was out of my body. I was gone! I was fuckin' somewhere else!

I was standing there, talking to myself, saying, "Where are you going? What're you doing? You gotta get back in there. You can't just lay there. You gotta move. Go back in there and move your body." I was talking to myself. Seeing myself so plain! It didn't scare me, but I felt like I had died.

I went back into my body and moved. I just told myself I had to. "You have to. Don't be stupid." And I went back in and woke up.

I was freaked out after because I remembered it. I turned to my friend and said, "Holy shit! You don't know what happened to me!" And he said the same thing had happened to him. Like, we both died!

Inevitably, a stripper will confront death. It's always there, of course, on a personal level, as a specter, a possibility. Strippers live with the fear of being the victim of a rapist or sex slayer. The stripper is a target for anger, hatred, scorn, exploitation, and abuse, and it all could lead to violence. But others may die around her. The ebb and flow of people in the bar stacks the actuarial odds in favor of an incidental death as well.

CRYSTAL ROSE: The gal who was doing the Love Act at the Garden of Eden was pregnant and she aborted onstage. She had a miscarriage. She was gushing blood everywhere. We grabbed bar towels; we called the ambulance. It was just the weirdest thing I've ever seen in my life. I'm sure all the customers were totally grossed out.

The thing about it was the ambulance got there, took her away, we cleaned the stage, and went on with the show.

BURGEONDY: A guy had a heart attack during my show. He was this old guy. He used to come in and I'd pick on him. I'd always tease him, flirt with him, and stuff. And he'd always take a deep breath and clap his hands. We'd wink at each other and blow kisses. And he'd say I was his little sweetie and tell me we were getting married next week.

He was walking by the stage and he had his hands in his pockets, and I was teasing him. I was shaking my boobs at him. And he took a deep breath and collapsed on the floor. And everybody started laughing, and I was laughing. We all thought he was joking. And then he didn't get up. He died on the way to the hospital. He didn't make it. That really freaked me for a while. I didn't dance for a while because I thought, "Kill people! God!" Shake your tits once and...

PEARL IDAHO: We went down to see this girl dance because she drank too much carrot juice in her time. She brings down her own portable shower. She fills up a Javel bottle with ice, pokes holes in it, wraps it up in pretty lace with a pretty bow, and sings, "I can't stop the rain, *oh, ohhh.*"

We sat there and right down below us was a table with these two guys and a lady. The dancer was just putting out her floor show mat and I was there in my costume and my cover-up because I was on next and I was just getting up to get some more ice and just as I got up, I heard this shot go off. It was pretty loud and the next thing I know everybody was on the floor. I ducked behind the bar stool, up against the bar, and then another shot went off. I crawled across the floor on my hands and knees. You didn't worry about the person beside you, you just went because the shots kept coming. One shot went wild and broke a whole bunch of glass that went flying all over us.

People were screaming and I thought, "This is a nightmare." I really thought it wasn't happening. I thought my hippie days had caught up with me, that I was having some kind of wild acid flashback. I figured the Lord's getting me for all the drugs I've done in my teeny-bopper years. I actually thought I was bad tripping. I looked around and saw everybody was on the floor and screaming, and then I realized, "No, this is really happening!"

I ended up under a table. The girl who was onstage ended up under the same table as me, nude of course, and there was this guy groping at her. She said to me, "Oh, hold my hand. Just embrace the air. Everything will be okay."

I hid under the table for about five minutes and it looked like everyone was filtering out. So I got up and I had to walk right by this guy with all the bullet wounds in him. I just froze. Then somebody pushed me: "Go! Get out of here! Get out of here!"

On the way upstairs I saw the guy that shot him and he was covered in blood, too. The three bouncers were on top of him and the gun was a couple of feet away. They were just beating on this guy. I went up through the staff door and tried to get the key in the door to my room. All the other girls were upstairs and we were all freaked out.

So they closed the bar down, of course: cops, ambulance, the whole bit. The first thing I said was, "Why couldn't this have happened at seven so we could take the ferry home? Now we're stuck here till morning."

I was still shaking. I mean, I've never heard a gun go off before. He only hit him four times. *Whew!* It was too much for my system.

And then the manager called us up at 11 and said, "Who's on next?"

I said, "What are you talking about? The club's closed."

He said, "No. We're reopening."

I said, "Yeah. Yeah. Right. Pull my leg."

He said, "No. The bar's open."

We ran down the fire escape into the pub and sure enough, it was open.

I went right over to where the guy was lying full of wounds and puking up blood and there wasn't a single mark. Not a single spot of blood. No signs that anything had happened.

They told us if we didn't work we wouldn't get our paycheck. They had 1,000 bucks of mine and I only had two shows left. They weren't just going to dock us two shows, they were going to keep our whole paycheck.

The manager said to me, "Do you think any of my staff wants to go back to work? I don't want to be here, either. What makes you so different?"

I said, "I'm a sitting duck. That's what makes me so different."

You know what the girl who was onstage said? "It always happens. Whenever you're having a really good show, somebody has to ruin it for you, don't they?"

Too much carrot juice.

14

Burlesque: The Exposure and the Vitality

It was a "wondrous experience in sex, an experience to anticipate, realize, remember and enjoy again."[1]

It was a "conglomeration of filthy dialog, libidinous scenes and licentious songs and dances with cheap, tawdry, garish and scant scenery and costumes."[2]

It was a "fairyland of lightness and alacrity, animation and vivacity, where the muses linger in a languor of love."[3]

"There is no element of truth in it. It has no element of goodness or of beauty, the three fundamental requisites of art in any form."[4]

"If vaudeville was once king, burlesque was the nation's raffish, rococo old queen."[5]

"Burlesque went from something to *nothing*."[6]

Deep within the social consciousness of stripping glimmers the razzle-dazzle of burlesque. A glitzy sideshow culled from the back streets of popular entertainment, burlesque was a hodgepodge of diverse elements—a kind of circus for adults—that found an uneasy common ground by virtue of their lack of sophistication or their outlandishness. In the early days the show girl, or cooch dancer—the forerunner of the stripper—played a small part in an extravaganza that included ever changing combinations of clowns, jugglers, mimes, acrobats, wrestlers, singers, magicians, freaks, strongmen, marksmen, animal tamers, ballerinas, and comics. As the format evolved, burlesque finally came to be known and remembered for three essential ingredients: the song-and-dance routines, the gags, and the all-important leg show.

It was this riotous mix of dance, humor, and sex that gave burlesque its unmistakable spirit. Crude, insolent, and naughty, bold, farcical, and painfully corny, burlesque was a caricature of refinement and ultimately of itself.

192

The gags, or bits, often pitted an authority figure (judge, policeman, politician, or business man) against a comic whose job it was to reconcile all social contradictions, such as status hierarchies, with a quick descent to the taboo.

> COMIC (Judge): Tell me, Mrs. Westfall, just where did you shoot your husband?
> MRS. WESTFALL: I shot him between the buttered toast and the cream pitcher.
> COMIC: It could have been worse.
> STRAIGHT (DA): It could?
> COMIC: Yes, if she'd shot him two inches lower...
> STRAIGHT: Yes?
> COMIC: She'd have caught him right in the percolator.[7]

Like the comic's last laugh in each bit, the wisecracks were often brash double entendres, crude plays on the genital and the scatological that required no effort to understand. A woman drops into the splits and the comic barks, "Don't stretch a good thing too far!" Or a woman walks onstage with a pair of oars and announces, "I just made the crew!" Or this routine:

> STRAIGHT: Are you getting a little on the side?
> COMIC: I didn't know they moved it.

The following is a list of stage lines banned by a burlesque circuit in 1929 in an effort to clean up the business:

> "I slept with the twins, but might as well have gone
>   home in the rain";
> "She had dimples on her hips";
> "Going to the livery stable for doughnuts";
> "Mother is home sick in bed with the doctor";
> "Didn't I meet you under the bed at the Astor?";
> "He's the father of a baby boy, but his wife doesn't
>   know it yet";
> "If I could go on the stage, I could be made";
> "That thing is sticking out again—flute player";
> "Hurry ... you're a little behind, Fanny";
> "I said relax, not Ex-Lax";
> "She calls her dog 'broker' because he does all his
>   business on the curb";
> "He's in the automobile business—last night he gave me an auto, and
>   tonight he's going to give me the business."[8]

This corner of burlesque humor appealed to the boy in the man, the latent scallywag, the part of him that never grew up, who, in spite of social grooming to the contrary, remains inwardly fascinated with genitals and feces. At the least, he is well aware of their potential for creating mayhem. Burlesque humor was precocious in its ability to turn the trappings of culture, status, authority, and decorum into dirty little jokes. It stripped away the mask of civilization to expose its vulnerable underbelly: the repressed regions of the genital and the anal, and the inescapable proximity—indeed the overlap—of pleasure and dirt.[9] Whether or not one laughed might have depended on one's personal stake in both the repression and the separation of these two realms.

Besides the song-and-dance routines, burlesque at the turn of the century retained at least one novelty act such as a juggler, magician, or strongman, but the main attraction was fast becoming the cooch dancer. Cooch is a derivative of hootchy-kootchy, the accepted euphemism of the times for the dance of female hips mimicking sexual intercourse. Hootchy-kootchy would eventually give way to bump and grind. The cooch dancer appealed to a wholly different entity than did the comic, as is evident from this 1915 review of Millie De Leon:

> Slowly, and in a manner hardly noticeable even through the transparent net which constituted the middle portion of her gown, the muscles of her body took on a wave-like motion. The undulations increased in rapidity. A purely muscular side to side movement, generally deemed the peculiar gift of horses, complicated the pattern and introduced a chaotic activity that probably lasted five minutes.
>
> Finally, Millie De Leon became unspeakably frank. From knee to neck she was convulsive. Every muscle became eloquent of primitive emotion. Amid groans, cat calls and howls of approval from the audience, she stopped. Standing suddenly erect, with a deft movement she revealed her nude right leg from knee almost to waist.
>
> A strut to the right, a long stride back, and the abdominal "dance" was resumed. The large pink rose in her belt nodded confusedly, and her hands clasped and unclasped spasmodically under the strain of the stimulated emotion. Streaked and sweaty, her face took on the aspect of epilepsy. She bit her lips, rolled her eyes, pulled fiercely at great handfuls of her black, curly hair.
>
> Indescribable noises and loud suggestions mingled in the hot breath of the audience. Men in the orchestra rose with shouts. A woman—one of six present—hissed. Laughter became uproarious. And then, sensing her climax, Millie De Leon gave a little cry that was more a yelp, and ceased.

Moving towards a box where two women were sitting with their backs to the audience, she once more showed the white expanse of her limb, put her hand to her throat as if further to display her person, but instead snatched a gaudy flower basket from the hand of an attendant and began to throw tiny blue garters into the pit.

Then the glowing gaze of a youth in a left proscenium box caught her attention. In both hands she seized his blushing face and kissed him on the lips. In three bounds she was at the box immediately opposite, and burying her fingers in the black hair of an older man, kissed him audibly. Those women who showed only their back were in that box. They blushed. The audience howled.

"Here, Sailor, come here!" The sailor came forthwith down the aisle between laughing hundreds and up the stage to the dancer's side. He, too, was kissed.

"Here, you! Come on up! No, you with the bushy hair!" This to a youth of obvious refinement, patently out of his element, about halfway back in the left section of the parquet. He squirmed and dodged. She pursued unmercifully.

"I mean you in the end seat of the twelfth row," she insisted.

"Aw, go on!" supported the audience.

The boy might have been nailed to his seat.

The air with which De Leon turned away was meant to be imperial.

As the woman's watery eye ran over the audience, many a man took refuge behind the seat in front. Some ignorant boys, desirous but fearful, nervously twisted their paper programs into shreds. Others, of a totally different type, hopefully made themselves conspicuous.

It was one of the latter class, a light-haired strapping fellow, who went to the stage next. He received kisses and more—the rose which adorned the dancer's belt was tucked beneath his own waist-band.

For her final dalliance, the woman turned to a youth whom she had evidently marked from the beginning. He was tall and slight, not more than eighteen years, and had been watching her with the eyes of a child from a box at the right.

He answered her call reluctantly, stumbled to the stage in confusion, and was completely taken aback when she seized his hair, kissed him, held him off for a moment and then applied her lips fervidly to his forehead.

With a taunting laugh she thrust him from her and called to the lantern man in the gallery: "Put the light on him!" Her laugh issued again from the wings and was echoed to the audience as the spotlight revealed on the troubled brow of the youth the scarlet impression of her lips. Ten minutes later the boy left the theater still troubled and still ignorant of the scarlet stains that seared his forehead.

As the chorus danced out for the final ensemble, the audience uproariously left the theater.[10]

The reviewer captures the heat and the commotion, the vibrations that jar ordinary reality into hypnotic spectacle. "Undulations," chaos, "primitive emotion," spasm, "climax"—there is no double entendre here—the words bring to life a powerful force before which a few of the daring or the delirious may choose to stand, but ultimately all men must resign themselves to the role of spectator. She is out of reach in both space and time; she has turned her admirers into a pack of blushing, squirming, ballyhooing neurotics, apparently without removing a stitch!

Obviously, Millie De Leon transcended the collective notion of femininity held by the audience. This was not your average woman on the street. This was the stuff of men's dreams: a woman refined of her nonsexual nature, a woman in whom the personality has succumbed to primal rhythms; but, nonetheless, a woman who wielded the power of arbitrarily seducing or humiliating her admirers: a sex goddess, a holy prostitute, a siren.

The cooch dancer was not funny. She was serious. She only became funny when she made a fool out of somebody. In that moment, she provided a release for the rest of the audience who were then able to project their inner conflict between desire and social control onto the boy in the spotlight and turn it to laughter. (One suspects that the reviewer projected his own inner trouble onto the lipstick-stained youth. Had he written *simulated* instead of stimulated emotion, the whole tone of the article would have shifted and he would have avoided adding to the sort of mythologizing that led another writer of the time to muse that Millie De Leon's large black eyes were "suggestive of the Odalisque of the East."[11])

If the essence of burlesque resided in its diversity of ingredients, its verve arose out of its rivalry of effects. Clearly, the fault line in burlesque ran between its eroticism and everything else about it. How did eros find a foothold among the variety acts? What common themes did they share?

The history of burlesque is the story of how the nude goddess image came alive and began to dance. Although she also found her way into Broadway revues such as the Ziegfeld Follies, it was in burlesque that she developed into a dance medium and subsequently rose to her most rankling notoriety.

Conceptually, the stripper is the physical manifestation of an idea resident in the minds of men. She is an image of femininity in which natural sentience and vitality have been replaced with a monolithic eroticism serving male fantasy. The power of the image lies in its resolution of men's deep-seated ambivalence about women, an ambivalence that appears to be primeval. The stripper rightfully takes her place in an age-old lineage.

From prehistorical talismans, through the statues of Ancient Greece, the sanitized icons of the Christian Middle Ages, and the Venuses in the age of oil painting to *tableaux vivants*, the nude goddess evolved through a succession of artistic vehicles appropriate to the spirit of the times. It has been suggested here that, in retrospect, it appears as though the goddess has pursued the path that will lead her back to her lost vitality. But the price has been the gradual erosion of her art and a simultaneous fall from grace. As soon as the image comes alive, it becomes invisible. The woman playing the role of the live nude goddess is assumed to have the properties of the image: infinitely gratifying and monolithically sexual. Many assume that if she is not ever available, she is at least available to many. From the perspective of community standards or family values, she has placed herself beyond the pale and threatens to infect us from within. From the viewer's perspective, the living, breathing woman holds within her the potential to shatter—at any moment—the properties of the goddess she plays and that drive his fantasy of her. From both the spectator's view and from that of culture, the living goddess is also very much a demon.

The story really begins after the close of the medieval period. In Western history the Renaissance is the designated watershed that loosened the political power of the Christian church and allowed eros a renewed, although circumspect, presence in art. Perhaps there is no greater icon of this age than Botticelli's painting *Birth of Venus* in which the goddess, nude and unsure of herself, is blown to shore by the winds of change after an eternity of exile. The painting signaled a major breakthrough in one aspect of the medieval public policy on eros, that of the inherent sinfulness of the naked body. Once the body as image had shed its ecclesiastical garments, the body's sensuality—the more grievous sin—was able to emerge by degrees in successive generations of renderings.

Body exposure and sensuality represent the outer and the inner codes of eroticism. To achieve the ideal of a vital and fully exposed image within a culture infused with vestiges of the medieval Christian fear of both the body and its passions, the goddess had to proceed cautiously. Too much exposure or too much sensuality and she risked being run out of town. This was especially true of the first experiments in live images that appeared in America in the early nineteenth century. Vitality had to be downplayed to further exposure and the more animated images could only go so far in displaying their bodies. Thus, the origins of the cooch dancer may be traced to the static nudity of the *tableau vivant* and the suggestive élan of the ballerina.

The appropriately named "living pictures," or *tableaux vivants*, represent the transition of the nude goddess from representative art to the stage. Imported from Europe, with a probable French origin, they made their American debut in New York during the 1830s. *Tableaux* presented simulations of various great works of art using live actors posed perfectly still with the appropriate props, drapery, and lighting effects, sometimes enclosed within a large picture frame. The first *tableaux* did not have an erotic intent, but once the motif had been established, imitations of classical nudes such as the three graces were inevitable. The illusion of nudity was effected by flesh-colored tights or body stockings that, while exposing to the public no areas of skin it was unaccustomed to, did, however, accentuate the body's outlines in novel ways. In an era when women wore an abundance of clothes that compressed their breasts and completely concealed their legs, when the sight of a mere ankle was an event, the presentation of women dressed in tights to the paying public was both sensational and scandalous. At the height of their popularity at the close of the century, one reviewer gulped that the revelations in some of the *tableaux* "were extreme enough to make an inexperienced, and perhaps more than ordinarily unsophisticated observer catch his breath for an instant in sheer amazement. Certainly frankness could go no further than did that of the 'Nymph of the Wave,' for there is no further to go."[12]

During their decline as main events, *tableaux vivants* were picked up by burlesque shows, where they were featured attractions until the 1930s, and, in keeping with the form, their elaboration gave way to their eroticism. By the time of their ultimate demise they had been distilled down to their one essential ingredient: a nude female posed against a dark background.

One might deduce that the dancing nude could have easily evolved directly from the *tableau vivant*. But to animate the Venuses in *tableaux* would have been too risky. Not only would an apparent nude in motion have had too much erotic content for nineteenth-century sensibilities (indeed, *tableaux* had sometimes been closed down for simply standing still), but she would have immediately dissolved the thin artistic veneer that had sustained the genre for the better part of a century. The predecessor to the stripper would have to emerge from a medium already in motion.

The ballet was introduced to New York audiences in 1827 by a French dancer named Francisque Hutin. Wearing nothing more revealing than "loose trousers gathered at the ankle and covered by a long silk skirt,[13] her pirouettes, which made her skirt fly up and her trousers hug her body, were said to have caused all the women sitting near the stage to leave the theater. After Hutin came Madame Celeste, Marie Taglione, and Fanny Elssler, among others, but by this time ballet had become coopted by high art. In Robert Allen's analysis, "Ballet became morally and socially acceptable (although, at first, only marginally so) by containing the ballerina within a silent, removed world; within plots that alluded to the settings of high-art literature and painting; and within a body that promoted rather than detracted from the illusion that the audience was watching a creature with the same materiality as a fairy."[14]

Ballet's costume, which exposed female ankles and, intermittently, thighs (in tights), acquired the acceptability of convention. Its relative exposure was seen to be necessary to the art but, as the following appraisal of the medium attests, it could go no further in either divestment or emotiveness without forfeiting its status as a high art. The quote originally appeared in a critique of the English ballet and was brought to bear on the American scene by Olive Logan, actress turned writer and tireless critic of the baser elements of the theater in the nineteenth century:

> The scanty drapery of the ballet, for the purposes of art, and art alone, is no offense against good taste or good manners; but if the ballet girl—not for the sake of art, but for the sake of attracting lewd attention—over-does the scantiness, and betrays the immodesty of her mind by her motions or gestures, she commits an offense, and ought to be hissed from the stage which she disgraces.[15]

While the *tableau vivant* and the ballet proved to be dead ends for the live nude goddess, female nudity and erotic vitality had become established, if precarious, theatrical motifs. The stage was set for a vehicle that would provide the fertile ground for the motifs to come together and flourish, safeguarded by a convenient alibi. That burlesque provided such a vehicle is a consequence of its eclecticism and its roots in travesty.

Long before it became synonymous with the leg show, burlesque was a popular literary and theatrical form that had no characteristic eroticism. The essence of legitimate or classical burlesque was to make fun of something by replacing its character with the incongruous. Lowly subjects acquired the mannerisms of the dignified and lofty subjects the habits of the uncultivated. The relation of the first device to the second is that of parody to travesty. Many chroniclers of American burlesque trace its roots to the plays of Aristophanes. Morton Minsky, for example, relates how his infamous older brothers (before Morton was old enough to become an active partner) borrowed heavily from the Ancient Greek dramatist in their frantic search for new material. Though not the most eminent of the literary arts, the list of its practitioners testifies to its comic finesse. After Aristophanes came Chaucer, Samuel Butler, Alexander Pope, Jonathan Swift, and W. S. Gilbert (of Gilbert and Sullivan) to name a few. And so it is of the utmost irony that classical burlesque evolved into a leg show, eventually to reinvent itself as a showcase for the female genitalia. Burlesque became a burlesque of itself.

And yet, the ascendence of eros within the spirit of burlesque might have been predictable. A genre whose métier was the unmasking of convention, propriety, and refinement with ridicule sooner or later had to lift the cultural lid on the libido (not to mention the processes of elimination). But by so doing, it fell. As the erotic component of the show increased, its artistic pretension shrank in proportion. The transition of legitimate burlesque to its eroticized derivative represented a shift away from a thing of the mind toward one of the body. It moved beyond the pale of moral standards and found itself situated more firmly in the camp of the lower-class audience. Since its audience *was* the lowbrow, it made sense that the gags were not at their expense but were rather aimed upward, at the masters, the high flown, the stuffed shirts. Thus, by the turn of the century, burlesque humor was essentially travesty. It was based on the unmasking of the refined by showing it and them to be ultimately corruptible by sex. In sex, moral authority collapses, pomposity cracks up, elegance dissolves, and the highly structured regresses to one simple compulsive rhythm. At any rate, if the predecessor of the stripper were to spring up somewhere, it could not have been in a more appropriate place than burlesque, which, previous to its reincarnation as the leg show, had been known for centuries as the art of the take off.

The origins of the American burlesque show are to be found in the amalgamation of travesty with the elaborate costumes, scenery, and stage effects of extravaganza, or musical spectacle. In his scholarly appraisal of the subject, Robert Allen names the 1860 stage production, *Seven Sisters*, as the point of departure for the new form. While it had been common for women to play some of the male parts in the travesties (in keeping with the spirit of reversal), *Seven Sisters*'s "major innovation was having nearly all parts—male and female—played by women."[16] A review of the show commented on the players' "tight-fitting clothes," their "shockingly low-necked dresses," and their "seducing and fascinating legs." Calling it "a tantalising piece," complete with "descending goddesses on aerial cars," the reviewer also made mention of its demonic properties: "The girls that figure in it do their prettiest to aid in the painful delusion and snare."[17] The unprecedented success of the show provided the inspiration for many imitations, which had the effect of raising "the moral and social concerns about burlesque for the first time."[18]

Seven Sisters was the first of five major milestones in the development of the American burlesque show. The second was Adah Isaac Menken's ride across the stage in pink tights and a short tunic strapped back to back with a live horse in the 1861 caricature performance of Byron's poem, "Mazeppa." Published in 1819, the poem was an idealized re-creation of the legend of a Cossack (Mazeppa), whose punishment for a sexual adventure with a count's wife was to be tied naked to a spirited horse and sent galloping into the wilds. The one scene, which became an enduring image in burlesque iconography, has been described as "a blur of equine movement played against a moving landscape drop and lighted by bursts of stage lightning. The clatter of the horse's hoofs on the narrow ramp was all but smothered by the orchestra's deafening accompaniment and sound effects suggesting a violent rainstorm."[19] It is said that Menken made an innovation on the style of tights worn by Madame Celeste by tailoring hers "nearer to the modern close-fitting body-stocking ... [and] assisted by sound, movement and light, [she] seemed, to the eager imagination of the audience, to be actually naked beneath her short, flimsy tunic."[20] *Mazeppa* played in New York for eight months and went on to draw large audiences in California and Nevada. In San Francisco Menken went a step further and abandoned tights altogether. Wearing only a blouse and a modest pair of shorts, she may have been the first woman in American theater to bare her legs. The poet Charles Warren Stoddard, obviously moved by a Menken performance, rhapsodized her as "a vision of celestial harmony made manifest in the flesh—a living and breathing poem that set the heart to music and throbbed rhythmically to a passion that was as splendid as it was pure."[21]

The third milestone in American burlesque was the 1866 stage production, *The Black Crook*. Originally conceived as a musical melodrama, it was rewritten to accommodate a company of over 60 tights-clad women assembled from London, Paris, Berlin, and Milan. They created such a sensation that the show ran for 16 months and took in over $1 million in receipts, a first in American show business. It was an unusually long spectacle, lasting over five hours with no intermission, linked together with a weak and often divergent script. Critics referred to its tedium and its incomprehensibility, but they also praised its scenery, lavish costumes, special effects, select performances in song, dance, acrobatics, and travesty and, inevitably, its "symmetrical legs and alabaster bosoms." Of the most popular piece in the play, the Pas de Demons (Demon Dance), a reviewer commented, "It used to be said that Menken's undress uniform 'took the rag off'; but these demons ... have scarcely a rag left upon them to take off."[22]

Not surprisingly, the play was denounced from many a pulpit, but the following account reveals that even moralists were susceptible to the performers' charms. Ostensibly firing a broadside at *The Black Crook*, a certain minister seemed to get caught up in his own description of the women's "beautiful countenances, regular busts, trunks and limbs chiseled out from head to foot by Nature's own hand with an exquisiteness of perfection far surpassing any that the finest art of man has ever wrought in Parian marble, with charms more bewitching and attitudes of softness and luxury most fascinating... Poor, dear, darling, charming, enchanting creatures; who could help loving them?"[23]

The *Black Crook* has often been referred to as the pioneer of the American burlesque show. Irving Zeidman, for instance, dubbed it "the acknowledged forerunner of modern burlesque because here, for the first time in the history of the American stage, female nudity was exhibited not as an integral part of the plot, but frankly and with bravado for its own crass and pleasant appeal."[24]

If the show signified a quantum leap in nudity on the stage, the corresponding leap in erotic vitality ensued two years later in the play *Ixion; or, The Man at the Wheel.* The first of many productions of Lydia Thompson and the British Blondes, who arrived in New York from London in 1868, the play was a travesty of the Greek myth of the Thessalian king whose punishment for having shown too much interest in Hera, the wife of Zeus, was to be bound spread-eagled to a fiery wheel and rolled eternally through the sky.

While the Blondes received rave notices for their legs, they were not often praised for their looks. One critic even went so far as to say, "If you would seek for corresponding features of beauty in their faces the disappointment is great. A more disastrous set of *ballet* girls, according to their facial index, it has not entered the hearts of men to conceive. In vain do we look for those touches of loveliness which make men fall down and worship the sex; scan them with a lenient eye, the result is the same."[25] The one exception was Venus, played by Pauline Markham, lovingly styled as "she who has found the long lost arms of the 'Venus of Milo,' and whose speech is vocal velvet."[26]

The appeal of the Blondes—and their controversy—derived more from their innovative rendering of the grand spectacle. *Ixion*, whose entire cast except one was female, represented a quantum leap in the participation of women in American theater. It was probably also the first play in which all the women—not just the chorus line—wore tights. Furthermore, perhaps more significantly, Thompsonian burlesque outstripped the artistic overlay on the female stage presence and brought her to bear more forcefully on the viewer. Having secured a place within the vehicle, the goddess commandeered the device already established in burlesque by male performers: intimacy with the audience. "Instead of whirling about in a removed realm oblivious of the audience's presence—as did the dancers in *The Black Crook*—the burlesque performer addressed the audience directly, aware, as one of Thompson's characters put it, of her own 'awarishness.'"[27] Thompsonian burlesque broke through the decorum of the ballet and gave sanction to erotic vitality in the dance. A critic of the time, obviously shocked by a burlesque show in the style of the Blondes he had witnessed in Boston, underscored the dancers' "abandon," their "infuriate grace," and their "fierce delight." The lead dancer, he wrote, "triumphed and wantoned through the scenes with a fierce excess of animal vigor. She was all stocking...; she had a raucous voice, an insolent twist of the mouth, and a terrible trick of defying her enemies by standing erect, chin up, hand on hip, and right foot advanced, patting the floor. It was impossible, even in the orchestra seats, to look at her in this attitude and not shrink before her." Later in the show a succession of women, apparently attempting to outdo each other, danced "to wantoner excesses, to wilder insolences of hose, to fiercer bravadoes of corsage... The frenzy grew with every moment... The spectator found now himself and now the scene incredible, and indeed they were hardly conceivable in relation to each other. A melancholy sense of the absurdity, of the incongruity, of the whole absorbed at last even a sense of the indecency."[28]

Thompsonian burlesque represents the point at which the image of the goddess fused with the person playing her. The dancers were no longer seen to be playing roles but expressing themselves. They were not mimicking erotic vitality, they were living it. "The nude woman of to-day represents nothing but herself," wrote Olive Logan. "She runs upon the stage giggling; trots down to the foot-lights, winks at the audience, rattles off from her tongue some stupid attempts at wit ... and is always peculiarly and emphatically herself,—the woman, that is, whose name is on the bills in large letters and who considers herself an object of admiration to the spectators."[29] To those with a stake in the repression of sexual passion, the apparent public exaltation of its release signaled an imminent chain reaction. Woman's sexual energy, the original sin, liberated from rational controls, would likely spread like the plague. Logan called burlesque dancers after the Blondes "a sort of fungus upon the stage." The *New York Times* used the word "epidemic." The dancers' foreignness, which enhanced their exotic appeal in the theater, only served to fortify the metaphor of contagion at large.

Once eroticized dancing had become an established motif in burlesque, more earthy forms became possible. The French cancan became a staple of the shows for a while, but its synchronized leg raises, kicks, and splits (in black stockings and white bloomers) were more in the spirit of choreographed fanfare than spontaneous primitive eroticism. What was required now was a form that appeared to come from below.

In 1893 at the World's Columbian Exposition in Chicago, the belly dance was presented to the American audience for the first time. A featured attraction in the Middle Eastern pavilions on the midway, the *danse du ventre*, as it was known, was performed by women wearing gaudy harem costumes, sometimes with exposed midriffs. An account of a performance witnessed in the Algerian theater describes its visceral vitality:

> The theme of the girl's dance is love, but it is the coarse animal passion of the East, not the chaste sentiment of Christian lands. Every motion of her body is in the illustration of her animalism, the languorous looks, the open lips, the waving hands, the swaying body, all are brutish; and as the shrill music passes into a noisy crescendo, the girl with undulating hips, protruding stomach, and wriggling frame, points towards the open mouthed Congo drummer, who shows his white teeth and red tongue and yells in chorus with the shrieking artists on the stage. Now the flushed face of the girl glows with passionate ardor, and she stamps her foot as she moves back and forth waving her beckoning hands. Then, in a perfect paroxysm of undulations, in which hips, stomach and torso are protruded and whirled, the girl rises on her toes and crouches in a series of wriggles towards the stage, like one in an epilepsy.[30]

Among the many belly dancers at the fair, only the name Little Egypt is remembered today. Speculations abound as to her true identity and some question whether she existed at all, but her name has nevertheless risen to mythic proportions. According to Bernard Sobel, the erstwhile press agent of Florenz Ziegfeld and a chronicler of burlesque given to some hyperbole, she so packed them in that she single-handedly saved the fair from ruin. Little Egypt would be remembered, however, not for saving the fair but for planting a crucial milestone in the development of the American burlesque show. Primitive erotic vitality in a solo dance performance without any pretension to high art was now an established motif. From the cooch of Millie De Leon to the vibrant hustle of Carrie finnell, all the headliners of the next century would owe their hurly-burly to the *danse du ventre*. As Robert Allen observes:

> The inclusion of the cooch dance as a standard feature of burlesque after the 1890s centered the form once and for all around undisguised sexual exhibitionism. The cooch dance linked the sexual display of the female performer and the scopic desire of the male patron in a more direct and intimate fashion than any previous feature of burlesque. Here,

all pretense that the performance was about anything other than sexual pleasure was dispensed with. The spectator's desire was not diffused among a company of performers or mediated by drama but focused exclusively on the body of a single woman. She, in turn, played only to him; her movements served no function other than to arouse and please him. Her dance was a pas de deux involving her body and his gaze. She was an exhibition of direct, wordless, female eroticism and exoticism.[31]

From this point on, it was simply a matter of refining the form. The belly dance became the hootchy kootchy, the hootch, the cooch, the shimmy, and the shake, and it was not long before the gyrations of the torso approached the resonance frequency in the costume and it began to unfasten: the striptease was born.[32]

Who actually performed the first striptease is a matter of much contention. The problem is mostly one of definition. Does removing one's clothes while standing qualify? Does removing them from behind form some sort of screen? How bare does the artist have to get? It is the lack of agreement on fundamental questions such as these that makes a definitive answer problematic. In the meantime, both the Americans and the French have made claims for the honor. On this side of the Atlantic, many believe the honor belongs to Hinda Wassau, whose costume inadvertently vibrated from her body during her frenzied hip shake in 1928 Chicago.

But there are other contenders. Herbert Minsky told the following story about Mae Dix, "a red haired beauty with a gorgeous figure and a great way of putting over a comedy song":

It was toward the end of that season [1917] that Mae had her lucky accident. On a stifling hot night she was working in a black short-skirt dress with a detachable white collar and cuffs. They were detachable so that they could be laundered daily, but Mae liked to save a little money and make them do for two days. As she went off at the end of her number, she pulled off the collar, trying to save it as much as she could. The audience saw her do it, and some gagster started applauding for an encore. Mae came back without the collar, raising a storm of applause, bowed, and pulled off the cuffs as she left the stage for what she thought was the last time.

But they wouldn't let her go. They clapped like crazy, this being a time when a woman on the stage was allowed to show no flesh at all. Between the heat and the applause, Mae lost her head, went back for a short chorus, and unbuttoned her bodice as she left the stage again.

Nick Elliot, our house manager, ran backstage to bawl out Mae and fine her ten dollars, since showing more than the script called for was a punishable offense. Then he ordered the house lights up, to quiet the audience, which was going crazy, and went out on the stage to bawl out the customers. The Minsky brothers, Nick told them, ran a decent theater. There was going to be no more of that, and if they didn't like it, they were free to leave.

Nick was one of our most loyal employees, but it took a lot of guts to try and calm down that audience. Once Mae's accident had happened and the effect of what was one of the first stripteases had been discovered, nothing could have held the audience back. Anyway, we didn't try. What, were we crazy?[33]

Herbert's brother Morton hints that it might have been a dancer named Mae Brown, billed as the Dresden Doll, but he doesn't elaborate.[34]

Irving Zeidman suggests that the first one to bare her lower torso by pulling her tights down just before she left the stage was Anna Smith, circa 1934.[35]

Anna Held, the first wife of Florenz Ziegfeld, is said to have changed in and out of costumes onstage behind the chorus line in a 1906 performance of *The Parisian Model* in New York.

A cooch dancer named Omeena is reported to have stripped off "almost all her clothing" in a midway tent at the 1896 St. Louis Fair.[36]

Meanwhile, a biographer of Adah Isaacs Menken maintains that her removal of her cloak ("partially shielded by actors") before her historic ride across the stage in 1861 was "the first public striptease act ever witnessed in a theater."[37] And so it goes.

On the French side, *Newsweek*, in an article on the Bobino Music Hall in Paris, states in passing that the first stripper was Blanche Cavelli, at the Bobino (apparently), sometime after the turn of the century.[38] But if this was the first striptease in the French theater, an earlier incident may have provided the inspiration. If the aftershocks of this event had been more subdued, the time and place might not have been recorded for posterity—midnight, February 9, 1893, at the Moulin Rouge. The occasion was the annual Four Arts Ball, a student-run affair, attended by artists' models, and noted for its mayhem. As the alcohol began to work its effect on the crowd, one of the models, feeling her oats, boasted at large that she had the nicest legs in town. Not about to be outdone, women began lining up to lift their skirts for the loudest applause (in what a reporter of the time could not have failed to pen "The Judgment of Paris").

As Paul Derval, owner-manager of the Folies-Bergère from 1923 until his death in 1966, tells the story in his memoirs, "The War of Legs became the War of Shoulders, then Thighs, and finally Bosoms... Suddenly, one of the models, justly proud of her generous charms, sprang to a table to claim victory. I'm sure there was no harm in Mona, as she was called, but this much is certain: she was as naked as Venus rising from the waves, as unadorned as Eve before she ate the apple!"[39]

When the authorities got wind of what had happened, they took immediate action. Mona was arrested along with a handful of others and fined 100 francs. In reply, the students rioted. They demonstrated for two days, often clashing violently with the police. Finally, when they surrounded the gendarmerie of the Latin Quarter, troops were called in and the revolt was finally quashed. All of this made good theater and the impresarios were quick to bring the motif to the stage. The next spring, a theatrical bit called "Yvette Goes to Bed" appeared:

> The stratagem was a simple one. Since it was out of the question to exhibit an entirely naked woman, and since an almost naked woman is never quite naked enough, evidently the thing to do was to rely on the spectator's lubricous imagination by presenting him with the spectacle of an actress undressing for bed by easy stages. Imagination being always one jump ahead of reality, the spectator would see her as already naked when she had not yet removed her last drapes. The strip tease was born.[40]

While some are reputed to have dared the first strip, other claims have been made for the originator of the tease. As the burlesquer Ann Corio said, "Anyone can strip, but few can tease." Corio names Carrie Finnell as the mother of the tease. Certainly, Finnell must hold the record for the most protracted tease of all time: she is said to have taken a full year to strip by either removing or shortening one piece of her costume each week. Finnell is also reputed to have invented the tassle twirl—tassles attached to each breast and rotated in opposite directions—which a performer of a later period turned into a memorable scene in the movie *The Graduate*.

While the quest for the first stripper makes for endless speculation into the hazy past, the striptease did not become a regular feature of American burlesque until well after the first World War. By this time, the nude goddess was represented in three motifs, the exposure of each being inversely proportional to its respective vitality. The chorus line, wearing lower garments approximating G-strings and sometimes bras, sometimes nothing at all above the waist, paraded down the runway, which had become an institution in burlesque houses, and worked themselves into a mass cooch dance. Following the cooch dance, the stripper, the star attraction, performed what was then known as the "teaser routine." This amounted to a litany between her and the audience where she would remove her costume piece by piece in response to applause. She would begin with a suggestive song, exit behind the curtain, wait for the roar from the audience to reach an appropriate level, return to the stage to remove one article of clothing, and exit again. This might be repeated five or six times until she was down to her last article of clothing, a G-string or skimpy skirt, which she would toss onto the stage after her final exit. Some strippers, such as Gypsy Rose Lee, took the concept a step further and, before their final exit, stood before the audience in full frontal exposure except for a piece of their removed costume held against their bodies. In the third motif the curtain was drawn to reveal a nude member of the chorus frozen in *tableau* fashion in the shadows, with one leg slightly turned and lifted or an arm strategically placed to conceal her lower abdomen.

Here we have all the components of the modern strip show but fragmented in respect of the law. Maximum exposure is still the province of the static and remote tableau. Maximum erotic vitality is still contained within a musical art form (such as it is) but has progressed to include bared breasts. Minimized distance (intimacy with the audience) combined with provocative disrobing is tempered with minimal vitality (to say nothing of the singing). Onstage, the stripteaser might not reveal any more of herself than the chorus coochers, but behind the curtain and in the minds of the audience she delivers the anticipation of her ultimate exposure.

While the nude in her various guises was elemental to the show, at the turn of the century it was the comic who was at the forefront of burlesque. The comic represented a man unbound by social conditioning, immune to social decorum, and irreverent of class distinctions. He was the incorrigible spoiler, ever reminding us of the undergarments of culture and etiquette and the absurdity of self-importance. In Ralph Allen's words, the comic represented "man stripped of his inhibitions, stripped of restraints of all kinds—free of moral pretense, innocent of education and, above all, lazy and selfish. He frequently appear[ed] to be a victim, but never a pathetic one, because in nine bits out of ten he blunder[ed] at the end into some kind of dubious success."[41]

A popular theme in the burlesque bits played on the unavailability of the goddess. Devices that made the monolithically sexual woman suddenly available to the comic were common fare: "Waving a 'whoozis' before a girl's face [played by the cooch dancer or the chorus girl] will cause her to stop in her perambulations and moan, 'Oh, daddy, give it to me.' Reading a magical line in a book will produce a beautiful woman out of the air. Another line will make her agree to 'take a walk in the woods.'"[42] But the shows also had a vested interest in underscoring men's antagonism toward women: "Women are 'bums' and 'tramps.' They are shoved about the stage. They are depicted as brazen, as 'gold-diggers,' as 'vampires.'"[43] The bits served to raise the profile of the goddess as a fantasy and simultaneously place in relief men's underlying fear of women.

The inner dynamic of the relationship between the erotic and comedic elements of the burlesque show rested on an outer dynamic of competition from other forms of variety and conflict with the law. Revue and vaudeville, for instance, were more socially acceptable, attracted more accomplished performers, and presented more sophisticated shows. In addition, the novelty of film was fast becoming a threat to the theater in general. Although burlesque had the monopoly on its signature inanity and irreverence, audiences looking for entertainment value could usually find it elsewhere. Revue, in particular, was also experimenting with its own brand of female nudity.

Competition also came from women's fashion. As the modern age began to unfold, the purpose of clothing shifted from concealment of the body to its accentuation. Dresses shortened and became more formfitting. As ankles and legs became more commonplace on the street, those in the theater lost their ability to draw.

Constantly threatened from all sides, burlesque, in order to remain burlesque, had no other option but to place more and more emphasis on its erotic appeal and to turn it increasingly toward the salacious. One might say that, in respect of the distinction between Helen and Eve, burlesque cornered the market on the theater of Eve. As a result, the comic's days were numbered. Reminiscing about the glory days, Max Furman, who capped his long career as a song-and-dance man with a role in the Broadway play, *Sugar Babies*, recalls the pain as follows:

> Toward the end, burlesque was often very demeaning. Audiences came to sleep—where could you get a flophouse for a buck-fifty? The stripper would come on, and they'd wake up. When the comedian came on, they'd yell, "Get off the stage!" Then they'd go back to sleep until the next stripper. Up, down, up, down. You'd hear snoring while you were on. It was killing you. Inside, your guts were turning upside down. You'd want to say, "*Please* listen to me."[44]

By the 1930s the striptease had become the dominant element in burlesque. Although still contained within the format of a variety show, the stripper had become its main attraction. And the Minsky brothers—Billy, Abe, Herbert, and Morton—had established themselves as her leading exponents. Ever exploring new frontiers of erotic display, they pushed the limits on body exposure, shortened the distance between the stripper and her audience, and moved her downtown. As a result, they garnered a corresponding share of police action. The infamous raid immortalized in the book *The Night They Raided Minsky's* was but one of many that brought the brothers to court throughout the 1920s and the 1930s.

While unembellished nudity was still very much taboo, the Minsky Girls became renowned for using various gimmicks to give the illusion of nudity or delivering quick, intimate glimpses of body parts in flashes. The gimmicks also served as alibis in the event of a raid. Margie Hart, for instance, is said to have worked with a Chicago G-string that could be stripped off in a trice during her show but would miraculously reappear in place if she were inspected backstage. In the same spirit, she is also said to have used a G-string with pubic hair glued to it.

Sometimes the alibis did not work. Morton Minsky recalls the following exchange at the License Commission hearing of 1933, presided over by Commissioner Sydney Levine. As always, the issue in question was indecent exposure, this time at brother Abe's New Gotham Theater:

> Joe Rose, who doubled as first comic and manager at the New Gotham up in Harlem, where they really did work quite "hot," appeared for Abe at the hearing. He told the commissioner that although the people out front thought they were seeing nudity, in fact they were not, and he set out to prove it. Rose pulled out four pieces of wardrobe while being questioned on the stand—two sets of brassieres and trunks. One of them was made of rubber and the other of net. The rubber ones, Rose explained, went on first, and the net ones followed. Then there was a coat of powder, and the stripper was all set to strip.
> "That's how they do it at the Gotham," Rose said with a straight face. But Levine was no dummy. "Isn't that powdering meant to give an effect of nudity?" he asked.
> "No, sir," Rose answered, "that's to keep them from *shining.*"
> Rose then proceeded to struggle into the strip garment over his suit to show the commissioner that it wouldn't fool anybody. Levine noticed that there were certain trimmings on the brassieres and asked what their purpose was.
> "Those," Rose answered, "are rosebuds. My girls are never without these rubber undies if I have anything to say about it. However, they may not be so careful when they are a little drunk."
> The commissioner was aghast. "You mean your actresses sometimes get drunk?"
> "Hell, yes!" Rose replied. "And when they're liquored up, they don't know *what* they got on! That's why I watch them."

Minsky then commented as follows:

Now I know Joe and I know what the Gotham was offering up there on 125th Street. If those girls were wearing rubber undies and fishnet leotards, I'm the herring on the wall that whistles for sure. Despite Abe's claims of being interested in highbrow burlesque, the New Gotham was notorious for running the rawest shows in town. Of course, we're dealing in a world of illusion, and if the customers at the New Gotham *thought* they were seeing actual nude flesh, then what's the difference, right?[45]

In spite of Rose's courtroom charade, the Gotham was forced to close temporarily.

The Minskys claimed to have installed the first runway in the United States in 1917.[46] A concept already in vogue at the Folies-Bergère (where Abe got the idea), the runway was an oblong extension of the stage that took the stripper right into the crowd. The transgressive force of this innovation is underscored by its eventual prohibition in New York in 1934. But the stripper's radical proximity to the audience was not as alarming as her rising profile in the glare of Broadway.

While the 1930s Depression just about wiped out mainstream theater, burlesque prospered. The Minskys and other promoters began moving into downtown theaters vacated by failed productions and, for the first time in history, burlesque established itself in the cultural heartland of New York. By 1937 seven major Broadway theaters had become burlesque houses. But what looked like the beginnings of the legitimization of burlesque ultimately precipitated its demise. The invasion of Broadway rekindled the old fears of cultural contamination, and on May 2, 1937, the city administration, fortified by hearings attended by various antiburlesque groups, revoked the licenses of all the burlesque theaters in New York. So thorough was the crackdown that the words burlesque, striptease, and even Minsky were forbidden to appear on any marquee. Although the theaters were eventually permitted to reopen, the new code of conduct and its regulation were so strict that most burlesque goers, primed on the very thing prohibited, stayed away. As the youngest Minsky summed it up, "If the audience couldn't have the old-fashioned strip, they were not coming back. And they didn't."[47]

Shortly after the closures, an epitaph for burlesque appeared in the *New York Times*. Lamenting the rapid decline of the once "venerable leg shows," it opined: "Since the striptease bit of midway hocus-pocus started turning burlesque into a peep show about ten years ago, the dank, dead attitude of the audience and the foulness of the comedy have very nearly destroyed the revelry that at one time was both coarse and wholesome and much prized for an occasional night out of bounds. Burlesque was at one time lively fooling." The writer's main objection was not the shows' eroticism (he compared the current alarms to those ignited by Lydia Thompson 68 years earlier), but its "debase[ment] into indecency by low art or even by the absence of art or by the sullen prurience of the audience." His summary of the most recent show he attended stated there was "No good singing, no good dancing, no ideas in the staging, no form or style in the comedy—no sense of vitality or enjoyment." The writer looked forward to "staying away from burlesque forever."[48]

The epitaph for burlesque, however, which has been written many times throughout its history, was once again premature (*Time* wrote one as late as 1970[49]). It represented the wishful thinking of its detractors as well as a belief that the limit had been reached and could be sustained no further. Similar epitaphs were written for striptease in later years. In the late 1950s, for instance, Lawrence Langner referred to the striptease as a "waning form of entertainment."[50] And a decade later even the media visionary, Marshall McLuhan, was moved to declare, "Gone are the thrills of striptease."[51] The rout in New York merely pushed burlesque back to the margins of culture, although in a refurbished, cleaner format. When asked by the *New York Post* in 1937 where he would "draw the line," Sam Scribner, a burlesque promoter since the 1890s and now an official censor of the newly chastened shows, replied: "Right above the navel. From that point upward a woman need wear nothing at all, as long as she stands still. If she moves about and shakes herself more covering may be required, but I see no harm in looking at a handsome bosom. Of course legs may be bared, but there must be a strip of something around the hips."[52]

Having discovered the limits of its expression, burlesque carried on through the 1940s and 1950s, but with a much lower profile. In 1943 *Collier's* reported that burlesque still thrived as "the biggest, daffiest, lustiest live-talent theatrical business operating today, packing houses from coast to coast without any of the names that made G-string a household word," but added: "And Mr. Izzy Hirst, who operates the Eastern burlesque circuit from New York, will thank you to keep your yap shut about it. The last thing he wants to see is a reporter. His slogan, apparently, is 'Burlesque is dead.'" The article confirms that the stripper's level of exposure had not increased since the New York crackdown: "The strippers don't strip as they once did. It is true that they take off the costume they appear in, but in most cities they end their acts wearing net pants and brassières. A few years ago this would have been regarded as fully clothed. The big change is that there is little teasing and not so many belly bumps and grinds. But the fishtail, a wiggling of the hips, has survived in full vigor."[53]

Those who celebrated the demise of striptease could not have foreseen the transformation in public attitudes toward sex that took place in the 1960s. Although there is some controversy about whether this remarkable decade actually witnessed an increase in sexual activity, it is true that most people thought it did, thereby lending an air of acceptability—even sanction—to prolific sexual behavior. This change in attitudes was reflected in a general liberalization of attitudes about fashion (the miniskirt, for example), erotica and pornography, movies (such as *Bob and Carol, Ted and Alice*, which extolled the virtues of swinging), rock and roll, and nude encounter groups. In 1964 the fashion mogul, Rudi Gernreich, unveiled the topless bathing suit. The use of mind-altering drugs, such as marijuana, mescaline, and LSD, regularly discussed in the media as sexual enhancers, became widespread among middle class Americans. It was a new age of sensuality that made traditional striptease look rather naive.

However, the 1960s also gave birth to a phenomenon that paved the way to the modern stripper: go-go dancing. Suspended in cages over the heads of discotheque and bar patrons, the go-go dancer signified the birth of the vitalized goddess as solo performer. While initially the concept was based on miniskirts, skin-tight tops, and high boots, the costume progressed toward more and more exposure. Carol Doda, who has the distinction of being the first topless go-go dancer (in San Francisco in 1965), is said to have drawn some inspiration from the Gernreich swimsuit.[54] A social scientist's notes on a Doda performance he saw refer to her as "a 'star' who descends to the stage as if she were some kind of heavenly spirit, and the lighting turns her into some kind of vision." Perceiving Doda's "enormous" breasts to be "symbols of 'mother,'" he also tells us that "the standard joke in topless places involves a customer asking a topless waitress for some cream in his coffee."[55] Toward the end of the decade, California go-go went bottomless and striptease found new life as a solo act in bars. And it allied itself with rock and roll.

It might have been predictable that bump and grind would merge with rock and roll. Both are intimately bound up with the imagery of dance and sex. Both describe actions descriptively antagonistic—reciprocating motion (bump and rock) and rotary motion (grind and roll)—brought together in a harmony of effect: like a piston and crankshaft, or the movements of the hips during sexual intercourse. Both turn dance into a metaphor, a theatrical euphemism for the sex act reduced to simple mechanics. Rock and roll provided the appropriate primitive beat for the new-age dance of divestment.

The 1970s' metamorphosis of the form from the theater to the bar proved to be the ultimate demise of burlesque. The times required—and permitted—the dancing nude goddess to be unencumbered by anything. The go-go phenomenon signified the final stage in the liberation of staged female eroticism from rational controls: from art, allegory, stasis, convention, choreography, comedy, and clothing. In retrospect, burlesque proved to be the vehicle that propelled stripping into the limelight and, like a rocket stage, was left behind in the relentless ascent to more ethereal forms of eroticism. Tease gave way to tantalize, levity to libido, and farce to explicitness. The leg show grew into the leg spread. Modern stripping is to burlesque what heavy metal is to bebop: whatever subtleties remain are all urgent.

The older dancers, reminiscing about the golden age, mourn not only the loss of the art but the loss of its spirit, pride, and respect; and they entertain faint hopes of a return.

DELILAH: The fifties were very conservative. We had pasties and full pants—that means your cheeks had to be covered. And in some clubs, you also had to wear nylon stockings because you couldn't expose any legs, or any flesh, as they called it then.

In '65, the pasties came off and the pants were cut into G-belts. They had to be two inches across at first; then they got skimpier and skimpier.

After that, in '69, in Los Angeles, there was almost like a revolution in that nightclubs went bottomless. Of course, a lot of them got busted and a lot of them stayed; there was a big turnover.

In the seventies, it started breaking out. The good dancers from the fifties and sixties were starting to get older and they either chose different occupations or they got married and raised kids. A very few stayed on, sometimes as "legends of burlesque." There weren't enough good older ones left for the younger ones to learn from.

A big thing happened between the mid-sixties and the late sixties. The biggest shock of my life. We always had live bands and then the tape machine came in. That was a big letdown for us. You always had the three piece orchestra—drummer, trumpet player, and piano player. The drummer was important because he always feels how you feel. He plays the mood. If you feel good, he'll speed up the music. If you don't feel good, he'll slow it down. But by the end of the sixties that was gone and we went to cassettes. It's something like selling a limousine and buying a Volkswagen. You cannot say, "Speed it up a little," or "Slow it down." You have no communication with the music. And if you have a power failure or the tape breaks, you're out of luck.

At the end of the seventies, beginning of the eighties, it was strictly go-go—topless dancing. You didn't have to have any talent. You didn't have to have any music, you didn't have to have any makeup on. You could come off the street as long as you looked cute and you could wiggle your butt and you could go up onstage. A lot of them didn't even care if their hair was done. It was just a shame. It was sad.

This generation doesn't have much of a sense of humor. It almost feels like their brains are not developed. It could be two things: they haven't been taught or they've done some very bad drugs when they were younger.

DANIELLE DEAN: Today, the whole atmosphere is different. When I started, they used to pay your transportation, your room, and board. When you came in, you had the red carpet rolled out. They treated you like gold. Now, you walk into a hotel and they tell you, "These are the house rules. You're not allowed in here. You're not allowed in there. You can't do this. You can't do that. Nobody is allowed in your room..." They think of you as a little kid, like you don't know anything, like you're a piece of garbage.

KARIN WEST: It's become a meat business. There's no vestige of art left in it. If you try to do something that is more of a theatrical performance than just fondling yourself in front of a bunch of men, people don't know how to take it. They don't understand it. It's always harder to improve yourself. It's much easier to get sleazy than it is to become a better dancer, a better performer.

TERI STARR: I think it's a natural progression, you know, like you get accustomed to anything in your life. One piece of pie for dessert and then first thing you know, you have a piece and a half and then you have two pieces...

But it will be entertainment again because you can take only so much of that. It's like the vicious murder and blood 'n'guts movies that we have. They just get worse and worse and now I'm tired of seeing that stuff. Then you want to see something that makes you think a little bit, so you can sit back and relax instead of being hammered with all the blood-splattered walls for entertainment. I think stripping is pretty much the same way.

15
Who's Zoomin' Who?

"Oh, yes—while they sit out there jerking, I'm the one using them."
Gypsy Rose Lee, quoted in June Havoc, *More Havoc* (p. 96)

Just who is using whom in the strip joint?

Most strippers feel, or will say—just like Gypsy Rose Lee—that it is *they* who are exploiting the men in the audience, and not the other way around. Fueling this conviction may be either a plausible need to reverse the low status and beleaguering stigma attending to the stripper, or a very real feeling of superiority over the men in the audience, who are often viewed from the stage as degenerate. But there are also a few strippers who articulate a politicized, if not a purely feminist, point of view.

> SARITA: The dancer is ultimately the loser. She's exploited. Of course, she's a willing participant, but that's neither here nor there. Most of these girls are young, like *very* young, and most of them are in need financially. The big picture is that young people nowadays have a very big problem. It's hard for these people. Something has happened where the older generation has not been able to provide for them. They have very little hope for the future. They are very depressed and they're hooked into being consumers, having things and living a certain lifestyle. They haven't been taught certain basic values. I can't talk to most of these girls now.
>
> I was telling them things like, "You're young! You're beautiful! And you go out there and do *that* for 20 bucks a show? These guys come in for the price of a lousy beer and they can see you degrade yourself. You're giving it away for nothing. And in such a degrading manner."
>
> There's almost something sacrilegious about it.

Nevertheless, the overriding point of view among strippers is one of freedom of choice.

TERI STARR: I feel that if you don't like where you are, get out. And the door is open both ways. Now if you're going to be exploited in any manner, if you don't like it, don't do it. But then, if you like it, you're not being exploited. You're doing it because you want to do it.

The men are there because of where their heads are. They like that type of thing. If they didn't like it, they wouldn't be there. And the women are there because it pays them a good living. And a lot of the girls resent it. They resent the fact that this guy is looking at them for their naked body. So then put your clothes on and go down to the 7-11 and get a job if you don't like it. I mean that's like saying, "I'll sing for you but you'd like it and then you're exploiting me."

PEARL IDAHO: We are exploiting the men because they are stupid enough to pay for it.

The issue of exploitation is a troublesome one. Since Karl Marx and the European revolutions of the nineteenth century, the subject has become a global concern. Rectifying inequalities between classes and categories of people (and lately between people and animals, people and trees, and people and the land) is now the subject of a daily public debate. Employer/employee, male/female, white/black, North/South, rich/poor, old/young, the strong/the weak: the use of another for selfish purposes, that is, without concern for the other's interests (as exploitation may be defined) feeds on visible differences (such as class, gender, race, and species) and legitimizes itself simply as the rewards of enterprise or of power. A reading of Marx (who had an interested party in Gypsy Rose Lee) is not necessary to seek out the psychic fuel for what manifests itself as exploitation. It is but one of—or a combination of—the lusts, such as that for wealth, power, or sexual gratification. Exploitation is the behavioral manifestation of self-serving habits, where in any kind of exchange between people (or people and animals, people and the environment), one party, usually because of its superior position, benefits more than the other.

But the judicious measurement of such relationships is difficult, given the nearly universal belief in both the need for superiors, leaders, policemen, priests, protectors, and other figures of authority, and in the rewards or privileges that such figures enjoy. Most, if not all societies, even if they do not ideologically subscribe to elites (such as communist ones), have them anyway. How much power should one individual or one class of individuals have over another without striking an imbalance or inequity that goes beyond what's fair?

On the face of it, the stripper seems to come out ahead in her relationship with the audience. *She* gets what *she* wants (wages, adulation, and creative self-expression), while most of the audience is left with an unfulfilled need. The stripper goes home merely exhausted; the men leave the club with libidos screaming for release. The men have been entertained, it is true, but the modern strip show, having left behind its comedy component, allows for no physical catharsis of stimulated urges except through expressions of male brouhaha (the club masturbator notwithstanding).

The professional stripper is in total control. She is in motion while the men remain glued to their seats. She is the manipulator; the men are clearly the manipulated. Who could possibly infer from the description of Millie De Leon's show in chapter 14 that she was anything but in complete control of her audience?

The distinction between the stripper and her audience is a function of both gender and sexual value. It is the relativity between these two categories that produces the conflicting responses to the stripper. In terms of gender, the woman who plays the stripper's role is categorically subservient to the men in the audience. As a woman, she has lesser status in several ways: she does not have the same access to the mainstream jobs and wages that men have; she does not have the same level of permission to experiment with her sexuality as the men do; she does not enjoy the same degree of protection by the law; and she is outmatched in a physical fight. As a woman, she is relegated, both in the symbolic and in the literal senses, to the realm of nature, feeling, and leisure, which, in any culture where the predominant ideology serves progress, is considered to be secondary to and less vital than the complementary male-associated realm of civilization, intellect, and work. This is the first and foremost relation and contradiction between the stripper and her audience: men versus women.

But the stripper is a special kind of woman. She is a woman refined, a woman transcended. She has been raised to an ethereal level, a sexual pedestal. She is a goddess, a fantasy. In this role she is a woman whose status is more elevated than that of most of her audience. The stripper rises also because she is a stage presence—a star—and that in itself serves to endow her with a superior position over her starry-eyed admirers. Coupled with her sexual prize, the stripper achieves much more buoyancy than her audience. Since the stripper's sexual value is enhanced, only a correspondingly enhanced value on the male side (measured in terms of wealth or power, the rewards of intellect and work) is capable of winning her affection or procuring her. This accounts in part for the sometimes extraordinary sums of money offered for the opportunity to go to bed with her. The overriding assumption in the audience is that the stripper is a more valuable score than they are. The crowd looks up to her, figuratively and literally.

Once again, here is the conflict between the stripper's image and her selfhood, the gender inequalities adhering to her person and the sexual considerations adhering to her image. When the focus is predominantly on the fantasy, the stripper holds the potential for manipulation and abuse. The men are in a trance state, disbelief suspended, and thus are fairly easy marks. But, paradoxically, were the stripper to exploit her superior position, she would risk dissolving the fantasy of her. If the audience begins to perceive some manipulation for its own sake on her part, if the issue of rejection becomes painfully overt, or if the dancer appears to be mean-spirited or to have a malicious agenda, the focus falls out of fantasy and occupies itself with psychic defenses. When the focus falls, so does the dancer, and the fantasy image of the monolithically sexual and infinitely gratifying turns into the nightmare image of the *femme fatale*. When this happens, the conflict resolved in fantasy—that arising out of the desire, fear, and control issues of the male viewers—may easily find its outlet in anger. Exploitive behavior on the performer's part can all too easily be turned back on her. The stripper can't use her audience in this way because she dances within parameters that do not support it. The professional stripper understands on some level that she does not have a free hand to arouse and reject male libidos. In fact, she has a vested interest in serving fantasy. Her show, her status, and her life depend on her catalytic generation of the alchemy of fantasy.

But she can't generate this pure state in everyone. Some of the men are just plain angry and abusive in spite of her efforts, and the alcohol makes them bold beyond the specter of the bouncers (if there are any). The stripper's license to explore the terrain beyond the pale, her brazen foraging of the taboo, lends some sanction to the release of repressed urges, some of which could at any time cross over into her realm. By publicly removing her clothes, the stripper symbolically removes her female defenses. She is not unlike the snake charmer in that the balance between spectacle and disaster is a function of rhythm. Become distracted, lose control, break the spell: and thus become a target. Her prospects for being overpowered, either physically or through emotional abuse, are far greater than that of the audience. So it would seem that the balance of power and the potential for exploitation actually tilts in favor of the men. Gypsy Rose Lee's affirmation of superior power at the head of this chapter would not mean much unless this were true.

But Gypsy Rose Lee was no ordinary stripper. She was, for one, at the pinnacle of her profession, "an institution," as one reviewer called her.[1] She had slugged it out on the vaudeville circuits from the age of six, often hungry and always on the move, eventually to become a featured attraction at the 1940 New York World's Fair. She hobnobbed equally with couturiers, authors, art collectors, movie moguls and gangsters. She had her own press agent. Gypsy Rose Lee didn't only *have* the power, she *was* the power. What about the run-of-the-mill stripper whose 15-minute limelight always borders on oblivion?

Lee voiced her affirmation of power over the audience during a conversation with her younger sister, June Havoc, backstage at a Minsky theater. Ostensibly giving her sister, a professional marathon dancer, the inside information on burlesque, Lee may have had a hidden agenda. In order to instill respect for the power she claimed, she first had to arouse awe for the forces she dealt with. But she seems to have been equally intent on creating a shock effect, to patronize with the privileged information of the insider, to take a swipe at naivete, and to overwhelm with the awe-inspiring intensity of shadowy images. In Havoc's re-creation of the exchange in her memoirs, Lee asks her,

> "Have you ever heard of any other public who sit with a newspaper covering their lap?"
>
> I was the perfect foil at the first hearing. "No," said I.
>
> "Oh, yes indeed." She told me later it was fun just watching my face. "You see, the reason for that paper is simple—it's because they're masturbating. That's right, and I guess they'd rather not be seen by the other Johns. God! All the stuff they bring in with them—it's an education! Milk bottles and raw liver, and—you don't believe me? Check the alley. See what they sweep out of here at night."[2]

The scene takes on the solemn tones of an initiation rite, a watershed of lost innocence. Havoc is awakened to a creepy world of furtive sex with gruesome devices. Some foreboding associations materialize. The milk bottle with its liver lining is the surrogate of the stripper. Its position beneath the newspaper (literally on the shadowy side of the evening news) can't help but be aimed at her, like a Reichian orgone accumulator tuned to the stripper's frequency. Bile, the main secretion of the liver, is an analogue of irritability and anger; and the milk bottle is a symbol of motherhood. The masturbator discharges into an anguished conflation of stripper and mother (sometimes vibrating "an entire row of poorly riveted seats."[3]). Once used, the bottle is discarded, a thing of the gutter, later to be replaced with another.

The Minsky's reinvention of the runway in America brought the girls right into the crowd. Morton, the youngest Minsky (who died in 1987), savored the event in his memoirs. Not only could the men "look right up [the girls'] legs," but "they could actually smell their perfume and hear their heavy breathing. It was sensational! Never before had an audience been able to get so close to the performers."[4]

Never before had the latent potential in the audience for mischief, misogyny, and malevolence come so close to the stripper. The runway was a *tour de force*, a swing of the pendulum that brought the visual event scandalously—and dangerously—close to the tactile.

The concept has always been to bring the men in the audience as close as possible to what is forbidden to them. The omega point, anticipated by those strippers who, in their floor show, spread their labia for the spectators in the front-row seats—the Sushi Bar—is to give the men a view right inside. The unavoidable implication of this relentless visual slide into the vagina is that the stripper has no private self, that everything about her is open to inspection and invasion, that her very soul is up for grabs, that she can be turned inside out, and that she has no boundaries, no conditions, and no limits on whom she lets in. She is simply transparent, like a milk bottle.

The stripper plays with some disturbing forces. She does not simply go onstage; she steps into an atmosphere of attitudes about her, most of which are predatory, consuming, and exploitive. Some of them are violent, twisted, and depraved. It is this psychic connection to male sexual fantasy that informs the stripper's experience. She can keep the men at arm's length, but the metaphysical reach of their plans for her has no boundaries. If only as a metaphor, at some level of consciousness being sushi to the hungry eye makes its impression. The fear of attack is sister to another fear, that of absorption into the underworld of aberrant passions.

SARITA: These businesses that pedal flesh pollute your soul. They poison your mind because they lie. They instill doubt and fear and weirdness into your space so that you can barely function sexually as a man with a woman or a woman with a man. What mystery is there left for you to enjoy? Can you become ecstatic any more about sex? Or have you become so sick in your soul that you can't explain that kind of joy and happiness, that gratitude that you can actually share your body physically with somebody else. The magic and the beauty and the romance and the mystery is gone. We've been deprived of that.

Backstage, the stripper has a business relationship with both her agent and the manager/owner of the club where she works. The agent books the dancers into the clubs. He (sometimes, she) is thus caught between the stripper's interest in earning maximum wages and the club owner's interest in paying out the minimum. Who the agent really works for is a matter of much speculation among both strippers and club owners. Unless the individual stripper is a feature or headliner or has a sizable local following, the club owner ultimately calls the shots. To book the run-of-the-mill stripper, he can play one agent against another to ensure he is getting the best for his money. All too often, it seems to the stripper that her agent is involved in a conflict of interest not in her favor.

Since the agent has a vested interest in making sure that his dancers show up for each show, he often finds himself trying to resolve the various personal problems that interfere. He gets to know his dancers on an intimate level; his role is invariably that of provider, fixer, and consoler. We might easily expect that he becomes a father figure to them, given the sociological absent father hypothesis. The agent, more than anyone else in strippers' lives, cannot interact with them in a disengaged way.

In the words of one agent: "You are the one solid focus in their life. A lot of them have come from nowhere, and they're going nowhere. They're just here for a short time. A lot of them don't have family because of what they do. Their family has disassociated from them and they don't want to have anything to do with them at all. They have lousy relationships with user boyfriends and you're the one solid thing in their lives. They know that, regardless of what happens to them, you are always going to be there. You become mother, father, sister, brother, doctor, lawyer, banker, psychiatrist, and baby sitter to them. You become everything to these people. And they tend to cling to you. And when you get a 100 of them clinging to you, you cannot help but care. This one just had a miscarriage or this one's boyfriend was just killed in a car accident and she comes to you because you're her one focal point, and you can't help but care. They become a huge family. And because you're the head of their family, you drown in their problems. You have to be a machine not to become emotionally involved. That's what drives you down. You get so tired of the problems. You have enough problems in your own life that when you get a free period with no problems you're like, "Aha!" But you never get there with dancers, because you've got too many of them and somebody's always got a problem."

This relationship has many benefits for the dancer who finds that her agent is the one person she can feel close to, but it also gives the unscrupulous agent extraordinary opportunities to tie the satisfaction of his libido to the dancer's livelihood. Or he may just want favors related to the business. In any case, the less than professional agent can take advantage of his patriarchal position to make the inexperienced and lonely stripper feel obligated to him.

> SARITA: I do believe that a lot of the girls are innocent victims. I remember what it was like for me. I really did not have a grip on what my values were when I was that age. It was easy to suck me in. Just trying to fit, trying to make a stand, trying to just be okay is a very important thing to young people. Belonging, being accepted, is part of the reason why they get into so much trouble. And they're vulnerable. That's why they are easy prey for these disgusting bastards [agents and club managers]. In some cases these people psychologically try to make you feel obligated to them because maybe they become the family that you didn't have. I had no family. I had nobody. I was very alone and very vulnerable. They come on like: "We care about you; we're your family." These young girls imagine that they really are their friends. But what they don't realize yet, and it takes time, it takes growing up to realize that anybody who would make you do that or encourage you to do something degrading to yourself for money is no friend, *ever*.
>
> That's what I mean by, "They're victimized." They are made to feel obligated to take on jobs they don't want to take, such as jobs in towns that have been known to be rowdy, where the facilities are very bad, the security is bad, or do stags where you're expected to do more than just take your clothes off and dance. The agents don't state it. It's a tacit understanding. They don't tell you, "These guys are pretty rowdy. When you take your clothes off, one guy's going to want to poke you with a dildo and another guy's going to want to have a little sex with you." Ninety-nine percent of them expect you to have sex with the groom. Sometimes they raffle you off without your knowledge. If you don't take these jobs, it is made to look like you are betraying your "friends," the agents. Your life is in the pot of the devil.

The stripper works under contract, but it is well understood in the business that whenever there is a problem the agent and the manager/owner usually prevail. Since the stripper is paid at the end of the week, the club owner can fire her on Wednesday and be in a fairly secure position to not pay her. Once she ceases to serve the image, perhaps because the club owner (or manager) doesn't like her appearance or her intelligence, because she is too demanding of her rights, or because she won't sleep with him or one of his friends, she falls. She becomes merely a woman, a female employee, and one who can be judged and dismissed out of hand for her degenerate display. These are the dynamics of the goddess-slut syndrome women live with on a daily basis, but which the stripper bounces between in radical shifts of perspective. The outlaw status of the stripper, together with her young age and inexperience in legal matters, almost always ensures that the perpetrator, usually male, will never be taken to court. In addition, strippers intuitively know that they do not have the same institutional safeguards as other segments of the population. (A current runs through society and the legal system that strippers, like prostitutes, get what they deserve.) There are many stories in these pages about such exploitation. Some strippers view such incidents as common, as part of an endemic attitude.

MARY: This hotel owner brought this guy upstairs and wanted me to talk to him. The guy was drunk out of his mind. Meanwhile, the owner had made me sign a paper saying, "No male visitors in the rooms." Now, my room was right next door to the bar so this guy could have hightailed back up there, broke the door down, and raped me and no one would have heard a damn thing.

Thursday rolled around and this guy was really drunk and he was throwing ping-pong balls 'cause Mitzi Dupree was coming the next week. I walked offstage, furious. The hotel owner took me into the back room and more or less told me to shut up, that I didn't have any rights. Later, he fired me.

BRANDI WEST: I worked once at a club in South Bend, Indiana. There was one stripper and about 4 or 5 go-go girls and they danced continuously, maybe 20 shows a night. And the dancers couldn't drink unless they drank champagne which someone bought for them. If someone bought you just a highball or whatever you get pop or juice. A drink cost $4 and out of that you got $1. A quarter bottle of champagne was $20, a half bottle was $40 and a full bottle was $60, and it was American champagne. The customers were not supposed to know that the dancer got pop or juice.

There were go-go pimps there and there was lots of soliciting in the place. The waitress would be giving guys hand jobs in the corners. And you were supposed to hustle drinks, which is just beneath me. I hated every minute of it.

There was a middle-aged black guy in the audience who said, "Could I buy you a drink?" So I sat down and had a glass of tomato juice and he bought me another one.

I got up to go to the washroom and the owner called me over and said, "You don't sit with niggers in my club."

That was the final straw. I said, "I don't subscribe to your religion. You want me to hustle drinks and now you're telling me who to hustle them from?" I went back and sat with him. I phoned my agent that night and screamed at him for about three hours and he finally got me calmed down and said I should finish the week there. The owner told me he didn't want me back.

MISS BRAZIL: The down side of the business is that there is no protection when it comes to holding down a job. Sometimes your contract has no validity. You can be fired at any time for the oddest reasons.

One of those reasons was that the color of my skin, my heritage (Brazilian and French), made me unappealing to the people who had hired me. They told me I needed to take dance lessons—a ludicrous reason. My agent told me later that the manager had told him that I looked too much like a Paki. I came home on the bus crying my eyes out because it was also my birthday. It was heartbreaking.

Sometimes you end up in a town and you find that you don't have a booking. And neither the hotel nor your agent will take responsibility for it. That's happened to me twice. One was a 12-hour drive to a smelly little town (there's a saw mill there). You get there—you're not on the list. You don't have a room. And nobody wants to know. Nobody wants to find out why it all went wrong. You're left out in the cold.

SARITA: The owner of this place, whom I will never forget—slimy people, man, slimy redneck jerks, real jerk-offs—came upstairs and assaulted me in my dressing room. I got out of it, but in a graceful way. I didn't make a big case out of it. I just kind of avoided it and got out of there. And then I had to go back and beg for my pay.

One club manager I knew was really pretty disgusting. Some of the customers there were allowed to go upstairs and peek on the girls getting dressed. He had been going out with one of the dancers, who was no more than a child, really. One day she related to me how she hadn't been paid in a month and she had a little boy at home and she had to buy food for him. My heart was breaking. I wanted to take her home with me and give her a good meal. I said, "What's the problem? Get your money. Do it for your child." I guess she started asking him for it and he started getting abusive and she started crying and then he started beating the hell out of her, naked, upstairs. I—he'll probably never forget me—went in there, and I'm not a tough person, but I screamed at him, "You stop it right now!" He just looked at me in disbelief. Like, who was this? He stopped and I put my coat over the girl and took her into the other room with me. That night I quit.

CRYSTAL ROSE: The worst thing was probably my experience in San Francisco. Just before I became a dancer I entered a topless contest and won. I knew how to go-go dance at the time and I started working at this club for two weeks. The guy who had recently purchased the club, a short little Jewish guy—and obnoxious—came up to me and said, "I want to fuck you."

And I looked at him and I said, "Well, you know, I really enjoy being your employee and perhaps your friend, but..."

And he said, "Then, you're fired! Get the fuck out of my club!"

I was absolutely devastated. I was so hurt by that I went and bought two pints of Southern Comfort and drank almost all of it in an hour. That was the only time I've ever gotten sick on liquor. And I can't stand the smell of that stuff today.

TONI: I worked at a club once in a small town. At the end of my week, the owner wanted me to give him five extra dollars for Performer's Rights Organization fees. I said, "No. I'm not giving you five dollars for the PRO fees. That's your responsibility."

He fought with me. He took my contract from me and said, "I'm not paying you because you don't have your contract."

I said, "Look. I know my rights. I'll sue your ass off if you don't give me that five bucks back."

He gave it back to me, but he said, "You're never going to work in this town again."

Few club owners are ever happy with a girl who knows her rights.

I sued my agent one time because he didn't pay me. And I continued to work for him. If you take a stance right from the beginning, they'll respect you for it. But they won't always give you the good bookings.

THISTLE DOWNS: The agents and the clubs work together. The agent feeds you so many lines, it's incredible. When you want to get more pay, he'll say, "The club will only pay you so much," when the truth is, the club owner will pay more, but the agent puts you in for a cheaper price, because it's good for the agent. And it's good for the club owner, too, because he's getting a girl that the agent has sucked in. The agent does not make as much money off the commission, but he keeps the club owners happy.

CITY LIGHTS: The agents and club owners all have terrible reputations. They're not professional, in that they don't protect their dancers at all. Sometimes there's a mix-up in the office and they send too many dancers or the bar owner changes his mind. The girl will show up and he'll say, "Sorry, we're not booking through that agent anymore." Or the bar owner will get drunk and fire everyone, or not like the look of somebody, or say this one's too short or too tall or too fat or too thin. The contracts don't mean anything. Sometimes dancers are booked for a certain amount of money and they get paid less. The agents don't insist that their dancers have proper dressing rooms. They have nothing to say about the staging.

MATA HARRIETTE: There's a lot of political bullshit amongst the dancers and amongst the agents. They can be really cruel. If the agent doesn't like you, the word will get around town and nobody will book you. For instance, I had a girlfriend who used to have buck teeth. She's not an exceptionally pretty girl, but she has a great personality onstage and she's very funny. She makes people laugh. And they wouldn't book her because of her buck teeth. She got the worst places all the time, even though she'd been dancing for three months. And because I knew everybody, I got all the great bookings, anything I wanted. So it was really kind of hard to be her friend. She eventually got her teeth fixed, but now she's pregnant and living at home. Those are the kinds of things that can happen.

But the agents have their stories, too. An agent in Vancouver related the following incidents:

The excuses we get for the no-shows on Monday mornings are every-thing from flat tires, "My husband beat me up," no babysitter, "I can't get my clothes out of the cleaners," to "There's a bomb in my car and I can't go to work today." That was a girl by the name of Phoebe [not her real name]. She phoned us one day and said, "I can't go to work today. I know this guy's out to kill me, and I know there's a bomb in my car."

There's maybe 10 or 15 girls out there who make this whole job worth-while. But the other 85, I really, deep down, don't have the time of day for. The other 85 are all takers. They'll use you.

The worst was when I lent a girl $700 out of my pocket. She'd been dancing for me for a while. And she didn't show up where she was booked. So I told the hotel owner that I'd try to track her down or find a replacement. She walked into my office. And I mean she was black and blue. Her eyes and her face were all swollen up and she had welts on her arms and her hands. Her one hand you could see was broken. She dropped her clothes in the office. She had welts all over. Her husband had beaten her with a stick. He used to walk with a cane. He had beaten her across the legs, front and back, on her back, her breasts, everywhere.

So I gave her $100 out of my pocket and told her to get over to Emer-gency. Whether she did or not, I don't know. She came back to the office the next day and said her husband had taken all the rent money and her landlord was going to throw her out in the street. So I gave her another $600 and told her to go home and get better.

I didn't hear from her for three or four days, so my partner and I went over to her place. She and her husband had moved out, lock, stock, and barrel. I think the whole thing was a setup right from the start. He beat her up and they used that to con money out of me. That was enough to get their plane tickets back to Toronto or Montreal or wherever they were from. The landlord said he saw them leave together.

From the strippers to the audience, agents and club owners, it is the lowest common denominator that sets the mood of this business. Most of the time it runs smoothly enough: the stripper does her shows for the week, the club pays her and her agent, and the next week it happens all over again with a different set of dancers and a new string of clubs. Nasty incidents are not the norm. But the combination of personalities involved in the business, together with its prevailing climate of attitudes and emotions—the guilt, greed, lust, anger, and desperation, along with the issues of control and dominance—ensures that some form of exploitation will occur. And most often it is the strippers who are the victims.

Most strippers come into the business in a state of need. They are often naive young women, disconnected and lonely, who are grateful for the opportunity to work. From the first moment they are in a position of indebtedness. And they are replaceable. If they don't toe the line, there are several more waiting in the wings who will. How the individual stripper fares in this realm depends on how quickly she becomes stagewise, for her individual strengths are her only reliable protection.

> REBECCA: There are some bosses or agents who prey on the girls and those are the girls who let themselves be preyed upon. Sometimes they're into drugs, sometimes they feel insecure; and just having the boss take an interest in you makes you feel better, that you're in good with him. I don't think they think a lot about what they're doing. But if you don't want it to happen, it won't. You just have to stick up for yourself.

One more issue must be addressed here, and perhaps it is the most pressing one of all. Does the stripper exploit the position of women as a whole? That is, does the presence of the stripper within a culture contribute negatively to the culturally held attitudes about women?

The study of the interrelationship between a culture's indigenous images and its prevailing ideology (or culturally held attitudes) is complex, convoluted, and obscure. Since ideology is an abstract and invisible phenomenon, its analysis has to come together eclectically. The areas of knowledge contributing to this subject have included semiology (the study of signs and symbols), psychoanalytical theory, Marxist analysis, film theory, art criticism, studies of advertising, feminist analysis, and, indeed, anything else that might pertain (such as anthropology). There is not nearly enough space or scope here to give this subject a thorough exposition. But, if it had to be summarized in two statements, they might be: (1) images arise out of a culture's prevailing ideology; and (2) images serve to reinforce the prevailing ideology.

Ideology is the term used for the all-encompassing sea of attitudes linking the people of a region, culture, or society. Ideology is the cognitive reinforcement for whatever bonds a group together. It comprises the complete system of codes or cultural agreements that defines everything from the hours of work, to what is considered proper dress, to how we communicate with each other. The codes are instilled by one's parents, by the educational institutions, religious institutions, the laws, and the mass media—by almost everything we come in contact with in our cultural environment. Ideology defines how citizens may affect government, the mores of social comportment, and the boundaries of good and bad, reward and punishment. It defines the familial—what is ours as opposed to what is theirs—and thus it is from ideology that we derive our sense of social stability, security, comfort, purpose, and privilege. Ideology is the cultural adhesive and, like water to a fish, not much thought is given to it because it is perceived as reality itself.

> Ideology is how the existing ensemble of social relations represents itself to individuals; it is the image a society gives of itself in order to perpetuate itself... Ideology uses the fabrication of images and the processes of representation to persuade us that how things are is how they ought to be and that the place provided for us is the place we ought to have.[5]

It would seem logical that images arise out of (and hence, reflect) the undercurrents of ideology, much as a building arises out of a blueprint invested with the needs and values of the community it will serve. Not only do the makers of images draw on their own internalized ideology to fashion them, but they must also bear in mind the internalized values of the people to whom they wish to communicate their message.

The interrelationship between image and ideology will be more comprehensible when we examine the public response to two very different images.

The first is the Marlboro cowboy. Of this image, one thing is certain: it is purely American (meaning the United States). It could not possibly emerge from Iraqi or Japanese ideology. Its endurance testifies to its comfortable assimilation within the U.S. mass consciousness, almost as though it has always been there. And indeed it has. The West, the frontier, the taming of the wilds, the dominion over nature, rugged (unemotional) masculinity, and enterprising individuality: all these are motifs animating the American dream that the Marlboro cowboy evokes with one picture. The Philip Morris Company, which markets Marlboro, must have thought that their cowboy had an intercultural affinity, if not a universal one, because they sent him off to Japan, horse and all, to sell cigarettes. As it was subsequently reported, "The campaign was a flop... The Japanese ... couldn't see the point of being like the Marlboro man—dirty and poor— so why would they want to smoke the same kind of cigarettes he did?"[6] In Japan the Marlboro horseman was a fish out of water, that is, it was an image uprooted from its ideological base. (Philip Morris subsequently changed the image to a younger, cleaner looking yuppie type in a pickup truck.)

The Marlboro cowboy didn't offend the Japanese; he just didn't register with them. What would happen if an image that was radically antagonistic to a culture's prevailing ideology appeared in the public eye? The Robert Mapplethorpe exhibition in Cincinnati is a case in point. Included among the artist's photographs, on display in Cincinnati's Contemporary Art Center in the spring of 1990, were several depicting homoerotic sex among adults and two of children with exposed genitals. One of Mapplethorpe's photographs was reproduced in *Penthouse*.[7] It shows the photographer himself dressed in black leather chaps exposing his buttocks to the camera, with the handle of a bullwhip inserted in his anus. The shock effect generated by the incongruous juxtaposition of these images and the prevailing heterosexual ideology (obviously more stridently championed in Cincinnati than in several other cities that the exhibition toured without incident) resulted in the first-ever indictment of a museum director on charges of obscenity in the United States (he was ultimately acquitted). The grass roots campaign against the exhibition was waged by a group called Citizens for Community Values.

One can see how far the Marlboro and the Mapplethorpe cowboys diverge in their respective affinities with the underlying American mass value system. One we accept as familial—it mirrors, and thereby reinforces, our internalized value systems—while the other was bound to antagonize some sizable segments of society. Some artists feel that the sole function of art is to produce precisely those images that jolt the internalized value system so that people become aware of how they have been conditioned.

As an image, the stripper is not as jolting as the more controversial Mapplethorpe photographs. And yet, she is clearly not as familial as the Marlboro cowboy. She has established a presence in most modern societies—including Japan—but it is a precarious one. Large segments of the population have attended her performances and are content with her containment within certain urban areas. Other segments would rather see her run out of town. She delivers a mixed message, enjoying an affinity with some aspects of the prevailing ideology and provoking a serious conflict with some others. As we have seen, this cultural ambivalence may easily exist within the same mind.

What messages then does the stripper image convey? What aspect of the prevailing ideology does it serve? What aspect does it antagonize? And how does it contribute to the prevailing ideological view of women as a whole?

The discussion of the stripper's image has concentrated on the following four characteristics:

1. It is usually at odds with the subjective self of the woman who plays the part.
2. It is constructed from the current format for the ideal female body animated by an infinitely gratifying and monolithically sexual persona.
3. It is a variation on the traditional goddess motif, distinguished by its being alive, its dancing, and its ritualized stripping.
4. As a live image, the stripper stimulates fears of rejection and manipulation in the audience and fears of contagion within society as a whole.

The most prominent feature of the stripper is that she is a modern Aphrodite or Venus image. The genre of her imagery is that of the inveterate goddess. She, like all the goddesses, conveys the theme of idealized femininity: a body refined according to the current vogue and displaying a disposition devoid of any nonsexual signals. As we have seen, this image has a long history serving a persistent male obsession: the appropriation and control of female sexuality. The goddess image is a male-inspired construct whose purpose is to pacify deep-seated male fears about women.

All the goddess images line up along a spectrum according to their body exposure and their erotic content. (Some of them, such as the video porn queens, move into a third area, that of sexual intercourse.) The beauty queen and the fashion magazine cover girl reside at one extreme and the stripper (where she can perform in the nude) and the porn queen at the other; the discreetly nude film goddess and the centerfold girl fall comfortably in between.

The ideological fault line will be found to cut across this spectrum at various places according to the regional attitudes about such public displays. (Cincinnati, for example, may have a more conservative fault line than, say, San Francisco.) It may be a feature of such a fault line that it always cuts through the general middle, the goddesses there being the ideologically ambivalent ones. They are not familial enough to blend in with the scenery and they are not controversial enough to provoke large segments of society. *Playboy* magazine, for instance, enjoys a circulation numbering in the many millions, but its nudes remain unsanctioned by family values. The middle represents the frontier of ideological acceptance.

The stripper delivers her jolt from the horizon of this frontier. She has the same basic relationship with the prevailing ideology as all the other goddesses, but she crosses the line with her unique format of unabashed sexual expression, nudity, dancing, and being alive. Thus it is her recognition as one of the goddesses that strikes a familial chord with many, while it is her specific variation on the theme that creates disharmony with many others. To put it another way, she incorporates all the codes necessary to an image designed for the pacification of male fears about women but her extremism places her beyond the middle ground.

Opposition to the stripper image comes from three main camps: moralists (essentially the religious right), feminists, and the business community. But their respective critiques of the image are different. Merchants and property owners oppose the stripper ostensibly not for reasons of morality but because of the perceived secondary effects accruing to her place of work. They do not have an interest in banishing her completely, only from their side of town. Their point of view stems from a belief that strip joints cause a decline in property values, profits, and the general spirit of the neighborhood. Strip joints are also believed to be a direct cause of increasing crime in the area. Steve Goetz, the mayor of Newport, Kentucky, articulated this view on a *Donahue* show. Speaking about the proliferation of strip joints on Monmouth Street, he said: "The people in the city of Newport, ... the people who live there 365 days a year, not just come in for one wild weekend—they don't want it. The people in the city of Newport want to get rid of that image. People can live in New York or wherever they want to across the country. And if all they remember of the city of Newport is Monmouth Street, then I'd rather they not remember us at all, because we're much more than just Monmouth Street."[8]

The moralist, on the other hand, takes direct aim at what the stripper does. Of all the characteristics of the stripper's image, the moralist is really only concerned with the third: her live presentation of unbridled eroticism and nudity. To the moralist, the stripper represents eros liberated from rational controls. She vibrates with the wickedness of the very first temptation, which teetered the divinely inspired order in Eden toward a world chaos of infernal passions, passions held in check solely by moral authority.

However, the moralist is not concerned with goddess images *per se* (the beauty queen, for instance, is not a target), only those whose sexuality crosses the fault line. That the goddess image panders to male control of female sexuality is not the issue, it is *how* that sexuality ought to be controlled. The campaign of the religious right has always been to contain eros, most crucially that of women, within marriage and behind closed doors.

Feminists, on the other hand, are most concerned with the first two characteristics of the stripper's image: the presentation of a false female sexual expressiveness that serves male fantasy, and hence the very concept of the goddess. To feminists, the stripper—like all the modern sex goddesses—symbolizes the male appropriation of female sexuality. Feminists object to the image on the grounds that it reinforces the prevailing ideologically based male fantasy about women.

The fantasy runs deep. The consequence of the goddess image for the general social attitude is its public exaltation over and above what it represents. This is a trap latent in all images and the rationale behind the Hebraic Second Commandment: "Thou shalt not make unto thee any graven image, or any likeness of any thing" (Exodus 20:4). The image of the feminine ideal, essentially an abstract and elusive concept, has enough of a semblance of reality, of possibility, by its living constructs—the film idol, the cover girl, the *Playboy* centerfold, the artfully cosmetized street goddess—to severely infect the general social view of women as a whole. The goddess has become an internalized template against which all women are measured.

The specifics of one aspect of this template (at least as it exists for American white male college students) have been quantified from research designed by Michael Cunningham, a psychologist at the University of Louisville in Kentucky. In the experiment, students were directed to rate pictures of women (mostly white, and over half of whom were Miss Universe finalists), for facial attractiveness. In spite of what we have learned about the commonality of internalized ideology, the results of the experiment revealed a remarkably consistent blueprint. The proportions of the ideal female face were so precise that minute variations in, say, the length of the mouth relative to the width of the face, made it much less attractive.[9]

In an article about his research, Cunningham commented on what the proportions mean: "The sum total of the features signify someone who is slightly young and helpless, though sexually mature and friendly. And men find that combination compelling."[10] "Compelling" is the key word, which implies compliant, compatible, and sexual, with a hint of availability.

The unavoidable result of the exaltation of an image is the relative diminishing of what it represents, in this case women. The presence of the goddess as a prevailing image in both popular culture and the internalized value system suggests to women what men want from them. Since they are not that way, the implication is that they must then be something other than what they are to be attractive, to be sexual, to have a relationship, and to bear children. This fact is reflected in the gargantuan success of the cosmetics industry, the current near worship of diet gurus, and the proliferation of cosmetic surgeons. The need to transform the body is symbolically attached to the need to transform the soul.

The internalized blueprint for the ideal in the opposite gender is reflected in the sexual marketplace, where value is measured by physical beauty for females and power for males. This results in an ideological assumption that the women a man finds himself attracted to will likely be attracted to males more powerful than him (and vice versa for women). That is, the ones he finds attractive inevitably will be unavailable to him. Attraction *equates* with remoteness. (The Freudian view is that this assumption, a feature of castration anxiety, is primally based in competition with the father for the mother's love.)

This effect alone guarantees that women will be inseparably bound up with fantasy in the male mind, and produces such effects as the proverbial thinking about someone else while making love to your lover. (This is also true for women, but note how the respective ideological gender images of beauty and power place all the world's resources in the domain of men; how females also become a resource; and how power conveys vitality, energy, and dominion while beauty is merely a visual image that, unlike power, depends for its vitality on the existence of a viewer, ostensibly male. Power is a subjective state; beauty is an objective one.)

In a consumer society the intelligent thing to do to sell your wares is to link them with the possibility of attracting one's goddess (or god). The implication is that a man has a chance of attracting his personal goddess without necessarily having to be powerful or wealthy, as long as he uses the right deodorant or smokes the right cigarette. A quick survey of advertisements in any men's magazine reveals the profuse use of the goddess in the marketing of products. A Seagram's gin advertisement, for instance, asks, "Have you found the hidden pleasure in refreshing Seagram's gin?" over a tall, bubbly glass containing a female bather worked into the shadows and curves of an ice cube. It is not hyperbole to suggest that the pursuit of the goddess fuels the economy. Because the goddess already resides in the internalized ideologies of men, it is not even necessary that she appear alongside a particular product to sell it. The implication of the Marlboro cowboy, for instance, is that he embodies the attributes (rugged, stoical, individualistic, and adventurous) of the masculine template in the goddess's mind.

Of course, the stripper is not respectable enough to fall into this category. Whereas the stripper inhabits the ideological frontier, capitalism picks its images from the cultural heartland. The dream is invested in the woman who embodies the ideal form but whose public demeanor—radiant, vivacious, friendly, and uncomplicated—only hints at a sexual passion beneath, and one that is reserved for the successful player of the capitalist game. The stripper caters to the ideological shadow (as it were): the sexual fantasies that smolder beneath the veneer of decency, family values, and middle America. The stripper does not represent the dream of a perfect life partner. Rather, she fuels the fantasy of the perfect sexual adventure, the ultimate one-night stand. Nonetheless, she contributes this disposable element (like milk bottles lined with liver) to the prevailing view of women. The difference between the beauty queen and the stripper, from the consumer's point of view, is simply one of quality or longevity: the beauty queen is good for a year, the stripper for a night.

The feminist labors to liberate all women—and ideally all society—from the exploitation inherent in both the pictorial representation of the goddess and its mirror image in the internalized template.

TONI: I hate to say this, but I have to because I'm a feminist: the industry of stripping plays a small part in pornography. We are not helping the women's movement. We are not helping the way the world is going. I think the basic exploitation in stripping stems from the fact that you are maintaining that stereotype of women as bodies. Women cannot be appreciated for anything but that. It's the same for women who do cosmetic commercials.

SARITA: I believe there's a part of a man's psychology where he worships the female form, the female sexual form. It's like a totem of their sexuality. I don't think there's anything profound about that at all. I don't think there's anything wrong with that. That's been going on since the beginning of time. I do think that, over time, it has taken on a stranger and stranger quality, where it has become a thing of violence, become pornography. And pornography isn't just sexual. There's all kinds of pornography. Pornography is being graphic about anything. Violence is pornography. Ripping away the mystery of anything that is beautiful is pornography. Dissecting a rose and getting into it even for the sake of science is pornography. When you rip the veil off the priestess, that is pornography. It deprives men of something and it deprives women of something, that intangible something that keeps things happening on a healthy level. I think that a woman who goes out there [onstage] and lets it all just be there for a price has given up something very special, very important. Once they've seen it, they've used you. They take you in. They devour you mentally. They use you over and over and over again.[11]

Notes

Introduction

1. Norman Mailer, "Like a Lady," p. 52.
2. Joseph Berger, "Strip Club Brings Out Protesters."
3. Nick Ravo, "'Quality' Topless Clubs Go for the Crowd in Pin Stripes."
4. Ibid.
5. Stéphane Mallarmé, "Ballets," p. 63.

Chapter 3

1. *Sun*, July 29, 1984.
2. "Pain and Passion" was a duo show—a leather, chains, and whips tribute to S & M—featuring Billie Jo as Pain and various others as Passion.
3. See Robert Geffner, "Current Issues and Future Directions in Child Sexual Abuse."
4. J. W. Mohr, R. E. Turner, and M. B. Jerry, *Pedophilia and Exhibitionism*, p. 114.
5. David W. Allen, *The Fear of Looking*, p. 36.
6. Circe (rhymes with mercy) was the mythological enchantress who turned Odysseus' crewmen into swine.
7. Allen, *The Fear of Looking*, p. 37.
8. Jacqueline M. Boles and Albeno P. Garbin, "The Choice of Stripping for a Living," p. 112.
9. Edwin E. Wagner, "Projective Test Data from Two Contrasted Groups of Exhibitionists," p. 131.
10. This point is now only regionally true. Strippers all over Canada and in many parts of the United States at the time of writing now show it all.
11. Wagner, "Projective Test Data," p. 139.
12. In a footnote, Wagner thanks his research assistant, who labored "under what must have been trying circumstances for a male graduate student."

13. Wagner, "Projective Test Data," p. 139.
14. James K. Skipper, Jr., and Charles H. McCaghy, "Stripteasers: The Anatomy and Career Contingencies of a Deviant Occupation."
15. Ibid., p. 396.
16. Ibid., p. 402.

Chapter 4

1. Collected from strippers and from personal observation.

Chapter 5

1. Erik Lee Preminger, *Gypsy and Me*, pp. 17, 18.
2. H. Allen Smith, *Low Man on a Totem Pole*, p. 85.
3. Burlesque routine, quoted in Morton Minsky and Milt Machlin, *Minsky's Burlesque*, p. 257.
4. Murray S. Davis, *Smut: Erotic Reality/Obscene Ideology*, p. 6.
5. James K. Skipper, Jr., and Charles H. McCaghy, "Respondents' Intrusion Upon the Situation: The Problem of Interviewing Subjects with Special Qualities," *Sociological Quarterly* 13, p. 239.
6. Davis, *Smut: Erotic Reality/Obscene Ideology*, p. 9.
7. A few strippers requested all references to illegal drugs be deleted from their narratives, but many who had been doing drugs for a long time simply didn't mention it, probably because for them being stoned was not an issue but a lifestyle.

Chapter 6

1. Rena Falmlen, "Here's What You Said," p. 25.
2. Dorothy Dinnerstein, *The Mermaid and the Minotaur*, p. 95.
3. Ibid., p. 33 (emphasis in the original).
4. Ibid., pp. 28-29.
5. Ibid., p. 166.
6. Ibid., p. 69 (emphasis in the original).
7. Ibid., p. 112.
8. Ibid., p. 66.
9. Ibid., pp. 66–67.
10. Ibid., p. 67.
11. Ibid., pp. 67–68.
12. Karen Horney, "The Dread of Women," p. 349.
13. It is perhaps significant that the term for the *hatred* of women—

misogyny—had been in use for more than 200 years before one denoting the *fear* of women was coined in 1866. And today gynophobia still has not found its way into the general public consciousness. Most of the discussion about gender issues remains focused on misogyny, while its roots in phobia are largely overlooked.

14. All quotes from the *Home Book of Quotations*. The sources are, in order of appearance: Homer, *The Babylonian Talmud*, Beaumont and Fletcher, Saint Jerome, Cyril Tourneur, Gelett Burgess, *Ecclesiasticus*, Euripedes, John Fletcher, Goethe, George Granville, John Home, John Masefield, Menander, Petronius, Stephen Leacock, and Leo Tolstoy.

15. Joseph Swetnam, quoted in Angeline Goreau, "Hers."

16. Paula Stern, "The Womanly Image," p. 87.

Chapter 7

1. Quoted in Horst de la Croix and Richard G. Tansey, *Gardner's Art Through the Ages*, p. 877.

2. René Huyghe, "Art Forms and Society," p. 16.

3. Una Stannard, "Adam's Rib, or the Woman Within," p. 25.

4. Ibid.

5. Desmond Collins and John Onians, "The Origins of Art," p. 14.

6. Ibid., p. 15.

7. Huyghe, "Art Forms and Society," pp. 19–20.

8. Ibid.

9. Collins and Onians, "*The Origins of Art*," p. 22.

10. Pliny, *Natural History*, ed. D. E. Eichholz, 10:17.

11. Kenneth Clark, *The Nude*, p. 74.

12. Ibid., p. 87.

13. Ibid., pp. 93–94.

14. John Berger, "Nakedness Veiled with Paint," p. 68.

15. See Pliny, *Natural History*, trans. Philemon Holland, p. 406.

16. Quoted in Paul Derval, *Folies-Bergère,* p. 108.

17. *Esquire*, Aug. 1990, p. 124.

18. Clark, *The Nude*, p. 17.

19. Quoted in H. T. Musper, *Dürer*, p. 36.

20. Clark, *The Nude*, p. 137.

21. Ibid., p. 94.

22. See Theodore Reff, "The Meaning of Manet's *Olympia*," p. 115.

23. John Berger, *Ways of Seeing*, p. 55 (emphasis in the original).

24. Ibid., p. 56.

25. Ibid., p. 51.

26. See, for instance, F. M. Crawford's *Saracinesca*, p. 6: "The French school had not demonstrated the startling distinction between the nude and the naked."

27. *New York Times*, March 28, 1878, quoted in Gordon Hendricks, "Eakins' *William Rush Carving His Allegorical Statue of the Schuylkill*," p. 394.

28. *Argus*, April 27, 1878, Quoted in Hendricks, "Eakins' *William Rush*," p. 394.

29. Donald M. Reynolds, "The 'Unveiled Soul': Hiram Powers's Embodiment of the Ideal," p. 412.

30. W. H. Cole, quoted in Linda Hyman, "*The Greek Slave* by Hiram Powers: High Art as Popular Culture," p. 220.

31. Quoted in Paul Ableman, *Anatomy of Nakedness*, p. 48.

32. Arnolfo B. Ferruolo, "Botticelli's Mythologies, Ficino's *De Amore*, Poliziano's *Stanze per la Giostra*: Their Circle of Love," p. 22.

33. Ibid.

34. Marie Tanner, "Chance and Coincidence in Titian's *Diana and Actaeon*," p. 536.

35. John L. Connolly, Jr., "Ingres and the Erotic Intellect," in Thomas B. Hess and Linda Nochlin, eds., *Woman as Sex Object: Studies in Erotic Art, 1730–1970*, p. 25.

36. William H. Gerdts, *The Great American Nude*, p. 40.

37. Ibid.

38. Clark, *The Nude*, p. 121.

39. Berger, *Ways of Seeing*, p. 88.

40. Kenneth Clark, *Feminine Beauty*.

41. Quoted in de la Croix and Tansey, *Gardner's Art Through the Ages*, p. 830.

42. Ibid., p. 845.

43. Quoted in Jorge Lewinski, *The Naked and the Nude: A History of the Nude in Photography 1839 to the Present*, p. 53. Much of the exploration of the early years of the photographic nude has been influenced by this book.

44. Ibid., p. 79.

45. "The Kilanyi Living Pictures," *New York Dramatic Mirror*, March 31, 1894.

46. See Jack W. McCullough, "Edward Kilanyi and American Tableaux Vivants," pp. 25–26.

47. *New York Clipper*, March 31, 1894, p. 31.

48. McCullough, "Edward Kilanyi," p. 27.

49. Quoted ibid., p. 28.

50. Ibid., p. 34.

Chapter 8

1. Robert Graves, *The Greek Myths*, p. 72.

2. *New York Times*, Oct. 21, 1868.

3. See Carl Jung, "The Practice of Psychotherapy," p. 174.

4. The Jungian perspective is that both men and women have masculine

and feminine qualities that, because of social conditioning, are out of sync with each other and may only be brought into harmony through an introspective relationship with the opposite gender.

Chapter 9

1. H. Allen Smith, *Low Man on a Totem Pole*, p. 82.
2. James K. Skipper, Jr., and Charles H. McCaghy, "Stripteasing: A Sex-Oriented Occupation," p. 280.
3. Clinton J. Jesser and Louis P. Donovan, "Nudity in the Art Training Process: An Essay with Reference to a Pilot Study."
4. From the U.S. Supreme Court judgment, *Barnes v. Glen Theater*, June 21, 1991.
5. Quoted in E. Louis Backman, *Religious Dances*, p. 191.
6. Ibid., p. 213.
7. *New York Times*, Feb. 5, 1869.
8. Quoted in Joseph Marks, *The Mathers on Dancing*, p. 67.
9. This and the following quotations are from U.S. Supreme Court judgment, *Barnes v. Glen Theater*.
10. This and the following quotations are from the trial transcript, Court of Appeal, Calgary.
11. See, for instance, Daryl Lembke, "Oil Crews Attract Prostitutes."
12. Sydney Biddle Barrows with William Novak, *Mayflower Madam: The Secret Life of Sydney Biddle Barrows*, p. 148.
13. Howard S. Becker, *Outsiders*, p. 9 (emphasis in the original).
14. Ibid., (emphasis in the original).
15. Edwin M. Schur, *The Politics of Deviance*, p. 68.
16. Ibid., p. 6.
17. Ibid., pp. 68–69.
18. *Newsweek*, Dec. 2, 1974, p. 43.
19. A surprising number of people who were well aware that I was interviewing strippers nevertheless kept referring to them as "prostitutes" and "hookers."
20. Some strippers make a distinction between those who work in theaters or clubs and those who work the so-called "titty" bars.

Chapter 10

1. Sophia Loren, "When Stripping, Look into a Man's Eyes," April 10, 1964 (emphasis in the original).
2. Gwendolyn, interviewed by Kim Derko, in Derko, "A High-Heeled Point of View," pp. 4-5.

Chapter 12

1. Charles H. McCaghy and James K. Skipper, Jr., "Lesbian Behavior as an Adaptation to the Occupation of Stripping," p. 268.

Chapter 14

1. Bernard Sobel, *A Pictorial History of Burlesque*, p. 9.
2. Attributed to Fred McCloy in Irving Zeidman, *The American Burlesque Show*, p. 43.
3. Attributed to Sam T. Jack, ibid., p. 39.
4. Attributed to the Catholic charities in Morton Minsky and Milt Machlin, *Minsky's Burlesque*, p. 274.
5. *Time*, April 27, 1970.
6. Max Furman, quoted in James Stevenson, "Takes," p. 59.
7. From the Broadway show *Sugar Babies*, quoted in Ralph G. Allen, "Bringing Burlesque to Broadway," p. 60.
8. From Abel Green and Joe Laurie, Jr., *Show Biz*, p. 348.
9. Sigmund Freud saw some significance in the fact that "the genital apparatus remains the neighbour of the cloaca," and actually "in the case of women is only taken from it on lease." Sigmund Freud, "Three Essays on the Theory of Sexuality," p. 187. Elsewhere, Freud described the vagina as "an organ derived from the cloaca." Sigmund Freud, "The Disposition to Obsessional Neurosis," p. 326.
10. *Philadelphia North American*, quoted in Zeidman, *The American Burlesque Show*, pp. 15–17.
11. Quoted in Zeidman, *The American Burlesque Show*, p. 13.
12. *New York Times*, May 11, 1894. quoted in Jack W. McCullough, "Edward Kilanyi and American Tableaux Vivants," p. 33.
13. Robert C. Allen, *Horrible Prettiness: Burlesque and American Culture*, p. 88. Much of the information on American burlesque in the nineteenth century is based on Allen.
14. Ibid., p. 91.
15. "Stage Morality and the Ballet," quoted in Olive Logan, *Before the Footlights and Behind the Scenes*, p. 576.
16. Robert C. Allen, *Horrible Prettiness*, p. 105.
17. *New York Clipper*, Dec. 8, 1860.
18. Robert C. Allen, *Horrible Prettiness*, p. 107.
19. Ibid., p. 99.
20. Wolf Mankowitz, *Mazeppa: The Lives, Loves and Legends of Adah Isaacs Menken*, pp. 18–19.
21. Quoted in Allen Lesser, *Enchanting Rebel*, p. 111.
22. *New York Clipper*, Sept. 29, 1866.
23. Rev. Dr. Charles B. Smyth, *New York Herald*, Nov. 19, 1866, quoted in Joseph Whitton, *The Naked Truth: An Inside History of The Black Crook*, p. 27.

24. Zeidman, *The American Burlesque Show*, p. 21.

25. *New York Clipper*, March 6, 1869.

26. Richard Grant White, "The Age of Burlesque," p. 261.

27. Robert C. Allen, *Horrible Prettiness*, p. 129.

28. W. D. Howells, "The New Taste in Theatricals," pp. 639–40, 641–42.

29. Olive Logan, *Apropos of Women and Theatres*, p. 135, quoted in Robert C. Allen, *Horrible Prettiness*, pp. 123–24.

30. Quoted in *Portfolio of Photographs of the World's Fair*, p. 3.

31. Robert C. Allen, *Horrible Prettiness*, p. 231.

32. Stanley Appelbaum suggests that hootchy-kootchy may be a derivative of Kouta Kouta, the Algerian version of the belly dance. See *The Chicago World's Fair of 1893: A Photographic Record*, p. 102.

33. Quoted in Minsky and Machlin, *Minsky's Burlesque*, pp. 33–34.

34. Ibid., p. 230.

35. See Zeidman, *The American Burlesque Show*, pp. 143–44.

36. "She Takes Off Her Clothes," *National Police Gazette*, Oct. 31, 1896.

37. Mankowitz, *Mazeppa*, p. 20.

38. *Newsweek*, Jan. 9, 1967.

39. Paul Derval, *Folies-Bergère*, p. 48.

40. Ibid., p. 50.

41. Ralph G. Allen, "Our Native Theatre: Honky-Tonk, Minstrel Shows, Burlesque," pp. 282–83.

42. David Dressler, "Burlesque as a Cultural Phenomenon," p. 68.

43. Ibid., p. 81.

44. Max Furman, quoted in Stevenson, "Takes," p. 52 (emphasis in the original).

45. Minsky and Machlin, *Minsky's Burlesque*, p. 184.

46. According to Robert Allen, the runway had been in use in New York in the 1860s.

47. Minsky and Machlin, *Minsky's Burlesque*, p. 281.

48. Brooks Atkinson, "On the State of Burlesque," sec. 11, p. 1.

49. *Time*, April 27, 1970, p. 58.

50. Lawrence Langner, *The Importance of Wearing Clothes*, p. 174.

51. Marshall McLuhan, *Understanding Media*, p. 121.

52. Sam Scribner, quoted in Henry Beckett, "Burlesque's Bosom Friend Draws a Fine Waist Line."

53. Harry Henderson and Sam Shaw, "Burlesque Is Dead," pp. 15, 39.

54. See Arthur Berger, "Varieties of Topless Experience," p. 420.

55. Ibid., p. 421.

Chapter 15

1. John Richmond, "Gypsy Rose Lee, Striptease Intellectual," p. 38.

2. June Havoc, *More Havoc*, p. 96.

3. David Dressler, "Burlesque as a Cultural Phenomenon," p. 161.
4. Morton Minsky and Milt Machlin, *Minsky's Burlesque,* p. 33.
5. Bill Nichols, *Ideology and the Image*, p. 1.
6. Tracie Rozhon, "Learning the Differences in the Language of Sell," p. 11.
7. *Penthouse,* Sept. 1990.
8. "Cleaning Up Sin City," p. 13.
9. Michael R. Cunningham, "Measuring the Physical in Physical Attractiveness: Quasi-Experiments on the Sociobiology of Female Beauty."
10. Quoted in Daniel Goleman, "Equation for Beauty Emerges in Studies," p. 17.
11. When interviewed, both Toni and Sarita—10 year veterans of the business—were no longer working as strippers.

Bibliography

Ableman, Paul. *Anatomy of Nakedness*. London: Orbis, 1982.

Allen, David W. *The Fear of Looking*. Charlottesville: University Press of Virginia, 1974.

Allen, Ralph G. "Our Native Theater: Honky-Tonk, Minstrel Shows, Burlesque." In *The American Theater: A Sum of Its Parts*, ed. Henry B. Williams. New York: Samuel French, 1971.

_____. "Bringing Burlesque to Broadway." *Horizon*. October, 1979.

Allen, Robert C. *Horrible Prettiness: Burlesque and American Culture*. Chapel Hill: University of North Carolina Press, 1991.

Appelbaum, Stanley. *The Chicago World's Fair of 1893: A Photographic Record*. New York: Dover, 1980.

Atkinson, Brooks. "On the State of Burlesque." *New York Times*. May 9, 1937.

Backman, E. Louis. *Religious Dances*. London: Allen and Unwin, 1952.

Barrows, Sydney Biddle, with William Novak. *Mayflower Madam: The Secret Life of Sydney Biddle Barrows*. New York: Arbor House, 1986.

Becker, Howard S. *Outsiders*. New York: Free Press, 1963.

Beckett, Henry. "Burlesque's Bosom Friend Draws a Fine Waist Line." *New York Post*. July 14, 1937.

Berger, Arthur. "Varieties of Topless Experience." *Journal of Popular Culture* 4, no. 2. Fall 1970.

Berger, John. *Ways of Seeing*. London: BBC, 1972.

_____. "Nakedness Veiled with Paint." *Harper's*. December 1985.

Berger, Joseph. "Strip Club Brings Out Protesters." *New York Times*. August 13, 1993.

Boles, Jacqueline M., and Albeno P. Garbin. "The Strip Club and Stripper-Customer Patterns of Interaction." *Sociology and Social Research* 58, no. 2. January 1974.

_____. "The Choice of Stripping for a Living." *Sociology of Work and Occupations* 1, no. 1. February 1974.

Clark, Kenneth. *The Nude*. London: John Murray, 1957.

_____. *Feminine Beauty*. New York: Rizzoli, 1980.

"Cleaning Up Sin City." Transcript no 3044, "Donahue." September 28, 1990.

Collins, Desmond, and John Onians. "The Origins of Art." *Art History* 1, no. 1. March 1978.

Connolly, John L., Jr. "Ingres and the Erotic Intellect" in *Woman as Sex Object: Studies in Erotic Art, 1730–1970*, ed. Thomas B. Hess and Linda Nochlin. New York: *Newsweek*, 1972.

Corio, Ann, with Joseph DiMona. *This Was Burlesque.* New York: Grossett and Dunlap, 1968.

Court of Appeal, Calgary, Alberta. *H. M. the Queen v. Michele Diane Pradia.* Trial transcript. September 14, 1984.

Crawford, F. M. *Saracinesca.* New York: Macmillan, 1893.

Croix, Horst de la, and Richard G. Tansey. *Gardner's Art Through the Ages.* San Diego: Harcourt Brace Jovanovich, 1986.

Cunningham, Michael R. "Measuring the Physical in Physical Attractiveness: Quasi-Experiments on the Sociobiology of Female Beauty." *Journal of Personality and Social Psychology* 50, no. 5. May 1986.

Davis, Murray S. *Smut: Erotic Reality/Obscene Ideology.* Chicago: University of Chicago Press, 1983.

Derko, Kim. "A High-Heeled Point of View." *Independent Eye* 12, no. 3. Spring/Summer 1991.

Derval, Paul. *Folies-Bergère*, trans. Lucienne Hill. New York: E. P. Dutton, 1955.

Dinnerstein, Dorothy. *The Mermaid and the Minotaur.* New York: Harper and Row, 1976.

Dressler, David. "Burlesque as a Cultural Phenomenon." Unpublished Ph.D. dissertation. New York University, 1937.

Falmlen, Rena. "Here's What You Said." *Spotlight.* October–November 1982.

Ferruolo, Arnolfo B. "Botticelli's *Mythologies*, Ficino's *De Amore*, Poliziano's *Stanze per la Giostra*: Their Circle of Love." *Art Bulletin* 37, no. 1. March 1955.

Freud, Sigmund. "The Disposition to Obsessional Neurosis." In *Complete Psychological Works of Sigmund Freud*, 12, trans. James Strachey. London: Hogarth, 1958.

_____. "Three Essays on the Theory of Sexuality." In *Complete Psychological Works of Sigmund Freud*, 7, trans. James Strachey. London: Hogarth, 1953.

Geffner, Robert. "Current Issues and Future Directions in Child Sexual Abuse." *Journal of Child Sexual Abuse* 1, no. 1. 1992.

Gerdts, William H. *The Great American Nude.* New York: William H. Gerdts, 1974.

Goleman, Daniel. "Equation for Beauty Emerges in Studies." *New York Times.* August 5, 1986.

Goreau, Angeline. "Hers." *New York Times.* December 4, 1986.

Graves, Robert. *The Greek Myths*, 1. Harmondsworth, England: Penguin, 1955.

Green, Abel, and Joe Laurie, Jr. *Show Biz.* New York: Henry Holt, 1951.

Havoc, June. *More Havoc.* New York: Harper and Row, 1980

Henderson, Harry, and Sam Shaw. "Burlesque Is Dead." *Collier's.* November 27, 1943.

Hendricks, Gordon. "Eakins' *William Rush Carving His Allegorical Statue of the Schuylkill.*" *Art Quarterly.* Winter 1968.

Hess, Thomas B., and Lind Nochlin, eds. *Woman as Sex Object: Studies in Erotic Art, 1730–1970.* New York: *Newsweek,* 1972.

Home Book of Quotations, 9th edition. New York: Dodd, Mead, 1964.

Horney, Karen. "The Dread of Women." *International Journal of Psycho-Analysis* 23. 1932.

Howells, W. D. "The New Taste in Theatricals." *Atlantic Monthly.* May 1869.

Huyghe, René, ed. *Larousse Encyclopedia of Prehistoric and Ancient Art.* London: Paul Hamlyn, 1962.

Hyman, Linda. "*The Greek Slave* by Hiram Powers: High Art as Popular Culture." *Art Journal* 35, no. 3. Spring 1976.

Jesser, Clinton J., and Louis P. Donovan. "Nudity in the Art Training Process: An Essay with Reference to a Pilot Study." *Sociological Quarterly* 10, no. 3. Summer 1969.

Jung, Carl. "The Practice of Psychotherapy." In *Collected Works,* 16. New York: Pantheon, 1954.

"The Kilanyi Living Pictures." *New York Dramatic Mirror.* March 31, 1894.

Langner, Lawrence. *The Importance of Wearing Clothes.* New York: Hastings House, 1959.

Lembke, Daryl. "Oil Crews Attract Prostitutes." *Vancouver Sun.* July 15, 1974.

Lesser, Allen. *Enchanting Rebel.* New York: Beechhurst, 1947.

Lewinski, Jorge. *The Naked and the Nude: A History of the Nude in Photographs 1839 to the Present.* New York: Harmony Books, 1987.

Logan, Olive. *Apropos of Women and Theatres.* New York: Carlton, 1869

_____. *Before the Footlights and Behind the Scenes.* Philadelphia: Parmalee, 1870.

Loren, Sophia. "When Stripping, Look into a Man's Eyes." *Life.* April 10, 1964.

McCaghy, Charles H., and Skipper, James K., Jr. "Lesbian Behavior as Adaptation to the Occupation of Stripping." *Social Problems* 17, no. 2. Fall 1969.

_____. "Stripping: Anatomy of a Deviant Life Style." In *Life Styles: Diversity in American Society,* ed. Saul D. Feldman and Gerald W. Thielbar. Boston: Little, Brown, 1972.

McCullough, Jack W. "Edward Kilanyi and American Tableaux Vivants." *Theatre Survey* 16, no. 1. May 1975.

McLuhan, Marshall. *Understanding Media.* New York: McGraw Hill, 1964.

Mailer, Norman. "Like a Lady." *Esquire.* August 1994.

Mallarmé, Stéphane. "Ballets." In *Mallarmé: Selected Prose Poems, Essays and Letters,* trans. Bradford Cook. Baltimore: Johns Hopkins University Press, 1956.

Mankowitz, Wolf. *Mazeppa: The Lives, Loves and Legends of Adah Isaacs Menken.* London: Blonde and Briggs, 1982.

Marks, Joseph. *The Mathers on Dancing.* Brooklyn: Dance Horizons, 1975.

Minsky, Morton, and Milt Machlin. *Minsky's Burlesque.* New York: Arbor House, 1986.

Mohr, J. W., R. E. Turner, and M. B. Jerry. *Pedophilia and Exhibitionism.* Toronto: University of Toronto Press, 1964.

Musper, H. T. *Dürer.* New York: Harry N. Abrams, n.d.

Nichols, Bill. *Ideology and the Image.* Bloomington: Indiana University Press, 1981.

Pliny. *Natural History,* ed. D. E. Eichholz. Loeb Classical Library, 10. London: Heinemann, 1962.

_____. *Natural History,* trans. Philemon Holland. London: Centaur, 1962.

Portfolio of Photographs of the World's Fair. Household Art Series, 4. January 1, 1894. Chicago: Werner, 1893.

Preminger, Erik Lee. *Gypsy and Me.* Boston: Little, Brown, 1984.

Ravo, Nick. "'Quality' Topless Clubs Go for the Crowd in Pin Stripes." *New York Times.* April 15, 1992.

Reff, Theodore. "The Meaning of Manet's *Olympia.*" *Gazette des Beaux-Arts* 63, no. 1141. February 1964.

Reynolds, Donald M. "The 'Unveiled Soul': Hiram Powers's Embodiment of the Ideal." *Art Bulletin* 59, no. 3. September 1977.

Richmond, John. "Gypsy Rose Lee, Striptease Intellectual." *American Mercury.* January 1941.

Rozhon, Tracie. "Learning the Differences in the Language of Sell." *The Press.* May 1981.

Rufinus. *Jousts of Aphrodite,* trans. Michael Kelly. London: Forest Books, 1986.

Schur, Edwin M. *The Politics of Deviance.* Englewood Cliffs, N.J.: Prentice-Hall, 1980.

"She Takes Off Her Clothes." *National Police Gazette.* October 31, 1896.

Skipper, James K., Jr., and Charles H. McCaghy. "Respondents' Intrusion Upon the Situation: The Problem of Interviewing Subjects with Special Qualities." *Sociological Quarterly* 13. Spring 1972.

_____. "Stripteasers: The Anatomy and Career Contingencies of a Deviant Occupation." *Social Problems* 17, no. 3. Winter 1970.

_____. "Stripteasing: A Sex-Oriented Occupation." In *Studies in the Sociology of Sex,* ed. James M. Henslin. New York: Appleton-Century-Crofts, 1971.

Smith, H. Allen. *Low Man on a Totem Pole.* Garden City, N.Y.: Doubleday, Doran, 1941.

Sobel, Bernard. *A Pictorial History of Burlesque.* New York: G. P. Putnam's Sons, 1956.

"Stage Morality and the Ballet." *Blackwood's* 105. March 1869.

Stannard, Una. "Adam's Rib, or the Woman Within." *Trans-Action.* November–December 1970.

Stern, Paula. "The Womanly Image." *The Atlantic.* March 1970.

Stevenson, James. "Takes." *The New Yorker.* August 31, 1981.

Tanner, Marie. "Chance and Coincidence in Titian's *Diana and Actaeon.*" *Art Bulletin* 56, no. 4 December 1974.

U.S. Supreme Court. *Barnes v. Glen Theater.* June 21, 1991.

Wagner, Edwin E. "Projective Test Data Form Two Contrasted Groups of Exhibitionists." *Perceptual and Motor Skills* 39, 1974.

White, Richard Grant. "The Age of Burlesque." *Galaxy* 8. August 1869.

Whitton, Joseph. *The Naked Truth: An Inside History of* The Black Crook. Philadelphia: H. W. Shaw, 1897.

Ziedman, Irving. *The American Burlesque Show.* New York: Hawthorn Books, 1967.

Index